Writing Muslim Identity

Also available from Continuum

An Introduction to Religion and Literature
Mark Knight

A Mirror For Our Times: The Rushdie Affair and the Future of Multiculturalism
Paul Weller

Muslims and Modernity: Current Debates
Clinton Bennett

Writing Muslim Identity

Geoffrey Nash

continuum

Continuum International Publishing Group

The Tower Building	80 Maiden Lane
11 York Road	Suite 704
London, SE1 7NX	New York, NY 10038

www.continuumbooks.com

British Library Cataloguing-in-Publication Data
A catalogue record for this book is available from the British Library.

ISBN: 9781441136664 (paperback)
       9781441124364 (hardcover)

Library of Congress Cataloging-in-Publication Data
Nash, Geoffrey.
   Writing muslim identity / Geoffrey Nash.
       p. cm.
   Includes bibliographical references and index.
   ISBN 978-1-4411-3666-4 – ISBN 978-1-4411-2436-4 1. English literature–History and criticism. 2. Islam and literature–History–21st century. 3. Muslims in literature. 4. Muslims–Ethnic identity. 5. Islam and literature–History–20th century. I. Title.
   PR149.I8N37 2011
   820.9'38297–dc23
                        2011016501

Typeset by Fakenham Prepress Solutions, Fakenham, Norfolk NR21 8NN
Printed and bound in Great Britain

For Stuart Sim, master at lending clarity to complex ideas

Note on Arabic words

No attempt has been made to follow a consistent system of transliteration of Arabic words. Proper names have been spelt according to common usage. Hence: Seyyid Hossein Nasr, but Sayyid Qutb, and Saddam Hussein. Words like jihad, hijab, and fatwa, now incorporated into English dictionaries, are not italicised. However, other less used Islamic terms, such as *umma, dar al-harb,* and *ijtihad,* are.

Contents

Introduction   1

Chapter 1   **Literature and the *Kulturkampf* against Islam**   7

Chapter 2   **British Migrant Muslim Fiction:** Farhana Sheikh, Hanif
            Kureishi, Monica Ali, Nadeem Aslam, Leila Aboulela   26

Chapter 3   **Fixing Muslim Masculinity, Saving Muslim Women:** Azar
            Nafisi, Azne Seierstadt, Taslima Nasreen, Irshad Manji,
            Ayan Hirshi Ali   50

Chapter 4   **Discoursing Muslim Modernities and Eschatologies:**
            V. S. Naipaul, Naguib Mahfouz, Jamal Mahjoub,
            Shahrnush Parsipur   70

Chapter 5   **Fixing the 'Islamic Terrorist':** Ian McEwan, Don DeLillo,
            John Updike, Mohsin Hamid, Laila Halaby   93

Conclusion   117

Notes   120

Bibliography   128

Index   137

Islam is the 'other' that we cannot embrace, even when we are at our most tolerant, because this other fails to accept the rules of the game – because it sees the game as a western game.

Bobby S Sayyid, *A Fundamental Fear: Eurocentrism and the Emergence of Islamism*

Islam is a mirror in which the West projects its own identity crisis.

Olivier Roy, *Secularism Confronts Islam*

All cultures and languages exclude – even the ones associated with modern science and humanism, and even the ones dedicated to tolerance, dialogue, and plurality.

Ashis Nandy, 'The Return of the Sacred: the Language of Religion and the Fear of Democracy in a Post-Secular World'

High mobility does play havoc with traditional religion. It separates people from the holy places. It mixes them with neighbours whose gods have different names and who worship them in different ways

Harvey Cox *The Secular City*

Introduction

If a tiny minority of militants are to be believed their religion, Islam, is today at war with most of the powerful nations of the world, pre-eminently the United States of America, Russia and western Europe. Whether or not we take the militants' words at face value, the overwhelming majority of their fellow religionists would refuse to endorse their sentiments – they do not wish to be involved in such a war. Yet willy nilly, Muslims the world over have become objects of suspicion and more insidiously, a war of words and images has been unleashed against them. Especially where they live as a minority with the status of quondam migrants, they feel themselves vulnerable to what might be called a *Kulturkampf* – a 'cultural struggle' that takes its cue from Bismarck's policies directed in the name of secularism against the influence of the Catholic Church in Germany in the 1870s. Both then, and now in the case of the campaign against Muslims which began to appear in the western media after the success of the Iranian revolution, the motive has been political. If Bismarck turned against the Catholic Church it was because the Papal States had supported France in the Franco–Prussian War of 1870–1. But Islam would appear to be an amorphous enemy which, as Ali Allawi argues in *The Crisis of Islamic Civilization*, from the late eighteenth century up until the mid-1970s entered two centuries of retreat. 'Bluntly put, Islam [as seen by the West in the 1950s] was a relic of the past and would survive only as a private faith and a loose set of moral and ethical principles. "Mosque-going" would follow church-going, and Islam would succumb to the laws of social, economic and cultural progress' (Allawi 2009: 63–4). Some (particularly nervous western political leaders) have repeated the mantra that Islam is a purely peaceful faith, that the overwhelming majority of Muslims are 'moderates' and that the so-called *jihadists* are aberrant extremists. However, the urge to reform Islam on the model of the early Muslim community which has been a feature of Islamic history since the eighteenth century means that – as the authoritative scholar of modern Islam Fazlur Rahman put it – 'It is the paradigm of the early Muslim history as an activist reform movement and bestowing upon Islam the character not only of religious and moral preaching, but also of religious and moral *action* leading up to the formation of a state [,] that must influence the ideals of a Muslim puritanical movement (although any puritanical movement is liable to adopt revolutionary methods)' (Rahman 1979: 211, italics in text). Puritan trends have certainly been in operation in the Muslim world since the

Wahhabi movement emerged in the eighteenth century; but arguably they did not begin to impact directly on the West until very recent times. As for the Muslim world of today, it has no defined political organization or leadership aside from individual states claiming to be Islamic.

I do not wish to go into the part played by the West in the creation of militant Islamist groups in Afghanistan in the 1980s – suffice to say that little attention was paid at the time to the prospect of awakening a sleeping giant. 'The Western support [in Afghanistan] reversed a thousand years of history, though it only lasted as long as it suited the global strategy of the CIA' (Huband 1998: 15). But Afghanistan, as everyone knows, gave Osama Bin Laden the opportunity to declare a jihad which in due course he extended to the one remaining superpower: 'The Soviet Empire has become – with God's grace – a figment of the imagination [he declared in 2001] [...] So we believe that the defeat of America is something achievable – with the permission of God – and it is easier for us [...] than the defeat of the Soviet Empire previously' (quoted in Desai 2007: 114). Fred Halliday emphasized that 'the goal of the fundamentalist movements' which began in West Asia but brought their agenda home to the western world on 11 September 2001, was 'not religious, in the sense of faith, nor cultural, in the sense of values, but political: it is to take power from those who control the states and, once they have power, to hold on to it' (Halliday 2002: 40).

The point I am seeking to make here is – whatever the politics of the moment proclaim, and whatever the secular and the believing practitioners of religious hermeneutics may say – Islam is a religion, not an ideology, and there is no point, ultimately, in making war with a religion. That is the premise upon which this book has been written. Except when using terms like 'Islamism' and 'political Islamism', I have no particular form of Islam in mind when using the substantive noun. (Generally speaking, newspapers such as *The Sun*, *Daily Mail* and the *Daily Express* have very restricted meanings in mind when they use terms such as 'Muslim' and 'Muslim Terrorists' in their headlines.) This book is therefore not intended as a defence of a specific form of Islam, either 'moderate', 'traditional' or 'radical'. My main task is to articulate and probe an image or set of images of Muslims and of Islam found in English writing published for the most part in Britain and America which though not entirely new, since the early 1980s have grown in intensity. This applies to both media discourse and to literary texts. In my analysis I am aware of the varieties of writing under scrutiny: ranging from the generically aesthetic (such as the fictional *bildungsroman*) to texts that are more discursive and subjective in orientation (travel writing, autobiography) to the avowedly polemic (journalism). I am in sympathy with David Spurr's method of 'at the risk of failing to show the proper respect for literary distinctions, [...] freely draw[ing] together examples from so many different kinds of text, treating them as moments in the production of a larger discursive phenomenon' (Spurr 1993: 11).[1] Nonetheless, I hope due allowance is given to these variations when interrogating texts for their 'truthfulness of representation'. I do not wish to adopt a reductive approach which assigns to each type of text 'testimonial value or the burden of representation', and as far as possible hope to avoid 'relegating the aesthetic to a secondary position' (Ghose 2007: 125). But I think it will become evident that reading texts for their play/pleasure (*jouissance/plaisir*) value is of less interest to me than what Edward Said pointed out, twenty years before the second attack on the Twin Towers, were the concrete effects of 'word politics' in the everyday lives of Muslims, and today we must say, of us all (Said 1981: xvi).[2]

Often studied and written about, negative images of Muslims in media stories, literary or pulp fiction, memoir and autobiography, travel writing, films and so on, have continued to acquire potency in the period covered by this book. Said and others have emphasized how political correctness may operate across the whole range of 'minority' groups, but that licence seems to apply towards the stereotyping of Arabs in particular and Muslims in general. Muslim 'fundamentalism' and Muslim 'terror' have not unsurprisingly, given the direction world events have moved in over the last two decades, become topics for filmmakers, novelists and dramatists to get their teeth into. Insurgencies that concern Muslims hardly at all, for example in areas of Africa or India, are less frequently reported than those which do. Deprivation of the human rights of Muslim women has exercised many writers and journalists; however, as the treatment of these issues seems to grow exponentially, not as many, in comparison, highlight, for example, the large scale channelling of girls and young women into prostitution in South-East Asia, or the incidence of child brides, forced marriages or honour killings among Hindus[3] and Sikhs, or the abandonment of aged widows in Hindu society. Islam is an easy scapegoat, in short, for cultural practices that have either been in existence for hundreds of years, or, like the child sex and adult prostitution 'industries' in countries like the Philippines (predominantly Catholic) or (predominantly Buddhist) Thailand, have developed over the last half century with the active participation of Europeans, Americans, and Australasians and no doubt Muslims too.

Undoubtedly specificities of the more recent and contemporary West–Muslim clash represent a change from the encounter of the Enlightenment/ Christian world-view that operated in modern times with previously nuanced (mainly traditional) Islams.[4] It is clear that there has been an important shift from the imperialist Enlightenment/Christian character of the *Kulturkampf* against Islam in the late imperial period (1880–1920s) as opposed to the secular democratic one of the late modern/postmodern period (1970s to date). Surprisingly, perhaps, a precise history of this changing encounter has yet to be written.[5] There has, for example, been a pronounced shift around the marker 'civilised' as applied to western values. 'In the 19th century, the West considered the wearing of clothes as the mark of civilization; it was "savages" who went naked. In the 20th and 21st centuries, however, semi-nudity became the signifier of western superiority' (Young 2003: 83).[6] The division over clothing, particularly the wearing of the hijab and *niqab*, has thus taken on an increasingly polarized, confrontational aspect. Some eastern writers see western civilization today as an aberration in the history of mankind. They argue that in its modern form it has been detached from Christianity and even more from the traditional, religiously oriented civilizations (Hindu, Buddhist, Taoist) with which Islam is also connected:

> The process of modernity has in the past destroyed the equilibrium of traditional societies and with its seductive, misleading and luciferian impulse, it now threatens their existence to the core. This force [of globalization] must be recognized as harmful [...] On the one hand it holds the material progress of the West as normatively superior to the rest of the world [...] and on the other hand it champions itself as the model for the 'backward societies' to emulate. It is like telling those 'Third Worlders' that you can never become like us, but nonetheless we would still like you to try and see if you can (Akram 2003: 100–01).[7]

Suffice to say, with the downfall of Communism and the end of the Cold War in the 1990s there arose a 'West v the Rest' binary which in real terms meant the West against the Muslim world. For one western Muslim thinker this 'is more than a clash of cultures, more than a confrontation of races: it is a straight fight between two approaches to the world, two opposed philosophies. [...] One is based in secular materialism, the other in faith; one has rejected belief altogether, the other has placed it at the centre of its world-view. It is, therefore, not simply between Islam and the West' (Ahmed, A. 2004: 264). As I argue in Chapter 1, the clash of western secularism and Islam is, if not a clash of fundamentalisms, at least a barometer of the distance the secular West (always excluding a significant proportion of the United States) has travelled from its Judeo-Christian origins.

Another phenomenon which emerges from this particular struggle of cultures is the way a section notionally belonging to one side peels off and joins the other. The so-called 'native informant', who we learn of in postcolonial theory, acquires a sharpened edge when s/he embarks upon campaigns against the traditional Muslim culture that ostensibly nurtured her in either familial or educational terms or in both. This is in part because the *Kulturkampf* against Islam disrupts the normal postcolonial periphery v metropolitan West battle-lines (if indeed these still operate) as it does the configuration of left/liberal politics. Postcolonial theory is yet to come to grips with Islam as a religious as opposed to a cultural category. In theorizing the Muslim subject as a politically resistant other and occluding or relativizing the role of religion, postcolonial thinkers may be distorting the subjectivity of Muslim men and women who are less likely to valorize as normative the values of rebellion (*fitna*) in comparison to communal conformity, and for whom religion is a primary identity marker. Similarly, the question of alliances between Muslim and socialist political groupings is often complicated by the extent to which the latter are wedded to secularizing and feminist narratives.[8] Academically speaking, postcolonial and cultural perspectives on Muslims are nevertheless the language games in which Muslim writers often feel they need to operate if they are to get published in the West.[9] I shall discuss in Chapter 1 the insertion of Islam within the discourse systems of postmodernism and Orientalism, as seen specifically in the work of Bobby Sayyid and Anouar Majid. On the other hand there are of course Muslim writers and intellectuals who are not wedded to working within the structures of western academe or to theoretical constructs of western prove-nance and therefore do not feel obliged to pay cognisance to western secular parameters of argumentation. As indicated earlier, I do not intend this book to be an apologia for Islam or indeed the actions or behaviours, economic, socio-cultural or political, of Muslims or Muslim states, either in the Islamic world or in diaspora. My focus will be on the discourse(s) used to construct Muslim identity, primarily in the West. While drawing upon standard theories, my primary aim is to demonstrate how, for political and ideological reasons, in recent writing, literary or otherwise, Islam has been singled out as the western world's Other.[10]

In addition, I wish to interrogate the conditions that might make it possible to speak of Muslim writing – that is writing that takes Islam or Islamic religious belief and culture(s) as its focus. Muslim writing might be said to constitute a domain outside the established nostrums of postcolonial theory. In his exploratory work, *Muslim Narratives and the Discourse of English*, Amin Malak sets forth a case for the term 'Muslim' as an identity signifier in English writings which does not exclude its participation alongside other identity signifiers. He situates his argument within the larger criticism that postcolonialism is the theoretical construction of a comprador intelligentsia who appropriate the literatures of non-western peoples in a way that is complicit with imperi-alist ideology. Malak's specific argument is that religion is shortchanged in postcolonial theorization. 'Another aspect, subtle but discursively serious, involves the dearth of useful "postcolonial" theoretical material germane to the issue of religion or the sacred as a key conceptual category, as compared to the valorized ones of race, class, gender, nation, migration, and hybridity' (Malak 2005: 16).[11] Of the women characters in Farhana Sheikh's *The Red Box* he states: '[T]he term *Muslim* represents the primary identity signifier, ahead of class, gender, or nationalism' (40). Malak's argument probes the predicament of Muslims living in diasporic 'exile' away from their countries of origin in a way we might expect characters from Africa or the Indian sub-continent to be represented in contemporary novels. The nub of his approach which makes it particularly valuable is his demonstration of how Islam features in both its purely religious as well as its cultural dimensions in the writings of a range of secular authors originating from Muslim nations or cultures, including non-believers like Abdulrazak Gurnah and Salman Rushdie.

One of the important things about Malak's position is his recognition that the multiple factors impinging on identity in today's globalized world impact upon Muslims too. He does not specify a vocation for the term 'Muslim' within these multifarious factors, but simply makes the argument for its place and its inclusion within our discussion of literary discourse. This seems to me an eminently sensible way of proceeding because it opens up a space in which Muslim identity can be discussed in its own terms while obviously not excluding other factors. For western writers for whom Islam represents an alien belief system, set of cultural practices, or political ideology in opposition to the West, this space may make little difference to their position. However, to authors whose origins connect them to Muslim identity of one kind or another, Malak's work is important because it valorizes some of the key parameters from within which they work. Moreover, his critique of Rushdie enables us to look, from a perspective different even from the postcolonial and Saidean anti-Orientalist ones usually employed hitherto, at 'native informant' type writers whose work is inherently hostile to Islam. Malak by no means proscribes writing critical of Islam – on the contrary, he accepts 'the dialectic of [Third World] literary discourse' will at times be 'critical (at times severely critical) of its cultural roots yet remain actively committed to them'. Those writers who set out to attack Muslims and Islam from inside, while sharing its cultural roots, can be considered 'alien to the "third world" view of itself' (110)[12] and complicit in the *Kulturkampf* against Islam.

Chapter 1

Literature and the *Kulturkampf* against Islam

'Their Religion is their Identity'

Throughout western Europe, in spite of policies of state-sponsored multi-culturalism – whether broadly or narrowly defined – the perception has arisen that the Muslim minority is a problem. In spite of their originating from a wide diversity of nations and cultures, there has been an increasing tendency among Muslim migrants to cohere around the signifier 'Muslim' as a commonality in response to their minority status within liberal societies in which, though cultural make-up is allowed to be diverse, the dominant view is secular. Before we even begin to probe the way in which Muslim identity has been constructed it is important to remind ourselves that such a discussion, or the terms in which it has been construed, is of quite recent provenance.

In late twentieth, early twenty-first century terms, Muslim identity has become an emergent category previously subsumed in classifications of immigrant populations in Europe that foregrounded race and ethnicity (Ansari 2004: 9). Since the 1980s individuals and communities have opted to choose the term Muslim as their primary, even sole identity signifier. The construction of a Muslim diasporic identity is a recent phenomenon. British sociologist Tariq Modood writes of his family's personal shift of identity from being considered Pakistani in the 1960s/70s, to Asian in the 1980s, and Muslim in the 1990s (Modood 2005: 4). According to Humayun Ansari, Muslims were subsumed within ethnic categories as part of the discourse of race relations until the 1980s, when the New Right's exclusion policies led to the adoption of religion as a signifier of identity. Battles over religious schools and onslaughts against Muslims as not belonging to British culture helped foster a British Muslim identity (Ansari 2004: 10–11). Philip Lewis (2002) locates 1980s Bradford as the nexus for the emergence of this Muslim identity in Britain, where self-sufficiency in the form of Muslim-owned shops and businesses and Muslim professionals flourished. The Bradford City council was among the first to set into motion the now much criticized machinery of multicultural policy by pledging that each community in the city had a right to its religious and cultural identity (70–1).

From the standpoint of cultural theory, despite its 'common sense' grounding in 'a recognition of some common origin or shared characteristics with another person or group, or with an ideal', identity is not a fixed sign, and it is invariably constructed with an Other in mind. As Stuart Hall puts it: 'It is only through the relation to the Other, the relation to what it is not, to precisely what it lacks, to what has been called its *constitutive outside* that the "positive" meaning of any term – and thus its "identity" – can be constructed' (Hall 1996: 2, 4–5). For Tariq Ramadan faith is the centre of Muslim identity: 'The first and most important Muslim identity is *faith* [...] In the many debates involving sociologists and political scientists, this dimension is often forgotten, as if faith and spirituality cannot be considered as scientific data with an objective "identity"' (Ramadan 2004: 79; italics in text). For Ramadan Muslim identity takes its point of departure from the *shahada* (declaration of faith): 'Muslims testify to their faith and state a clear foundation for their identity: they are Muslim, believe in God, in His messengers, in the angels, in the revealed Books, in fate, and in the day of judgement' (ibid.: 74–5). In relation to non-Muslims, from the early days of its inception Islam contained the concept of *dar* (house, dwelling) defining a society in which Muslims lived and practised their religion. In the past this constituted 'a line of demarcation between them and non-Muslims [...] on the basis of considerations of space' (75). 'The old binary geographical representation, with two juxtaposed universes', that is the *dar al-salaam* (abode of peace) of Islamic territories and the *dar al-harb* (land of conflict) where non-Muslims dwelt, amounted to 'a schema of two "houses" living the reality of a "confrontation"' (75–6). The operation of Self and Other is thus tacitly recognized by Ramadan; he is aware of the construction of Muslim identity according to its 'constitutive outside', the *dar al-harb*. However, in relation to a modern Muslim identity, according to Ramadan the former conditions no longer apply: the old binaries are re-configured in the modern world of globalization which has its centre in the West with the rest of the planet its periphery. Now, by reason of their migration, Muslims settled in the West find themselves 'at the *center*, at the *heart*, in the *head* of the system that produces the symbolic apparatus of Westernization' (ibid.: original italics). Since this society accords them rights to practise their religion it must not be considered as *dar al-harb*. Ramadan calls for western Muslims to view their new situation as constituting an area of responsibility and testimony. In terms of identity it requires a re-orientation: for Muslims living in the West their identity must be protected and actualized 'not as Arabs, Pakistanis or Indians but as Westerners' (83).[1]

Muslims as a Non-Western Other

In the liberal West, as among Muslims, the Other has been construed both in relation to what it is not and to what it lacks. During the last two decades a shift has also occurred in the way Muslims have been viewed by mainstream society:

this embodies a change in attitude in which Muslims have come to be judged as constituting a distinct religious grouping rather than (as was largely the case beforehand) an ethnic minority or collection of ethnic minorities. In Britain the public awareness of the Muslim presence coincided with the agitation against Salman Rushdie's novel *The Satanic Verses* which, it has been argued, was fanned by an Islamist agenda of international proportions (Kepel 1997: 126–45). As a result, a *Kulturkampf* against Islam has been invoked with the aim of refuting and nullifying the perceived 'Islamic threat' to western values, in the process re-asserting these values as universals constitutive of the entire programme of modernity.[2] The *Kulturkampf* operates as an articulation of the binary of ourselves and the Other, asserting the pre-eminence of a secular self that is culturally and politically hegemonic. However, in the process this clash of cultures has precipitated anxieties and inconsistencies that undermine that secular self. The successive impacts of the Rushdie Affair, the wars in Bosnia and Chechnya, and the terror attacks of 9/11 each added their inflection to how Muslim identities have been perceived. Integral to this shift in attitudes were the events surrounding the publication of *The Satanic Verses* and the 9/11 attack on the New York World Trade Center. The latter event in particular intensified the 'clash of civilizations' theory at a time when one third of the world's Muslims live as members of minorities outside of the Muslim world (Roy 2002: 18). In the West Muslims as a group are stigmatized for cultural backwardness and religious fanaticism. Outmoded stereotypes emphasize religious and cultural separatism/antagonism. Increasingly identification by religion has been imposed upon Muslims by a variety of factors including political, societal and media pressure, cultural chauvinism, and Muslims' own perceived need for self-definition.

Coverage given to Islam in the western media has tended to set it apart as a religion, and has all too frequently turned its followers, the Muslims, individually and collectively into oddities or deviants from the norms of modern civilization – the 'barbarians at the gates' (and in this linked to Communists and Nazis) in the words of a recent book.

Liberal secularist Sam Harris believes that the West is not at war with terrorism, nor even with Islamic terrorism, but with 'Islam itself', with 'the vision of life that is prescribed to all Muslims in the Koran'. The distinction between moderate and fundamentalist Muslims is irrelevant because 'most Muslims appear to be "fundamentalist" in the Western sense of the word'. 'Is Islam compatible with a civil society?' asked Harris. 'Is it possible to believe what you must believe to be a good Muslim, to have military and economic power, and not to pose an unconscionable threat to the civil societies of others? I believe that the answer to this question is no' (Malik 2009: 206).[3]

Harris equates *all* forms of Islam with fundamentalism. This is done in such a way as to make Islam out-fundamentalize every other type of fundamentalism

(Christian, Jewish, Hindu or whatever). At a moment in history when attacks of a religious, racial, or national kind are assiduously policed in the West, such licensed invective against a religion that has existed for over 1400 years, contiguous to and for more than 600 of those actually within parts of western Christendom, might cause us to consider: what is it about Islam that makes it so distinctive and unacceptable in some people's eyes?[4] The most prominent contemporary codification of criticisms against Islam derives from the secular, liberal, pro-Enlightenment, pro-freedom of speech, ideology that is prevalent in much of Europe and the United States of America. John Esposito (1995) sums this up as a stereotype that sets 'the modern, developed, secular, rational Western mind versus the traditional, underdeveloped, religious, emotional, irrational Muslim mind' (xx).[5] A related antagonistic perspective often espoused by the Christian Right (and invested in by Jewish conservatives) argues that western civilization is founded on Judeo-Christian values to which Islam (in spite of its obvious connections with Christianity and Judaism) is somehow inimical. These ideas underpin Italian Prime Minister Silvio Berlusconi's remark: 'We must be aware of the superiority of our civilization, a system that has guaranteed well-being, respect for human rights and – in contrast with Islamic countries – respect for religious and political rights.'[6]

Why mark out Islam and its followers in such a way among all the other problems that beset modern humanity? First of all, it is important to probe contexts before we can answer this question. According to Edward Mortimer, after the removal of the iron curtain and collapse of the Soviet bloc, westerners identified with liberated eastern Europeans, who in part had been led by Christian dissidents and the Churches, as 'sharing our culture and religious heritage and aspiring to share our freedom and prosperity'. That led westerners to emphasize 'what we had in common with them, but not with others: human nature is such that a group has to be defined by what it is not, as well as what it is. Many even felt the need to discover a new threat to replace the Soviet one. For both purposes "Islam" lay ready to hand' (Mortimer 1991: 10). Especially in the United States some Cold War warriors seamlessly transferred their attention from Communism to a global Muslim threat. 'Charles Krauthammer, in the midst of the unravelling of the Soviet Union, spoke of a global Islamic uprising, a vision of Muslims in the heartland and on the periphery of the Muslim world rising up in revolt: a "new 'arc of crisis'"' (Esposito 1995: 208). An historical enmity between Islam and Christendom was thus incorporated into 'a new myth':

> The impending confrontation between Islam and the West is presented as part of a historical pattern of Muslim belligerency and aggression that is now viewed as a potential domestic threat, given the significant presence and growth of Muslim communities (ibid.: 209).

The 1990s saw a huge outlay of journalistic and academic expertise seeking to give credibility to this notion, in many ways crystallized in Samuel Huntingdon's 'clash of civilizations' paradigm, about which Dale Eickelman wrote: 'A principal difficulty with [his] "West versus the Rest" formulation is that, having reintroduced culture and religion to thinking about politics, he overstated their coherence and force, in addition to treating the Muslim world as a monolithic bloc' (Eickelman 2000: 122–3). Nonetheless, the critics of Islam, with the aim of demonstrating what was wrong with Muslims, focused on how their religion and culture disabled their embrace of modernity, especially democracy and human rights, and made them a threat to the civilization created by the West, with its universalist principles. Such axioms could be demonstrated by the aid of those rational 'scientific' tools that in themselves testified to the superiority of the West or, depending on your point of view, were the latest version of Orientalist mumbo-jumbo. One political scientist set out to test empirically the 'extent to which democracy and Islam' were 'mutually exclusive [...] with implications for civilizational conflict and democratic peace' (Midlarsky 1998: 485). While claiming to be empirical, the model starts with Huntingdon's presumption of Islam's proclivity towards 'civilizational conflict', and Middle East Studies expert Bernard Lewis' thesis that Islam is oriented towards theocracy – and therefore by implication unsuited to democratic politics.

Thrown in for good measure is the Enlightenment nostrum that modernization and secularization demote the public role of religion while leaving it to the sphere of the individual; ergo, a society which is guided by 'revealed truth' 'tends to be more autocratic'. While building in a number of variables such as colonial influence, income, and land (as opposed to sea) borders, the study proceeds on the a priori assumptions that 'Islam is negatively related to democracy'; the larger the Muslim population the greater the likelihood Islamic law will be adhered to, and thus the greater will be the likelihood of autocracy (ibid.: 492–3). One of the more bizarre observations thrown up by this pseudo-science is the following inference derived from rainfall patterns:

The amount of precipitation can distinguish between the more Islamized Middle Eastern countries that have little precipitation, hence a presumed tendency toward autocracy, and the less Islamized countries such as Indonesia and Malaysia with abundant rainfall that might be exempt from this environmental constraint (ibid.: 496).

Articles like Midlarsky's, we might interpose, are out of the archive. Their provenance is Orientalism. But as the *Kulturkampf* against Muslims as a non-western Other intensified in the late 1990s, so did animosity against Islam as a religious faith. In spite of its apparent grounding in belief in the superiority of Judeo-Christian civilization à la Berlusconi, this animosity represented a deepening of the trend, which I've already pointed out in the introduction, away from faith per se, and towards secular materialism.

Secularism Confronts Islam

Dale Eickelman points out: 'The prevailing secularist bias of many current theories of society has alternately marginalized and demonized religious forces and religious intellectuals [...] trends in the Muslim world [...] have been characterized as especially resistant to "modernity"' (Eickelman 2000: 132). In secular western societies inscription of Muslim culture is seen for the most part to proceed on the basis of binaries already set out above, in which values of modernity, rationality, liberalism and toleration are set against intolerance, fundamentalism, fanaticism and patriarchal chauvinism. The latter are deemed by western writers and their native converts to be inherent to Muslim belief and practice. The fact that diasporic or ethnically hybrid writers with Muslim connections appear to endorse invective against Islam and Muslims may or may not obscure their desire and ability to adopt a 'liberal' position with regards to the racism and violence often directed against migrants in western societies. In terms of representation, however, while the sympathies of such writers may be with the individual migrant (a Shahid in *The Black Album* or a Nazneen in *Brick Lane*) these usually do not extend to migrant communities, and their fiction more often than not incorporates two-dimensional versions of Islam and Muslim fundamentalists. Writers such as Salman Rushdie, Hanif Kureishi and Monica Ali do not present migrant Muslims' beliefs and attitudes from the inside, but instead promote a western secular agenda. This may be because the supposed bifurcation between 'Islam and the West' forces such writers, consciously or unconsciously, to make a choice between two competing narratives. Overwhelmingly, they identify with a West 'allegedly defined by a set of values[:] freedom of expression, democracy, separation of church and state, human rights, and, especially, women's rights' which is in itself partially constructed and iterated with a Muslim opposite in mind (Roy 2007: vii). What is rarely acknowledged or even understood is that 'the paradigms and models mobilized in Western debate over Islam hardly reflect the real practices of Muslims.' That is to say: 'the political debate over the potential danger allegedly represented by Muslims [...] more or less inspired by the intellectual debate about the "clash of civilizations"' is a model that needs to be abandoned 'in order to understand how it is possible to practise one's faith as a Muslim in a secularized Western context' (ibid.: x). This is connected to what, in *Secularism Confronts Islam*, Roy posits as a bind within western secularist discourse: western ways of managing immigrant Muslim populations, be they militantly secularist (*laïcist*) in the French mode, or multicultural in the Anglo-Saxon, both posit 'a link between religion and culture'. But, among the young at least, 'today's religious revival [...] develops by decoupling itself from cultural references. It thrives on the loss of cultural identity [...] Islam is not seen as a cultural relic but as a religion that is universal and global' (xi). When Roy likens the universalizing and globalizing Muslim faith of young immigrants and indigenous converts to evangelicalism and Protestantism, he is both naturalizing and demystifying it within a western context. It is no longer alien and other. But secularists, be they proponents of laicism or multiculturalism, still perceive this Islam of second/third generation migrants as a threat. Both types converge in their disquiet over public wearing of the veil which they decode as a sign of religious extremism. For Roy, however, what is at stake is the more profound issue of 'the articulation of religious identity within the public space and therefore the questioning of secularism' (xii).[7]

Although Mortimer contended that secularism 'is not synonymous with godlessness, or with hostility to religion as such' (Mortimer 1991: 7) recent denigration of religion in the West suggests otherwise. As long ago as 1965, Harvey Cox made a distinction between the process of *secularization* and the formulation of what we might today term a fundamentalist *secularism*. The triumph of secularization over God and the creation of a 'godless society', linked to the arrival of the modern 'technopolis', forced Christianity out of the public arena into a private space (Cox 1966: 164). Cox, however, made a clear distinction between secularization and secularism. Secularization delivered culture and society from tutelage to religious control and a closed metaphysical world-view and was 'basically a liberating development'. Secularism, on the other hand, is an ideology, 'a new closed world-view which functions very much like a new religion [...] Like other isms it menaces the openness and freedom secularization has produced' (21).[8] Since the 1960s a religious challenge to secularism has emerged, initially in the form of Christian fundamentalism, and later by the appearance of a revivalist Islam demanding a presence within the de-sacralized western public space. The secularist triumphalism of the 1960s, which seemed to have rolled back the traditional religious establishment in Britain, was shaken by the Rushdie Affair of the late 1980s, and by the so-called jihadists of the early 2000s, revealing the 'uncertainties and insecurities of Western societies about the worth of basic liberal values' (Malik 2009: 208).

The perceived threat posed by Islam to the cultural values of western societies by the Muslim immigration accompanied the moment Islamism made its appearance on the political stage in the form of movements endeavouring to rectify the powerlessness of Muslims who had no super-state to protect them or express the 'transnational but invisible bond which connects the world of Islam [...] itself a type of virtual empire' (Allawi 2009: 142). The political element within Islam has not of course gone unrecognized by western writers, many of whom argue, as does Bernard Lewis, that Islam aims at 'a polity ruled by God' – a theocratic state. 'For believing Muslims, legitimate authority comes from God alone, and the ruler derives his power not from the people, nor yet from his ancestors, but from God and the holy law' (Lewis 1993). That implies Muslims do not do normal secular, democratic politics, but remain caught in the bind of autocracy and dictatorship, secular or religious.[9] Ernest Gellner, on the other hand, saw revivalist Islam as the winning out of 'High Islam', the puritanical, scripturalist Islam of urban scholasticism and the traditional bourgeoisie, which supplied the function of nationalism in the struggle against western colonialism. In modern Muslim nations reformed Islam 'confers a genuine shared identity on what would otherwise be a mere summation of the underprivileged' and defies the secularization thesis that religion withers away in modernized societies (Gellner 1992: 15,18). However, other western writers and political theorists now see in the Muslim Brotherhood (founded in 1928), the Jama'at Islami formed around the ideas of Abul Ala Mawdudi in the 1940s, and the more recent Islamist parties influenced by figures like Sayyid Qutb and Ruhollah Khomeini, a politics derived from modern European totalitarian movements. John Gray (2007) goes so far as to categorize radical Islam as 'a recent western construction' and 'a by-product of late modern globalisation' (xvii). Al-Qaeda specifically, for all its apparently anti- or pre-modern tenets, is 'a modern organisation' in which 'modern western influences are fused with Islamic themes' (ibid.: 79). Writers like Gray and Malise Ruthven see Islamic fundamentalism as a kind of oriental Frankenstein's monster, a flawed response to the McDonaldization of the world (Ruthven 2002: 26–5), and 'a symptom of the disease of which it pretends to be a cure' (Gray 2007: 26). But where Meghnad Desai (2007) separates Islam as a religion from Islamism by categorizing the latter as a political ideology, Gray defines the war between Al-Qaeda and the West as 'a war of religion' in which the 'Enlightenment idea of a universal civilization, which the West upholds against radical Islam, is an offspring of Christianity [and] Al-Qaeda's peculiar hybrid of theocracy and anarchy is a by-product of western radical thought' (Gray 2007: 116–17).

Nonetheless, secularists' fears and anxieties remain directed against Islam as a religion, particularly in so far as it represents a challenge to the secularized public space. The Muslim is not so much a new figure as the return of a repressed earlier type many in western society believe has disappeared. That is, the Muslim has a lot in common with a previous bogeyman, the Jew. This habit of separating out one section of society as different, as outside of civilized codes or engaged in diabolic practices ought to ring alarm bells in Europe. In *In Bluebeard's Castle*, a series of lectures delivered little more than a generation after the opening of the Nazi concentration camps, George Steiner proposed, among other things, that the new Europe had not yet exorcized the ghosts of its millions of Jewish dead, nor begun to recognize the cultural erasure their deaths had brought about. For Steiner, though he admitted in holding this opinion he was in 'minority one', Europe hated the Jew because:

> In his exasperating 'strangeness', in his acceptance of suffering as part of a covenant with the absolute, the Jew became, as it were, the 'bad conscience' of western history. In him the abandonments of spiritual and moral perfection, the hypocrisies of an established, mundane religiosity, the absences of a disappointed, potentially vengeful God, were kept alive and visible (Steiner 1971: 41).

'When it turned on the Jew, Christianity and European civilization turned on the incarnation – albeit an incarnation wayward and often unaware – of its own best hopes' (ibid.). In its belated guilt-ridden attempts to atone for the holocaust the West has incorporated aspects of modern Jewish experience into its sanctioned narratives: denial of the historical fact of the holocaust becomes a criminal offence; *The Diary of Anne Frank* is afforded the status of a sacred secular text; the Jewish right of return to Israel is upheld without question. In this way the West exorcizes (or believes it has exorcized) its bad conscience over the Jews. Support for the State of Israel founded upon a Zionist ideology that is secular (however deeply under threat from within that secularism may be today) lends to western governments and societies the illusion that the religious claims of a Judaism Europe spent most of its history seeking to extirpate, have now been laid to rest. For secular Jewish voices, now situated at the centre of western narratives about liberty, freedom of conscience and so on, the recrudescence of a creed that keeps alive a potentially vengeful God with a religious law that in many ways appears a simulacrum of the Judaism of their ancestors, can only bring alive anxieties they would prefer kept dead and buried.

Islam as a religion is the unwelcome guest at the feast of western secularism. For all its supposed, easily derided pre-modern crudity it stands, like Steiner's earlier ugly Judaism, as a reminder that humanity in its entirety has yet to throw off the lendings of transcendental longing and embrace the brave new world formed upon liberty, hedonism and a mind-numbing obsession with electronic technology. From a political point of view, Ashis Nandy, a self-confessed secularist and agnostic, has cast doubt upon the project of enlightenment secularism and its attitude to religion, both in civilizational terms and those of post-secular democracy. Emphasizing the comparatively brief existence of enlightenment secularism in contrast to the 5000 years of civilization built upon religious belief, he castigates the growing tendency of secular states to look upon the followers of religion as 'demonic others that need to be de-fanged'. The elites who run democracies of both East and West may fear and bemoan the unenlightened religious individuals and parties democratic elections produce, but the language of religion is 'still a living reality and a crucial vector within contemporary political cultures' (Nandy 2006).

Islam, Postmodernism and Fundamentalism

Critics of the critics of Islam invariably start out by drawing upon Edward Said's catalogue of western stereotyping of Islam set out in *Orientalism*. Said's work has been vital in so far as it demonstrates a long persisting Othering of an historic enemy. However, Bobby Sayyid goes further than Said in positing an Islam that is outside the monolith of Orientalism, indeed outside of the West; he also decouples the unique connection between the West and modernity by building on the arguments of Gianni Vattimo and Robert Young that diasporic writers

decentred and decolonized European thought and culture and established
the postmodern critique of modernity. 'The postmodern critique of modernity
seems to disarticulate the West from modernity [...] The decentring of the West
means the weakening of narratives that constructed western identity [...] If the
West is no longer a unified entity, it cannot provide the unity to modernity'
(Sayyid 1997: 110). For Sayyid there is no one modernity ('modernity is not just
the rationality of the Enlightenment but also the savagery of the Holocaust').
A West that is no longer the centre cannot hold court over the Rest (à la
Huntingdon) – 'If the West is decentred, it must be decentred in relation to
the non-West; without a centre, there can be no periphery [...] If there is no
one Europe there can be no one modernity' (ibid). Sayyid's interest in Islam is
focused on its modern political expression Islamism, and in particular on the
Iranian Islamism of Khomeini. Postmodernity's decentring of the West opens
the way for Sayyid 'to understand Khomeini's political discourse as a manifestation of the decentring of the West' (ibid.: 113). It is not necessary to endorse
this form of Islamism in order to appreciate the value of Sayyid's argument as
a critique of the western critics of Islam that shifts the discussion away from
the obvious Orientalist methods adopted by Midlarsky et al., and focuses on
the 'fundamental fear' that activates such critics. As the blurb on Sayyid's
bookcover announces: the fear and anxiety which the so-called Islamic threat
arouses is tied up with how Islamism contests the notion that 'West is best' and
forces the need to 're-think Western identity'.

Anouar Majid has continued Sayyid's work in a number of ways, particularly
in the opposition he raises against the dominance of secular western humanism
which he argues should no longer exercise dominance in the world. Majid's
critique of Edward Said the postcolonial intellectual is that – in spite of his
championing of the Third World – he continued to think in terms of liberal
western humanism. Such a frame of thought needs to be critiqued in terms of
its putative universality. In practice, Orientalism (or secular western thinking)
as Said pointed out, only provides a 'reading of Others, especially Islam, as
a list of "absences" – capitalism, cities, civil society, democracy etc. – and the
transfer of the West's anxieties of the Orient. Viciously solipsistic in its textu-
alistic approach, [Orientalism] is remarkably immune to global changes and
remains "captive to a metahistorical schemata" in which the "homo islamicus" is
frozen into an unchanging past' (Majid 2000: 67–8). Despite global capitalism's
seemingly inexorable spread throughout the world, bringing in its wake the
deculturation of non-western societies, for Majid: 'One simply cannot find hope
in the expansionist agenda of a Eurocentric modernity, since it is premised on
an un-negotiable intolerance of Others and a polarizing, wasteful and unsus-
tainable economy' (ibid.: 136). Given that 'the secular structures fit badly into
cultures in which human agency is constantly negotiating its boundaries with
those of Revelation, in which accommodation to the divine intent is a fundamental principle' there is a need to create non-capitalist spaces 'at a time when
the reigning ideology of capitalism has de-sacralized all of human life' (118).

For Majid both Arab nationalism and Islamism are effectively products of Orientalism in reverse – the rhetorics of anti-Semitism and anti-Muslimism were introduced respectively into the Arab world by Maronite Christians and into Israel by Zionism, and both are of European Orientalist provenance. Moreover, Arab nationalism and militant Islamism 'have been unable to articulate a different position that takes the collective fate of humanity into account' (72). The nation-state has had catastrophic effects in the Third World; the separation of religion and state is a tenuous proposition in the world of Islam. Islam is cosmopolitan, but has been unable to eradicate inequalities based on class, gender and religion. Like Said, Majid believes that the problems of the Arab and Muslim world cannot be solved by a return to the seventh century. The challenge of the universalizing ideology of modernity cannot be resisted by a return to a historically bounded sharia or by proving the infallibility of the Qur'an. The 'Historical conditions of [...] an Islamic community that lived more than a thousand, five hundred, or even fifty years ago cannot be recuperated, even by Muslims speaking the same language and using the same religious and literary texts' (147). Equally however, he finds little attraction in Salman Rushdie's postmodern project of the 'dismantling of traditional convictions and the redeeming of people into a liberating hybridity'. An invention of a specific set of historical circumstances in the West, secularism has to be rejected by the Muslim world as 'part of Muslims' struggle for self-definition' (39, 42). Much as the Jews were hated by Europeans for maintaining their faith in a transcendent God, today Muslims cannot be accepted because they uphold the same creator and reject secularism. Moreover, notions of human rights and the individual packaged up in western modernity are not universally applicable. Modern notions of civil society and freedom presume pre-Muslim states were despotic when in fact these societies left a lot of open spaces as seen in Bedouin, Sufi, and other traditional social arrangements. Western-inspired human rights assume the sovereignty of the individual, not the community (124). Majid calls for a third way for modern Islam that charters a route outside of the failed modernist ideologies and clerical Islam and which is both indigenous and progressive. He finds hope for this in the still largely unread manifesto of Mahmud Muhammad Taha, *The Second Message of Islam* (126). Furthermore, Muslims and other members of non-western traditional cultures have to delink themselves from the expanding and intensified process of capitalist exploitation. 'A postnationalist, Islamically progressive identity can contribute not only to Muslims' autonomy but also to the forging of new cultural solidarities in a polycentric world' (72).

Sayyid and Majid both have a place alongside critics of Eurocentrism and the Enlightenment epistemological tradition who have also been influenced by postmodernism, such as poststructuralists and postcolonialists. Sayyid as we have seen uses poststructuralism to aid his own deconstruction of the West's image of Islam. Nonetheless the persistence of what are basically Orientalist attacks against Muslims well into the postmodern period suggests either a continuation of modernist modes of thinking, or that postmodernism has its own bone to pick with Islam. The most likely answer is that both propositions are correct. Kenan Malik demonstrates a near fundamentalist commitment to Enlightenment secularism and a vitriolic distaste for the relativistic postmodern multiculturalism of those who have no stomach for confronting Islamism on a modernist platform. But as for postmodern thinkers such as Derrida, Baudrillard, Žižek – and Foucault himself – each of these, as Ian Almond demonstrates in *The New Orientalists: Postmodern Representations of Islam* (2007), has followed the Orientalist practice of 'producing discourse about Orientals, but never includ[ing] them or allow[ing] them to speak'; and of maintaining 'the peripherality of the Islamic world and Western thought's equally peripheral consideration of it' (164–5). Almond shows how 'from a non-European perspective […] postmodernity to a large extent inherits in an altogether subtler way many of the Orientalist/imperialist tropes that had been so prevalent in modernity' (4). Certainly, from the point of view of Muslims themselves postmodern theory has its own axioms that remain antagonistic to Islam. As Bryan Turner puts it: 'In epistemological terms postmodernism threatens to deconstruct all theological accounts of reality into mere fairy tales or mythical grand narratives which disguise the metaphoricality of their commentaries to a (false) authorship' (Turner 1994: 92).

The so-called clash of civilizations between the West and Islam is often articulated as a confrontation between fundamentalism and modernity in which Islamic fundamentalism manifests as an anti-modern reaction to the licence, immorality and cultural decadence of western modernity. Stuart Sim defines fundamentalism as 'the search for purity of thought and deed' (Sim 2004: 212). Ruthven sets Islamic alongside Christian, Jewish and Hindu fundamentalisms, defining the fundamentalist mentality as '"a religious way of being" that manifests itself in a strategy by which beleaguered believers attempt to preserve their distinctive identity as a people or group in the face of modernity and secularization' (Ruthven 2004: 8). Within the context of Middle Eastern and other Islamic nations, fundamentalism may function as a code of resistance to westernizing modernity, which is perceived as 'wholly materialistic, devoid of spiritual values'. Muslim students studied by Susan Waltz '"come to see their lives bifurcated between an Islamic culture that provides moral values, community and spiritual satisfaction, and a Western culture that provides access to the material improvement of their lives".' As embodied in fundamentalist Islamism, this frame of mind sees itself through the eyes of the West in a type of Orientalism in reverse – 'the West "continues to serve as the standard by which Muslims evaluate their own culture"' (Ruthven 2002: 120–1).

In contrast to a Muslim living within a majority Muslim state who on account of globalization still might feel Islam to have been 'minoritised', a Muslim migrant is ascribed a distinct Muslim identity (Roy 2002: 19). Such a migrant's response to western modernity can be even more pressured than his or her counterpart within the Muslim *umma* if Roy is to be believed:

Especially in times of political crisis (such as 9/11), ordinary Muslims feel compelled (or are explicitly asked) to explain what it means to be a Muslim [...] This task falls on the shoulders of every Muslim, rather than on legitimate religious authorities, simply because [...] there are so few or no established Muslim authorities in the West. Each Muslim is accountable for being a Muslim [...] To publicly state self-identity has become almost a civic duty for Muslims (ibid.: 24).

Moreover, Roy's taxonomy of 'globalised Islam' in the twenty-first century establishes that Muslim 'fundamentalists' (or 'neo-fundamentalists' as he terms them), living within the traditional Islamic spaces, do not seek to 'articulate an antimodernist reaction from among traditional sectors of society. They are actors of deculturation and change inside traditional societies [...] contribut[ing] to the collapse (or the adaptation) of traditional societies and pav[ing] the way for other forms of westernisation and globalisation' (ibid.: 262). The deterritorialization of Islam, which Roy emphasizes has nothing to do with Islam itself, helps bring about a universalized form of Islam delinked from the specificities of local cultures. Not only does this constitute a form of religious reformation, it also challenges the construction of Muslims within a simple binary of opposition to modernity and the West, however much this may be re-iterated by those who continue to wish to assert the superiority of western civilization above Islam.

Muslim identities Pre- and Post-9/11

The main contention of the remainder of this chapter is that, as far as Britain is concerned, Muslim identity as we know it today arose in the context of the rise of Islamism and its perceived threat to 'the West'. This activated dormant Eurocentric notions of Muslim otherness embedded in western culture by the colonial narrative of the superiority of European civilization over non-European, backward, traditional, pre-modern areas of the world. It will be useful to sketch out the period from the late eighties up to the present in so far as this pertains to the key issues informing the representation of Islam and Muslims. These relate to whether Muslims were seen primarily as an ethnic minority or a religious grouping, and to what extent they were stereotyped as dangerous and fanatical.

In its December 2006 issue, the *Journal of Muslim Minority Affairs* published three articles devoted to media representation of Muslims in Britain, France and Australia, and to attitudes towards multiculturalism in the European Union. To varying degrees the articles provide evidence for the propositions that: (a) during the period mentioned a shift occurred in the way Muslims were viewed by mainstream society; (b) this embodied a change in attitude in which Muslims came to be judged as constituting a distinct religious grouping rather than part of ethnically constituted minorities; and (c) as a group Muslims were deemed to be prone to (often dangerous) religious fanaticism. While views of Muslims during this period continued to draw on Orientalist stereotypes long prevalent in the West, according to Brown (2006) fanaticism and delinquency came to be privileged over exoticism and sensuality. Brown's article is indeed structured around what he considers 'the "paradigmatic shift" from an exotic, sensual stereotype of Islam to a stereotype of Muslim fanaticism (predominant at the time of the Rushdie affair, for example), which prepared the ground for responses to 9/11' (297). In her study of Australian media representations of Muslims in the early 2000s, Nahid Kabir tests Muslim Australians' belief that 'the Western media [...] aggravated anti-Muslim sentiment since the 1990–1991 Gulf Crisis, and after September 11, 2001 and the Bali tragedy in 2002, effectively divid[ing] the world into Muslim terrorists ("bad") and civilised Christians ("good")' (313). Among her conclusions is the clear sense that 'contemporary media representation of Islam and Muslims focuses on Islamic militants, effectively demonising all the Muslim people' (326). Finally, in an article entitled 'Muslims and Multiculturalism in the European Union', H.A. Hellyer underlines the shift from categorizing Muslims according to ethnicity to viewing them as a religious grouping (2006: 329).

In the case of Britain the growth of a Muslim community can also be studied as an historic development distinct from singular events like the Rushdie Affair and 9/11. Winter (2002) connects the emergence of a British Muslim identity to a process of 'embedding Islam in Britain' which from an Islamic perspective can be seen as 'another chapter in a long story of accommodation of minoritarian Muslim communities, a process for which there is ample precedent in Islamic law and in [Islamic] history' (21). Adopting a diachronic perspective, he presents the Muslim presence in Britain as a grafting onto earlier indigenous religious traditions according to a 'process of assimilation to aspects of Britishness' (6). What is interesting for our argument is how Winter discerns this change of consciousness as involving a dropping of ethnic forms of Muslim practice ('rooted in rural particularities') in favour of more global ('universalised') forms: 'It is clear that aspects of South Asian rustic pieties of the supernatural, even of the magical, are giving way here to various scripturalisms, both normatively traditional and Salafist' (6–7). Malise Ruthven (2002) confirms the view that modern Islamism is universalist in its pretension and markedly opposed to localized Sufism and nationalism (266–7). The relationship between Islam and ethnicity is specifically foreground by Ruthven in his probing of the issues behind the *Satanic Verses* controversy. Describing the Hyde Park demonstration of 27 May 1989, he describes the Muslim protestors in the following terms:

They came in their thousands from Bradford and Dewsbury, Bolton and Macclesfield, the old industrial centres; from outer suburbs like Southall and Woking; from Stepney and Whitechapel in London's East end, from the cities of Wolverhampton, Birmingham, Manchester and Liverpool. They wore white hats and long white baggy trousers with flapping tails. Most of them were bearded; the older men looked wild and scraggy with curly, grey-flecked beards – they were mountain men from Punjab, farmers from the Ganges delta, peasants from the hills of Mirpur and Cambellpur. After decades of living in Britain, they still looked utterly *foreign*: even in Hyde Park, a most cosmopolitan part of a very cosmopolitan city [...] (Ruthven 1991: 1; original italics).

Ruthven proposes one explanation for the demonstrators' injured sensitivities in the 'Indo-Muslim identity, forged in centuries of conflict with the polymorphous expressions of Hindu pantheism, [being] still unsure of itself [...] It thrives on conflict and persecution, for only through such can it reinforce its sense of distinctiveness' (9). But while Muslims of South Asian origin were calculated as constituting around 80 per cent of the more than two million Muslims in Britain in the early 1990s, by no means all of these were as ethnically exotic as the Ruthven quote implies. Literati such as Tariq Ali, Hanif Kureishi and Farhana Sheikh, while of Indo-Pakistani origin, describe elitist family backgrounds which in both Ali and Kureishi's case were secular if not atheist in orientation.

As for Muslim migration into Europe, Olivier Roy sees a similar process of Muslim movement away from ethnic particularities towards new streamlined forms facilitated by the process of globalization. The deterritorialization arising from globalization means that diasporic Muslim communities 'have to reinvent what makes them Muslim' with the result that the 'common defining factor of this population is the mere reference to Islam, with no common cultural or linguistic heritage' (Roy 2002: 18). Far from contradicting Winter's assertion that the late twentieth century saw a refocusing of a traditional Islamic metanarrative based on texts accepted throughout the Sunni Muslim world, Roy, like Winter, seems to be emphasizing Islam's adaptability, its capacity for reformulation outside of traditional Muslim heartlands (the lands of the *dar al-Islam*) according to conditions of modernity. Such a process presented the conditions – especially for British-born Muslims for whom their parents' traditional cultural Islam held little attraction – to engage with what 'an all-encompassing ideology seeking an imaginary space beyond a lost territory' (ibid.: 107). For these young offspring of migrants the inability of Muslims to impact on the contemporary world combined with a refusal of the civilized, secular West to accord Islam respect helped make identity an issue of religion rather than ethnicity. For white society 'Muslim' connoted adherence to an Islam expressed in conservative, fanatical, fundamentalist values and beliefs. Malik seems to think this was inevitable given the self-appointed leaders who stepped forward to represent the entirety of British Muslims during the Rushdie Affair (Malik 2009: 165). Needless to say, the racial prejudice of the indigenous white society had hardly gone away. Describing the in-betweeness of Muslim youth born in Britain who experienced the countries of their Asian parents as 'a largely alien world', Ansari (2004) writes: 'It is Islam, they assert, that perhaps plays the most important part in their lives.' Feeling themselves 'as part of a maligned minority', their Muslim identity empowers them to identify themselves 'with global Islam [...] to see themselves as part of a potentially powerful community' (18–19).

The Rushdie Affair: Inscribing a Conflict of Cultures

From Fatwa to Jihad: The Rushdie Affair and its Legacy – the determinism is of course enabled by hindsight, but nonetheless the title says it all. Kenan Malik's logocentric narrative of barbarian intrusion into a Europe whose power of resistance has been hopelessly weakened by several decades of multiculturalism starts with an endorsement: Huntingdon's sermon on the unbridgeable gulf between two different civilizations and the impact this has on their views about 'the relations between God and man, the individual and the group, the citizen and the state, parents and children, husband and wife, as well as differing views of the relative importance of rights and responsibilities, liberty and authority, equality and hierarchy.' Huntingdon 'wrote those words' in 1993, but according to Malik in 2009 the binaries were still straightforward:

> [A]lready, four years earlier, many had seen in the battle over *The Satanic Verses* just such a civilizational struggle. On one side of the fault line stood the West, with its liberal democratic traditions, a scientific worldview and a secular, rationalist culture drawn from the Enlightenment: on the other was Islam, rooted in a pre-medieval [sic] theology, with its seeming disrespect for democracy, disdain for scientific rationalism and deeply illiberal attitudes on everything from crime to women's rights. 'All over again,' the novelist Martin Amis would later write, 'the West confronts an irrationalist, agonistic, theocratic/ideocratic system which is essentially unappeasably opposed to its existence.' Amis wrote that while still in shock over 9/11. The germ of the sentiment was planted much earlier, in the Rushdie affair (Malik 2009: x–xi).

As far as Muslims were concerned, putting aside for a moment the sense of grievance many of them felt at what they perceived to be Salman Rushdie's attack on the character of their Prophet, the honour of his family and the foundations of their faith, the agitation that was raised against the book proved formative: from having been beforehand migrants split into different groups who were often vulnerable to racism, they emerged in Britain at least as visible cohesive communities strengthened by their experience. The President of the Bradford Council of Mosques gave Malise Ruthven the impression in June 1989 that 'in some ways [...] Salman Rushdie had done the Muslim community a favour [...] Bradford was definitely on the Islamic map, a Mecca of the north.'

The city's disparate mosques had acquired an umbrella organization, Muslims were becoming more united, and the community realized it had put down roots; people now had no intention of returning to Pakistan (Ruthven 1991: 82). The Rushdie Affair succeeded in confirming old antipathies, but in the process it bolstered the identities of both sides by gathering them around two clashing narratives: western secularism's 'civilizational struggle' with Islam; and migrant Muslims' sense of an emerging global Islamic identity that over-rode the cultural particularisms of the past.

The struggle between the contesting narratives has largely obscured the issues raised by *The Satanic Verses* as a text. Amin Malak poses a question about author motivation that some purists would consider theoretically irrelevant – 'Was it blasphemy? Offense? Self-hate? Racism? Or simply bad taste?' (Malak 2005: 101). Supporters of Rushdie might demur at this – not because of the impropriety or theoretical naivety of raising author intention – but because they deem an author's right to compose and publish what they like sacrosanct, whatever their motivation. Rushdie's own shifting encapsulations of the novel's meaning, such as his claim that he wrote it as 'a secular man's reckoning with the religious spirit', would do as an answer, but whichever way he accounted for the novel's genesis the anger of his (mostly) Muslim critics was barely shaken. Shabbir Akhtar was among the first of these and we might at least sympathize with his argument that in Rushdie's biography of 'Mahound': '[T]he events and characters [...] bear so striking a resemblance to actual events and characters in Islamic history that one has grounds to doubt its status as merely fictional.' *The Satanic Verses* was no less than 'a character assassination of the Arabian prophet [...] a calculated attempt to vilify and slander Mohammed' (Akhtar 1989: 4–5, 6). Two literarily sophisticated Muslims claim the Rushdie Affair was 'a confrontation brought about by a postmodernist author in true postmodernist fashion, trying to write a traditional worldview out of history. The author is vigorously defended by postmodern secularists, whose position his text vindicates' (Sardar and Davies 1990: 7).

Vindications and condemnations of *The Satanic Verses* usually disclose more about the ideological preconceptions or sheer emotionality behind their writers' respective discourses than they do about the qualities or otherwise of the text. As Margaret Scanlan points out, each side either neglects to read the other's sacred/ esteemed text, or fails to read it in the prescribed way (Scanlan 2001: 21). In *Distorted Imagination: Lessons from the Rushdie Affair*, Muslim writers Sardar and Davies contextualize their outrage by earnestly setting out the tenets of Islam and the authentic facts of Islamic history (not Rushdie's travesties of them), as well as by invoking Said's *Orientalism*. The approach is effective in demarcating the offence in the eyes of Muslims and in part useful, at least in postcolonial terms, in situating Rushdie as a 'native informant' (or 'Brown Sahib', a term they borrow from Ashis Nandy). But on those who view the work as a masterpiece of postmodern mimicry and an emblem of western cultural sophistication, such rectification is only so much spent ammunition.

The rawness of M.H. Faruqi's response has probably not diminished: 'It doesn't matter if it's a fiction, a serious book, a dream – [...] the problem is the abusive and insulting way the Prophet is described in the most filthy language' (Appignanesi and Maitland 1989: 33). For Kenan Malik too the issues have certainly not gone away, though he is regretful that the Rushdie campaign has since foundered. On the notorious Bradford book-burning incident, while remaining sceptical concerning the afterthoughts of quondam anti-Rushdie activist Inayat Bungawalla, now respectable representative of the British Muslim community, he argues: '[T]oday, the radical, secular clamour, which found an echo in *The Satanic Verses*, has been reduced to a whisper, largely because it has been strangled by multicultural policy' (Malik 2009: 165).

One therefore cannot see Ian Almond's chapter in *The New Orientalists*, entitled 'The Islams of Salman Rushdie', balanced and considered as it is, either assuaging the anger of M.H. Faruqi or satisfying Kenan Malik. If anything, Almond's position is a revisionist one that satisfies neither side. He argues that there are at least four Islams in Rushdie's fiction and essays: (a) the Islam that the 'Enlightenment Rushdie' represents in *Midnight's Children* and *Shame* as backward-looking and 'unable to keep up with the pace of modernity'; (b) The 'entrepreneurial Islam' in *The Satanic Verses*, which owes not a little to Rushdie's argument with Mrs Thatcher; (c) The Islam that 'facilitates the nationalisms' of Pakistan and Bangladesh (again in *Midnight's Children* and *Shame*); and (d) Rushdie's 'positive portrayal of suffering, marginalized Muslim minorities' in *The Moor's Last Sigh*. Together with statements made in some of his essays concerning Sufi versions of Islam, overall, Almond argues, while seeking 'the identity of Islam through conflict rather than correspondence' Rushdie's struggle is against the idea of 'a single signifier for Islam'. Indeed at times he appears to endorse an alternative Islam which he sets against fundamentalist 'misrepresentations' of the Prophet's original liberal intentions (Almond 2007: 97–109). Almond's analysis, as I've already implied, does not detract from the point about the two narratives of cultural conflict I have been making so far. A notable feature of his chapter is that it says very little about *The Satanic Verses* whereas it is of course this text that has caused most of the furore concerning Rushdie's onslaught against Muslim identity.

For those like Kenan Malik the Rushdie Affair set things on a trajectory that led in slightly more than a decade to the events of 9/11. From having flexed its muscles over Rushdie, an emergent Muslim identity (linked or not with the attack of 9/11 – Malik hardly makes his case that there was a logical or causal connection) found itself confronted by a state-prosecuted militancy. Only partially satiated by the invasions of Afghanistan and Iraq, this reaction was characterized for the most part by an active demand, if not for vengeance, then at the very least for putting Islamism in its place. Inevitably, this impacted on the writing of Muslim identity to an unprecedented degree, and in the process scaled up the *Kulturkampf* against Islam exponentially. There were unleashed in print (and film) a plethora of fictional and non-fictional representations of 9/11 and the lessons that should be drawn from it. In post-9/11 fiction especially, images of the Muslim Other are seen to be fed by political and cultural neuroses afflicting western postmodernity which help account for a growing fixation on the 'Islamic fundamentalist' and 'Islamic terror' threat against the West.

Chapter 2

British Migrant Muslim Fiction: Farhana Sheikh, Hanif Kureishi, Monica Ali, Nadeem Aslam, Leila Aboulela

In this chapter I intend to focus on fiction from the 1990s and early 2000s that is about Islam and Islamic culture in a British context.[1] Since the Rushdie Affair, writing concerned with Muslim identity has become increasingly polarized. On the one hand the majority of texts incorporating Muslim identity from the '90s onward might be characterized as being written by what Spivak terms the westernized 'native informant' and Ashis Nandy 'the brown sahib'. Authors belonging to this category possess connections – usually through race – with peoples of Muslim culture, but they construct Islam and Muslims – whether traditionalist or revivalist – by employing recycled Orientalist tropes cast in the insider's voice. Muslims are represented largely in terms of female-disabling, fanatical, and aggressive characteristics. Hanif Kureishi's *The Black Album*, Monica Ali's *Brick Lane* and Nadeem Aslam's *Maps for Lost Lovers* are notable examples of this type of writing. On the other hand, neo-Muslim writing, such as that of Leila Aboulela, re-writes traditional, ethnic views of Islam and Muslims in terms of a twenty-first century global Islam that attracts believers from many different backgrounds including converts of hybrid non-European and European ethnicity. Despite their strongly opposed codification of Muslim identity, I intend to approach both sets of writer within the category of Muslim fiction.

Muslim authors Sardar and Davies argue of Salman Rushdie's fiction: 'A [Muslim] believer who stands within his or her own tradition is a character that never receives close, let alone sympathetic or empathetic attention in the artistic vision of Rushdie [...][He] is writing about Islam while censoring the majority of believing Muslims out of all his tales' (Sardar and Davies 1990: 138).[2] While we can hardly expect the informant type of writers to represent the varieties of Muslim immigrant practice in contemporary Britain with the religious commitment of Leila Aboulela, we might ask why it is not enough for them at least to do so without inscribing the 'clash of civilizations' stereotypes so clearly within their work. To actually embrace the religious mindset of the Muslim Other, debilitating though it might be in terms of one's cultural credibility – 'committing profession suicide' as a character in one of Aboulela's novels puts it – was and is still a possibility as her work testifies. In the broader context, statements on Islam by white British writers such as Fay Weldon (made during the Rushdie controversy), Martin Amis, Jeanette Winterson et al. (after 9/11) contribute to what amounts to a hegemonic literary discourse on Islam[3] to which the 'native informant' has been eager to connect him/herself.

From Ethnic Minority to Muslims: British Asians in Farhana Sheikh and Hanif Kureishi

In the final chapter of Bali Rai's novel *(un)arranged marriage*, the experiencing-I narrator, Manjit, looks back over his adolescent struggle to break free from his Punjabi Sikh family and make his own choices:

> I did confuse being a Jat Punjabi in the way that my old man saw it, with being a Sikh, which is something totally different. I've been reading up on it lately and I've found that Sikhism preaches tolerance and equality towards everything [...] Men, women. Black, white. All the same. The problem is that people like my old man tie in all these old traditions to the religion – arranged marriages, all that racist shit, the caste system stuff, things which are nothing to do with religion and more to do with culture and politics and social norms. My old man and his mates are the ones who are really confused; they're too ignorant to change their ways or even realize that they don't know what they are on about (Rai 2001: 270).

Rai's book is by no means unusual in its assault on the traditional practices of an ethnically based immigrant community living in the UK in the name of liberal western values. What is perhaps notable is the manner in which the narrator distinguishes between ethnically and culturally located practices and beliefs, and an essentialist religious idealism. Even allowing for the naïveté of the narrative voice, such a distinction could be invoked as a form of dissociation from hostile critics who conflate religion and ethnicity in their attacks against an ethnic community. In the case of Muslims, however, it might be argued there has been a growing tendency for hostile critics to refuse to make a similar separation between traditional practice and religious ideal. Equally, writers of Muslim background who began by conflating ethnicity and religion, have later on moved to writing about Islam in its modern de-cultured 'fundamentalist' form – indeed both approaches can be seen in the work of Rushdie (Almond 2007: Chapter 5).

I shall trace the movement from ethnicity to Muslim identity in 1990s British fiction by looking at Farhana Sheikh's *The Red Box* (1991) and Hanif Kureishi's *The Black Album* (1995). Sheikh's novel is set around 1980, and centres on Raisa, a young Anglo-Pakistani woman who as part of her Master's degree in education holds a series of interview/discussions with two pupils at an East London comprehensive, Nasreen and Tahira. From a privileged middle class Pakistani family, aged twenty-seven when the novel begins and thirty-one at its end, Raisa has a not so fresh memory of seeing *Women in Love* at sixteen. She is both attracted to the girls on account of their common gender, national and religious background, and at the same time guiltily aware of the class differences between herself and them. Sheikh is concerned with a number of intersecting issues: class, race, gender and culture as well as religion in *The Red Box*. The gulf of class and religion that separates secularized literati from the ordinary Pakistani at home and in diaspora has in the novel not yet precipitated into a bifurcation of a favoured narrative of western secularism as opposed to a disfavoured Islamist narrative. On the contrary, the aim of the author appears to be to unite her Muslim characters by emphasizing their similarities but without downplaying their differences. This is possible because the political atmosphere that pervades the novel concerns the racism of the 1980s rather than the anti-Muslim climate of the 1990s. The sessions between Raisa and the girls take place against a backdrop of racial tension between Asian and indigenous white students in the school. The common enemy is racist thuggery, and behind it an unjust system of immigration controls against which Asians of all religious persuasions and Afro-Caribbean (and even a small minority of white) students at the school can march and demonstrate in unity. The otherwise self-effacing Nasreen throws a chair at a white racist pupil while both girls express solidarity with Palestine. These causes, connected to the liberation and human rights narratives of the 1960s, '70s and early '80s, make the girls feel 'part of a bigger thing' (Sheikh 1991: 87).

While race is a key issue in *The Red Box*, gender concerns are equally if not more important. Patrick Williams (1995) categorizes the novel as 'a very woman centred text, a narrative of women talking to women, of the making of female identity via the discourses of family, community and religion.' He is correct in saying 'the central question of the text remains: "What is it to be a woman, and a Muslim, in such conditions"?' (48) The motive behind Raisa's research is a feminism which operates neither in opposition to or in tandem with her Muslim background. Rather than religion the divisive threat to feminist solidarity between Raisa and the girls is class. Raisa's independent, educated status impacts on both of them, but especially upon Tahira, the one more rebellious and open to experimentation. In contrast, because she comes from a more pious family Nasreen conforms to Pakistani norms, notably with respect to traditional construction of gender. The implied criticism is directed against the narrow, ethnically constituted moral judgements of these norms, as well as the migrants' in-fighting and the shame of poverty unrelieved by the working conditions of the women in Mr Khan's clothing factory where Tahira's mother works. Breaking the strict gender codes that confine Pakistani women by conducting a separate social life in Southall where she enters a dangerous liaison with an Asian boy, it is Tahira who eventually discovers 'you aint just one thing anyway' (181).

For Raisa, the pressures imposed on the girls by their families is a throw back to her mother's life back in Pakistan. She sees high class Pakistani women as having had to face the same kind of problems over *izzat* (honour) at home in the 1960s and '70s as the girls must in London in the early '80s. The implication is that migrants' lives are lived in the shadow of values of home of an earlier generation. But what is intended as the novel's telling twist at the end – Raisa's discovery of her mother's secret work history in the red box – reinforces the pretext for Raisa's interest in the girls. Contrived and unconvincing as it is, the device serves to emphasize the co-joining of gender and class such that, as Williams points out, identity is constructed 'not as a kind of essence, but as historically, culturally and gender specific, born of the factors of social existence' (50). Despite its composition in the early '90s, Sheikh's decision to set her novel a decade earlier means that ethnicity is not delinked from religion. The British Asian female characters are not pressurized to achieve '"self-liberation" from culture and community' and there is no appearance of the 'hyper-masculinised' young Muslim male (Ahmed, R. 2009a) both of whom feature in the post-9/11 discourse of the era of *Kulturkampf* against Islam. More significantly, in spite of the criticisms she makes of the class discrimination and exploitation of women within the British Pakistani community, Sheikh is not tempted to condemn these practices by turning on Islam as a set of values.

The few years that separate *The Red Box* from Hanif Kureishi's *The Black Album* may be considered a gestation period for the fallout from the Rushdie Affair to settle. Kureishi's *The Buddha of Suburbia* (1990) is an epitome of the ethnic experimentation of the 1980s which Kureishi himself had been instrumental in implementing. Already well-known for his screenplay *My Beautiful Laundrette* (1986), according to Ruvani Ranasinha (2007) Kureishi's early work constituted 'an artistic response to the diversity and complexity of British Asian experiences' that progressively deconstructed 'received, conventional assumptions of minority communities and [led] to a broader self-definition [of these]' (238). In turning his attention to the impact of Islam on the new generation of British-born children of Asian immigrants, Kureishi's writing became focused on the binary between western liberal discourse and Islamic fundamentalism, with an emphasis on Muslim violence and the promotion of the values of secularism. In an article written in *The Guardian* in August 2005,[4] Kureishi implied that through practical research in the early 1990s he had foreseen the extremist attacks to come and he located them firmly within the fundamentalist mindset. Ranasinha agrees that *The Black Album* (1995) and 'My Son the Fanatic' (1997) now appear 'prescient in view of the scrutiny of this community in the context of 9/11, global warfare, and 7/7'. Nonetheless, she also opines 'these texts crudely and uncritically reflect and embody rather than question predominant fears, prejudices, and perceptions of British Muslims as "fundamentalists", a group already constructed as particularly threatening in the West' (Ranasinha 2007: 239). We might want to ask how, with his previous access to Pakistan, outlined in the essay 'The Rainbow Sign' (Kureishi 1996), where he expatiates at length on the deadening spread of Islamic orthodoxy in that country, the emergence of Islamism among the British Asian community came as such a shock for Kureishi. Why, as Ranasinha charges, did he succumb to the standard western fears about Islamic fundamentalism, so much so that he 'never explores any forms of Islam that are not "fundamentalist"?' (Ranasinha 2005: 244).

The Black Album is set in 1989 when, Kureishi later told Kenan Malik, the fatwa against Rushdie 'created a climate of terror and fear [...] Free speech became an issue as it had not been before. Liberals had to take a stand, to defend an ideology they had not really had to think about before' (Malik 2009: 202). It seems the cause outweighed art when it came to the composition of *The Black Album*. According to Kaleta, the novel 'pit[s] consumerism again fundamentalism' and on an ideological level stages a 'violent conflict between fundamentalism and western progress', with Kureishi taking pains to exhibit 'his strong political liberalism' (Kaleta 1998: 6, 137, 123). Sheila Ghose writes of a critical position that sees 'the binary opposition that the text seemingly cannot avoid [...] pandering to a white mainstream liberal discourse of professed tolerance and multiculturalism' (Ghose 2007: 122). While *The Satanic Verses* adopts a style of postmodern fragmentation to signify the immigrant's experience of disconnection, Kureishi, Ghose suggests, has written a realist *bildungsroman* that by implication buys into liberal humanism and berates British Muslims for refusing the multiple/fluid identities favoured by postmodern authors. In other words, the challenging of racial and communitarian stereotypes that had operated performatively in *My Beautiful Laundrette* and *The Buddha of Suburbia* has given way to a pedagogic postmodernist message in *The Black Album*. This can be seen in the Kureishi type protagonist Shahid's final rejection of his former Muslim companions:

> How could anyone confine themselves to one system or creed? Why should they feel they had to? There was no fixed self; surely our several selves melted and mutated daily? There had to be innumerable ways of being in the world. He would spread himself out, in his work and in love, following his curiosity (Kureishi 1995: 274).

Moore-Gilbert argues that *The Black Album* and 'My Son the Fanatic' 'see the rise of "fundamentalism" in the contemporary era as a reaction against the threat to "local" cultural tradition which the homogenising tendencies of globalisation represent' (Moore-Gilbert 2001: 5). If that is the case, Kureishi, like many others, has misunderstood the potential globalization has conferred on 'fundamentalist' Islam over 'local', particularist Islams. However, Kureishi is hardly solicitous of the subcontinent's local village-style Islam threatened by a spreading westernization – in his writing he frequently dismisses this kind of Islam as the province of the vulgar and ignorant. What worries him much more is the emergence of a viable Islamist challenge to those freedoms he holds dear in Britain. In *The Black Album* the Muslim student leader Riaz does not actually endorse the veracity of the holy writing which the ordinary believers discern inside the aubergine; instead he organizes a public exhibition of the vegetable as a means of uniting those he sees as downtrodden Muslims, asking Shahid:

> 'Are you not with your people? Look at them, they are from villages, half-literate and not wanted here. All day they suffer poverty and abuse. Don't we, in this land of so-called free expression, have to give them a voice? Aren't we the fortunate ones, after all?' (Kureishi 1995: 173)

Kureishi demonstrates quite clearly here his grasp of the political challenge of groups like Riaz's, who he represents as self-proclaimed defenders of the Muslim community with an agenda that extends to the creation of an opportunist ideology which uses multiculturalism to advance its programme of intolerance and violence, as seen in the firebombing of the bookshop at the end of the novel. What clearly upsets him in *The Black Album* and 'My Son the Fanatic', where the Asian taxi-driver's son rejects his father's latitudinarian attitudes in favour of a fundamentalist religiosity, is that a new generation of British Asians should choose to adopt an identitarian position that is polar to the one he has chosen for himself.

As a writer of mixed race the issue of Kureishi's creation of a space for himself within an expanded code of British cultural norms is therefore a crucial element in our discussion of his attitude towards the assumption by many British Asians of the identity marker of Muslim. In probing this connection I intend to argue that the emergence of this marker disturbs not only the negotiation he had already made with immigrant ethnicity in the 1980s, but his even more individualized stance, adopted after *The Black Album*, of a successful writer who has moved beyond ethnicity. In an article on Kureishi's short fiction of the late 1990s, in which she argues that Kureishi has 'moved away from the issues of race and ethnicity that are dominant in his early novels and screenplays', Rehana Ahmed proposes that Kureishi's characters of this period seek 'autonomy from categories of ethnicity and from the traditional nuclear family', and concludes that this desire 'tends towards an individualist rebellion that actually operates comfortably within the limits of contemporary liberal multiculturalism and hegemonic social formations' (Ahmed, R. 2009b: 28).

The licensed individualist rebellions of his fiction are variations on Kureishi's own life, as laid out in his memoir, *My Ear at His Heart: Reading My Father* (2004). Ostensibly an exercise in excavating family relationships by re-constituting the fragments of autobiographical fiction left behind by his deceased father, Rafiushan Kureishi, a writer manqué, Hanif's composing of the memoir serves to accentuate the career success and eventual individual acculturation within late twentieth-century British culture of the son, in comparison with the dislocation of his Indian family and the social disorientation in Britain experienced by the father. In discussing Kureishi's films and novels critics often light on the term 'ambiguous'; but while there may be ambiguity concerning Kureishi's political orientation in a work like *My Beautiful Laundrette*,[5] there is none when it comes to his and his characters' 'obsession with pop, youth, music' and their invariable accompaniments (Kureishi 2004: 165). In *My Ear at His Heart* Kureishi sets his father's ancestral religious faith against cultural freedom and confirms *The Black Album*'s 'strong belief in art as a survival strategy for the Asian British character' Shahid (Ghose 2007: 131). The statement in the memoir, 'it wasn't belief I was looking for: I already believed in culture and love as the only possible salvation' (Kureishi 2004: 167) also reiterates the hedonistic creed of Deedee Osgood and Shahid. In the memoir, the author's many little rebellions against a family life from which his father was never able to extricate himself accompany the progress of the son towards ultimate self-realization as a writer. Kureishi specifically marks out his own position as an individual, self-achieved, writer: 'Ambition was self-belief and hope. I wanted to be able to say, "I write for a living"' (ibid.: 145). As writers the failure of the father and the success of the son develop around the former's reluctant incarceration within monogamy and the apparent availability to the latter of unremitting sexual gratification; but they are also tied in with Kureishi's final decoupling from Islam – something his father was never entirely able to do.

The father's death becomes a watershed in the son's life and also precipitates the struggle between the writer's libertarian artistic creed and his father's family's residual Islam. Kureishi records a diary entry from this period: 'Drink and drugs all week, plus a visit to the mosque' (166). We are not certain about the connection intended here: is the visit an attempt to escape the despondency within himself brought on by his father's death (with undertones of guilt?), to lay to rest the visceral claim of ancestral religion, or to test the possibility of its consolatory power? His father's reminiscence of 'the childhood monotony of having to learn the Koran by rote, and of being hit with sticks by the Moulvis' is then invoked, followed by a report of one of his uncles' surprise and sadness to learn that he had given up all allegiance to Islam thus 'depositing myself in a kind of spiritual limbo' (167). In rejecting even the submerged cultural Islam of his father and his uncle, Kureishi wants to make it clear he is putting behind him the darkness and ignorance of traditional Islam ('no one intelligent could swallow the superstition'), and the irrationality and violence of the new, politicized form he has encountered in a West London mosque. He also appears to clear up the matter of the motivation behind his mosque visits when he writes: 'I think I was looking for solidarity, to see whether there was a Muslim part of me that existed apart from my father, to see whether being part of this group could be significant, or therapeutic in any way' (168). Not only was this possibility erased by his exposure to politicized Muslims, it actually galvanized him to write *The Black Album* and the film 'My Son the

Fanatic' (169). So negative was this experience that he writes in his *Guardian* article about rushing 'into the nearest pub and drinking rapidly, wanting to reassure myself I was still in England'.[6] Nevertheless, these passages go further than simply disclosing a leave-taking from a religion that was never endorsed and had only ever held a distant, ancestral claim on the writer. They confirm both Kureishi's exorcism of his father's influence (including his criticized attachment to family life) and a final separation from the ethnic community to which his father had belonged. In addition, they lay the ground-work for an ideologically configured *Kulturkampf* against Islam by a writer strongly staking out his credentials as an upholder of English culture as defined by his dedication to art, free speech, rational thought, free love and the consumption of drugs and alcohol.

The arrangement of *The Black Album* demands that Shahid develop an attraction towards a group of Muslim students which Kureishi presumably never entertained himself. Although the dilemma presented to Shahid of choosing between their beliefs and London's late 1980s hedonism is scarcely tenable given his obvious predilections for the latter (which are of course his creator's), his temporary adherence to the group recalls the question Kureishi poses for himself in the memoir. Here, however, it is interesting to note that the writing largely accounts for Shahid's initial fascination with Riaz and his cronies in ethnic rather than religious or ideological terms. His sense of being personally 'invisible' in the city contrasts with the warmth and intimacy of the student group (Kureishi 1995: 5). Unlike the terrorists we shall meet in post-9/11 Anglo-American novels and essays, Riaz is made particularly believable as a thirties something activist with a hybrid Muslim-Yorkshire accent. Meeting him on a staircase in the student residences where they exchange greetings in Urdu, Shahid ends up eating spicy food with him in an Indian café. Riaz inspires Shahid with feelings of familiarity and recognition: attracted first by his 'gentleness' and bookishness (which he associates with 'goodness') he sees in Riaz a combination of J.B. Priestley and Zia Al Haq (ibid.: 2, 14, 6). Riaz and his henchmen Hat and Chad become '*the first people he'd met who were like him*, he didn't have to explain anything [...] he was closer to this gang than to his own family' (my italics, 57). Riaz even writes poetry – 'songs of memory, adolescence and twilight' inspired by his home village in Pakistan – connecting him more closely to Shahid than his own philistine, upwardly aspiring Asian family (68). This intimacy appears to be cemented when Shahid comes home stoned on drugs and Riaz cleans up his vomit.

It is evident too that alongside ethnic brotherhood, Kureishi means us to see Shahid's involvement with the group as an extension of the fight against racism, which so excites him when he hears Deedee Osgood lecturing on racial discrimination in America. Anti-racism is constructed not so much as an ideological issue as a sign of the novel's time location on the cusp of the Rushdie Affair. The defining incident in this section is the group's defence of the Bangladeshi family terrorized by racist thugs with which Shahid's commitment to his new friends coincides. While on duty in the family's flat he experiences a bout of self-recrimination for his depraved behaviour with Deedee; soon after the fanatical Chad presents him with a white cotton salwar kamiz and watches him change, 'for the first time, into "national dress"' (131). This is meant as a peace offering for an earlier argument over Chad's intrusive questioning of Shahid's personal life during which the following interchange had occurred:

> Chad's voice rose: 'Earlier, did you say Paki to me?'
> 'Yeah, I was trying to say—'
> '*No more Paki. Me a Muslim.* We don't apologize for ourselves neither. We are a people who say one important thing – that pleasure and self-absorption isn't everything!' (128, my italics)

For an Asian, formerly known as Trevor Buss and brought up by a white family as Chad was, to choose to affirm a Muslim identity over an ethnic one is particularly telling in the late 1980s context. Kureishi clearly understands the significance of Chad's outburst even if he displays little sympathy for his character. The transition from ethnicity to Islam – or more properly revivalist Islam – has been staged. The novel's representation of the flare up over *The Satanic Verses* is now all that is needed for Kureishi to deconstruct the negative implications behind this emerging identity.

Kureishi's various accounts of his encounters with the new generation of Asian Muslims foreground their to him mindless belief that 'they had access to the Truth as stated in the Qur'an. There could be no doubt – or even much dispute about moral, social and political problems – because God had the answers [...] I found ideology and fundamentalism, and young people holding extreme, irrational and violent views [...] It was puzzling: there was no attention to the inner life; it had been politicized. Behaviour, rather than thought, was all.'[7] This emphasis on the poverty of the individual's inner life and the directed, group-centred consciousness of the young fundamentalists is re-iterated in *The Black Album*, where it becomes the grounds for the fundamentalism versus tolerant liberalism dichotomization which forms the choice Shahid must make. The Muslim students group he encounters has as its leader Riaz, the initially attractive figure who we later learn has been ejected from his home after condemning his father – rather like the young man in 'My Son the Fanatic' – for drinking alcohol and for 'praying in his armchair and not on his knees' (109). Riaz has a symbiotic relationship with the group centred around him – he appears to be weak when without them while they 'become childish, forgetting the reasons for their actions without him' (129). Armed with his doctrinal certainties, Riaz identifies with the emerging global warfare between Islam and the West, connecting the defence of the local Bangladeshi family with the torture of Muslims in Palestine, Afghanistan and Kashmir (82). Represented at first as humorous farce – '"We should call ourselves the Foreign

Legion," Shahid told Hat on the stairs, getting into the spirit of the thing. His blood was warming; he felt a physical pride in their cause, whatever it was' – the group's activism eventually becomes physically threatening when they burn Rushdie's book and throw a petrol bomb at a bookshop (82–3, 273).[8]

Rehana Ahmed sees signs of 'Kureishi's liberal antipathy towards monoculturalism "from below"' in his writing as early as the mid-1980s. She locates his antagonism towards Asian Muslim 'fundamentalism' in Slavoj Žižek's positing within a late-capitalist liberal democracy of 'the tension between "open" post-ideological universalist liberal tolerance and the particularist "new fundamentalisms"' (Ahmed, R. 2009b: 33). Kureishi's obvious distaste for what she calls 'the binary homogenous collect' which Asian Muslim fundamentalism constitutes for him, calls forth a re-assertion on his part of 'heterogeneous individuality'. This however masks the racial discrimination and class inequalities that in reality produce such 'monoculturalist' reactions as Islamic fundamentalism in the West. By aligning himself with the individual he has opted to situate himself within 'a largely normative liberalism' (ibid). Added to this, I have also argued Kureishi's writing on Islam is further inflected by his need to identify himself as a successful writer, which in turn is defined by his commitment to freedom of speech and the multiple 'truths' of postmodern aesthetics. In order to signal such an identity it was necessary for him to cut himself off entirely from his ethnic and religious ancestry. His fictional work of the 1990s recognizes the shift from ethnicity to religion as an identity marker; in repudiating the latter Kureishi also appears to take the stance that race and ethnicity are matters that no longer concern him.[9]

Secular Writers and Britain's Asian Muslim diaspora: Monica Ali and Nadeem Aslam

In the national struggles against colonialism religion could be suborned into the service of the national struggle (as it was during the war for Algerian independence in Algeria and France) or identified as an obstacle to national self-determination (as in the first decades of the twentieth century in Egypt.) The emergence of political Islamism has often caused the elites that once acted as the leaders of national movements to make common cause with former colonizers, their nationalism now superseded by their apparent identification with western values of freedom and democracy. Sayyid's adoption of the term 'Kemalism' confirms the identification of the secular elites that ruled in the countries of the former Ottoman empire with the watchwords of western-led modernity: secularization, nationalism, modernization, and westernization. 'Accounts of Islamism tend to make a major distinction between the Islamists of today and other political movements which came to power as the European empires retreated. These movements have variously been described as "nationalist", or "secularist" or "modernizing"; another way of describing them is to use the category of Kemalism' (Sayyid 1997: 52). Within this value-system Islam seems unable to find a place. Kemal Atatürk himself 'repeatedly described Islam as "the symbol of obscurantism", as a "putrified corpse which poisons our lives", as "the enemy of civilization and science"; and so on' (ibid.: 65). In the process of establishing their modernizing nationalist credentials, the intellectual elites of postcolonial national societies often took up a position that relegated religion to the role of object.[10] But after the Iranian revolution of 1979 the emergence of Islamism has pressurized the secular space even in persisting Kemalist states. Those from the secular intellectual elites, who have removed to the shelter of western societies and have been able to access the powerful publishing media there, have however frequently adopted anti-religious positions, attacking the Islamic beliefs, practices and cultures of the lands to which they notionally belong. Postcolonial axioms of writing against colonial models are replaced by neo-Orientalist ones. Sometimes non-authoritarian forms of Muslim culture such as Sufism or local traditional Islams are appropriated to attack revivalist Islam.

The first decade of the twenty-first century witnessed the emergence of a new generation of novelists with links to the Muslim cultures of the sub-continent, writing about Muslim subjects. In *Brick Lane* (2004) and *Maps for Lost Lovers* (2004) migrant Muslim communities (rather than the individual Asian Muslims we find in *The Satanic Verses* and *The Black Album*) are writ large. *Maps for Lost Lovers* has been critically lauded for the way in which, through the eyes of its migrant population, an English town is imaginatively re-mapped as though it were in the Indian subcontinent. *Brick Lane*, on the other hand, in purporting to present a portrait of the Bangladeshi community of London's East End, became embroiled in debates over the politics of authenticity and the burden of representation. Jane Hiddleston encapsulates the controversy behind the novel: 'While some readers congratulated [Monica] Ali for pulling back the curtains of the residences of Tower Hamlets and depicting the injustices and dissatisfactions suffered by their inhabitants, others were shocked by her boldness and offended by what they considered to be a gross misrepresentation of Bengali culture in London' (Hiddleston 2005: 57). Hiddleston's discussion of the novel proceeds to probe the artifice of the text and the difficulties of representation attaching to the enterprise of revealing (or to use the Orientalist trope, 'unveiling') the lives of the immigrant inhabitants of Brick Lane. However, while she brings out both Ali's equivocal positioning vis-à-vis the Bangladeshi community (viewing them, in Ali's own words, 'neither [from] behind a closed door nor in the thick of things, but rather in the shadow of a doorway')[11] she seems to take at face value Ali's claim of authorial self-effacement: 'she has no determined argument, no personal hold upon the work, but uses the space of fiction to exhibit and perform a series of culturally and rhetorically produced figures' (70–1). This might be the case if it could be argued that Ali had no investment in creating in her central protagonist, Nazneen, a character who certainly is a 'culturally and rhetorically produced figure' to the extent that she fulfils the function of the Muslim woman who is liberated from her native culture to achieve freedom and independence in the West. While Hiddleston is doubtless right in her observation that narrator intervention and character discourse become confused at sensitive moments in *Brick Lane* (thus troubling our sense of the authenticity of the voice given to Nazneen) there can be no doubt concerning Nazneen's conformity to this stereotype.

Ali's programme for Nazneen is that she escape the 'fate' that women such as her mother have to endure in Bangladesh. For much of the novel the mother's death remains unaccounted for – the reader surmises it may have been a suicide, or faked as an accident by her husband who ironically dismisses her as coming from 'a family of saints'. For Nazneen, however, despite 'being left to her fate' as a newly born by her mother, destiny intervenes. Fortuitously married off at eighteen to Chanu, a gentle garrulous failure twice her age, who she grows both to despise and feel affection for, Nazneen is gifted her green card to self-discovery. In Britain she slowly outgrows her mother's fatalism. That she accomplishes this can be explained in part by her natural intelligence, but more crucially, by her creator finding for her the way to move beyond the mental confinement of her East London Bangladeshi enclave. (Her beautiful rebellious sister Hasina is less fortunate for although she exercises her right to choice and elopes with her lover there is no room for feminist enfranchisement at home in Bangladesh. Her fate is to be conquered by Third World poverty and patriarchy.) Nazneen's conscious sense of agency is, by the end, enlarged to the extent that she resists her husband's demand for her and her daughters to return with him to Dhaka, separates from the young lover she has collected along the way without drawing upon herself the opprobrium of her community, and successfully sets up on her own account in the textile business.

Perhaps what is most surprising about the impact *Brick Lane* has had is that it should ever have been received as anything other than it is: a first novel by a Cambridge English graduate of hybrid Asian extraction, consciously writing out of the tradition of migrant and mainstream canonical English fiction. Critics and commentators have discerned the influence of Rushdie in the account of Nazneen's birth; Dickens and Naipaul in the character of Chanu; Zadie Smith's Millat in Nazneen's lover Karim; and Smith and Kureishi's portrayal of home-grown Islamic fundamentalism in the agitations of the Bengal Tigers.[12] That some among the Bangladeshis of East London should have been upset by the novel's representation of themselves is clearly an outcome of *Brick Lane*'s reception by reviewers and the media in general as a real life exposé of their community.[13] (Admittedly, there is shock value in the married woman, Nazneen's, adultery; the provocatively named Mrs Islam's usury; and Mrs Azad the doctor's wife who dresses as a tart and who fishes out a five pound note to give her daughter to spend at the pub.) Nevertheless, Ali's work hardly purports to be engaged, as *The Black Album* clearly is, in an ideological struggle with religio-political fundamentalism. The presence of

Islam as a discrete entity in the novel may be no more than a fortuitous result of the date of its composition and the intertextual field outlined above. In fact two Islams feature: in the first half a traditional, quietist (though not really local) one submerged within Ali's overall project of delivering Nazneen from the clutches of Asiatic fatalism. This Islam functions within Nazneen's initially deferential behaviour towards Chanu and is a part of the dulled, subservient, oppressed female consciousness that Ali may have as easily derived from classic Marxist Orientalism as from feminist Orientalism. The second Islam, which is Ali's attempt to re-write Islam into the migrant experience, is more closely connected to the intertexts already mentioned.

As a newly married wife for Nazneen the Qur'an represents a point of reference linked to her childhood in Bangladesh, 'she began to recite in her head from the Holy Qur'an one of the suras she had learned in school [...] Nazneen fell asleep on the sofa. She looked out across jade-green rice fields and swam in the cool dark lake' (Ali 2004: 21). She invokes the Qur'an's teaching of divine omnipotence and omnipresence – 'To God belongs all that the heavens and the earth contain' (20) – in order to control her desire.[14] Prayer acts upon Nazneen as a form of opiate, reinforcing the interiorized resignation to fate of her mother, the saintly Rupban, who held that: 'If God wanted us to ask questions, he would have made us men' (80). However, it loses its efficacy in dulling pain during Nazneen's pregnancy: 'she recited in her head her favourite sura [...] But the pain in her knee and her hands and her ankle destroyed the verses' (57). This experience leads her to question her religion – it tells her it was created for (and was the creation of) men:

> There was a special dispensation for pregnant women. If she chose to, Nazneen could do namaz from her chair. She had tried it once and it made her feel lazy. But it was nice that the imams had thought of it. Such was the kindness and compassion of Islam towards women. Mind you, if any imam had ever been pregnant, would they not have made it *compulsory* to sit? That way, no one could feel it was simply down to laziness (69; italics in text).

Here Ali is implying that in prescribing as the norm namaz on one's hands and knees, with pregnant women obtaining a concession almost as an afterthought, Islam underwrites the masculine as primary, while the feminine is almost an afterthought.

From this traditional, fatalistic Islam Nazneen is progressively disconnected by virtue of her British residence. Alone in the flat, she undergoes a crisis engendered by the contradictory impulses of natural desire, awakened within her new, non-Bangladeshi situation. 'Every morning before she opened her eyes she thought, *if I were the wishing type, I know what I would wish* [...] Was it cheating? To think, *I know what I would wish?* Was it not the same as making the wish? If she knew what the wish would be, then somewhere in her heart she had already made it' (18; italics in text). Nazneen's wish, which Ali does not concretize, is nevertheless set up in opposition to her acceptance of her fate, which is to be married to frog-faced Chanu. At this stage desire and nurtured self-constraint come into conflict when she glimpses ice-skaters on television; the dual fetishes of the Arabic Qur'an kept wrapped in cloth on a high shelf (sanctified above the mundane, and rendered otiose by the fact that she is unable to understand Arabic), and the flicker of the male–female paired ice-skaters' figures subliminally compete for her soul. 'Sometimes she switched on the television and flicked through the channels, looking for ice-skating [...] The old Nazneen was sublimated and the new Nazneen was filled with white light, glory [...] But when it ended and she switched off the television, the old Nazneen returned [...] She was glad when the ice-skating came no more. She began to pray five times each day' (41). Later, now mother to a new baby, she misses both morning prayers, only to experience an epiphany in which she imagines herself as the female skater holding and squeezing the male skater's hand. We are intended here not only to sympathize with Nazneen as an individual woman with desire, but also to naturalize her as a part of a universal female consciousness. Nazneen aspires to her true natural state – struggling to free herself from the Asiatic, backward culture of arranged marriages and suppressed female desire, in which Islam plays a complicit role.

The second Islam is the Islam of Karim. Since the focalization throughout the novel is Nazneen's, the new Islam comes across to her as a liberating force. 'Radical', direct, purposeful, and authoritative – it is the opposite of Chanu's weak, ineffectual anti-colonial (but peasant-hating) Bengali nationalism. However, Karim's Islam is undermined because it is entirely associated with the romantic/sexual fixation that for the moment takes hold of Nazneen, but which at the end she rejects along with Karim as an image of her own construction. In spite of finding space in her mind for the *umma* and the martyrs of Palestine and Chechnya, where before it had been filled with angels, the impact of the new Islam on Nazneen is rendered superficial and meretricious on account of its conduit via a sexual affair founded upon Nazneen's mistaken assumption of what Karim represents. While not entirely a tailor's dummy, Karim's signal function in the novel is to play the part of Nazneen's lover, to exemplify the faction that even Asian Muslim women in semi-purdah can have love affairs. One of the reasons why Karim impresses Nazneen is that she believes that he, as a second generation Bengali immigrant, has found a settled identity which she as a migrant lacks. 'The thing that he had and inhabited so easily. A place in the world' (264). 'The reader begins to understand that Karim is the first person Nazneen has met who seems to "fit in" with his location. Even his extreme religious orthodoxy is denuded of its original meanings and rendered a performative hybrid. He receives "Salaat alerts" on his mobile phone, and when he begins to pray, Nazneen finds the experience erotic' (Cormack 2006: 704). However, as Sara Upstone points out, Karim's apparent self-assurance is erroneously decoded by Nazneen: eventually 'Karim's status as one who has "a place in the world" is revealed as a fiction and replaced with a final judgement of him as "born a foreigner", beholden to the reality of his parents' (Upstone 2007: 342). For this critic, Ali's novel vacillates between a postmodern Rushdie-style vision of the Bangladeshis of East London as migrants who are 'itinerant wanderers', and the more optimistic note picked up on by some reviewers as evidence of a new black/ Asian British-born confidence. Though Upstone is undecided as to which view predominates, we can certainly say that Karim's Islam, for all its contemporary razzamatazz, posturing self-conscious militancy, sloganizing and attitudinizing, is ultimately dismissed by Ali as reactive and contingent. Ali's projection of Karim as leader of the Bengal tigers is effected with the same note of narrative irony and detachment as that used to convey Mrs Azad's shocking acculturation to women's liberation and the pub. Where Kureishi's more comical ironizing of young Muslim activists turns to ugly confrontation in the book-burning scene, Ali's militants end up dissipating their energies in rioting and attacking one another as the novel reaches its cinematic climax. Nazneen's interest in the new Islam has already evaporated, before, in the thick of the battle, she comes across the ludicrous praying Multicultural Liaison Officer who declares to her: "'I is praying to Allah to save all these boys. Can't get up now'" (Ali 2004: 471).[15] Salaat, whether in its authentic prone masculine or concessionary female form, is wholly jettisoned from Nazneen's life. She has decided to stand up for herself as a successful business woman, without Chanu, but with her two British-born daughters to evidence her claims of belonging. Thus Islam, old and new, goes the same way as Chanu, Karim and the ice-skating couple: the self-re-birthed British Nazneen has no further need of them.

In Nadeem Aslam's contribution to the *Granta* issue, 'God and Me', a dichotomy is staged which is redolent of the fabric out of which his novel *Maps for Lost Lovers* is woven. The soft and sensitive weave is the canopy of a tall tree in his grandparents' garden out of which leaves and flowers emerge. From 'the blue haze of its flowers' rises a young woman – his sister – who is then pulled away by her mother, leaning out of a window before the ladder supporting her daughter falls. In contrast to the preserving custodianship of his mother, the behaviour of the author's uncle is harsh and destructive: he smashes children's toys because he considers them idols; he chants loudly the Arabic words of his prayer. For his nephew these connote the violence and pain he received as a child when he was 'regularly slapped or beaten with a cane on the hands and body by the clerics for not having memorized the [Arabic] verses [of the Qur'an]'. The uncle – 'a follower of a strict unsmiling sect of Islam' – also deprecated performances of devotional Muslim music, and in fact his 'version of Islam was the same kind practised by the Taliban' (Aslam 2006: 66–7).

In one short section of *Maps* Aslam sets up this hard-line, puritanical Islam against the Sufi music of Nasrat Ali Khan. But what might have turned out to be a novel mixing the varieties of Muslim practice from the very diverse Islamic societies of Pakistan and India is instead constructed as a representation of a community ruled over by harsh religious edict. In the northern English town re-named Dasht-e-Tanhaii (desert of solitude) by its diasporic Asian Muslim inhabitants the fanaticism of Aslam's uncle is transferred to the mother-character, Kaukab, while Jugnu, the fictional uncle, is obsessed with butterflies and moths. Other characters who are possessed of delicacy and feeling devote their time to thoughts of love or the flora of the local park. Otherwise superstition, bigotry and cruelty are the ubiquitous norms. Kamila Shamsie writes in her review of the novel: 'In this book, filled with stories of cruelty, injustice, bigotry and ignorance, love never steps out of the picture.'[16] It could be argued that the novel's main topos is that in Pakistani culture religion is the enemy of love. If love is a universal given, Aslam does not feel obliged (as for instance Rai does) to disentangle a 'pure/ideal religious essence' or even a more smiling version of Islam from local traditions; instead the religion practiced by the ethnically based community is almost entirely derived from the Taliban-style Islam of Aslam's uncle. In effect, Aslam takes the quasi-universal pretensions of this so-called 'fundamentalist' Islam at face value. By inscribing it in the way he has he has paid homage to it, or credited it as a dominant form, in a similar way to how négritude credits white racism, or Occidentalism (or 'Orientalism in reverse') pays homage to Orientalism. He is not so much resisting it as re-inscribing it.

The novel performs this activity by incorporating a series of major/minor stories/incidents that function collectively to build up a dark picture, if not of Islam as a religion, then certainly of Islam as the formative factor behind a range of beliefs, superstitious ideas and practices. Transported from Pakistani culture to Britain these have as one of their main outcomes the thwarting of human love. Kaukab, the fanatically religious wife of the main protagonist Shamas, and mother of their three children, Mah-Jabin, Charag and Ujala, is at the centre of several of the incidents. The overarching one concerns a couple missing, presumed dead. It transpires that lovers Jugnu (Shamas's brother and Kaukab's brother in law) and Chanda (Shamas and Kaukab's neighbour) are victims together of an 'honour' killing perpetrated by Chanda's brothers. Early on we also learn how Kiran (a Sikh woman) was stopped from contracting a love match with the brother of Kaukab by their family and, later, how Kaukab's daughter Mah-Jabin was, age sixteen, taken to Pakistan and married to her first cousin, Kaukab admitting she would have tied her daughter up and taken her there if she had resisted. Focalizing this and a series of Mah-Jabin's other experiences of childhood and adolescence, the narrator informs us: 'Trapped within the cage of permitted thinking, this woman – her mother – is the most dangerous animal she'll ever have to confront' (Aslam 2004: 110–11). The statement is born out by Kaukab's admission to Shamas that she had (preposterously) made their baby son Ujala fast at Ramadan. She is therefore either directly involved or complicit in incidents that lead to the murder of two people, the thwarting of a love marriage, the endangering of the life of one of her children, and the threat of violence to another.

Suraya, another female character faithful to her religion, is forced according to Islamic law to marry and divorce someone else before she can re-marry her former husband who had previously divorced her while drunk. In desperation she proposes to Charag, a few years her junior, citing the Prophet's marriage at nineteen to 'a woman of forty'. Charag's immediate inner response is: 'And he was in his sixties when he consummated his marriage with a nine year old' (132).[17] Soon after this unsuccessful proposal Suraya coincidentally encounters Charag's father Shamas, who, fearful of her being seen talking to him, in his mind recalls 'a Pakistani man mounted the footpath and ran over his sister-in-law – repeatedly, in broad daylight – because he suspected she was cheating on his brother'. His meditation continues, 'according to the statistics, in one Pakistani province alone, a woman is murdered every thirty-eight hours solely because her virtue is in doubt' (136). A further violent end is inflicted on a young girl who has 'a secret Hindu lover' and is beaten to death over a period of several days by a holy man called in by her parents in a fruitless attempt to exorcize her djinns (185–6). Besides these incidents, the novel incorporates a copious inventory of religious injunctions or religiously indoctrinated axioms and notions. The following expression of Kaukab's personal world-view through free indirect speech typifies the polemical content of so much of Aslam's novel:

> Some vulgar people ask that if a pious man will get seventy-two wives in Paradise, how many men will a pious *woman* receive? That of course is the height of ignorance and indecency: a pious woman cannot bear the thought of letting a man other than her husband touch her – so in Paradise, where there is nothing but ease and satisfaction, why would she be put through the torment of being groped and fondled by strange men [...] There will be no urine, no faeces, no semen, no menstruation; erections and orgasms will last for decades, and men will often hear their earthly wives say, 'By the power of Allah, I could find nothing in Paradise as beautiful as you' (ibid.: 266–7).

How successful a novel then is *Maps*? As the repetitive accumulation of anti-Islamic detail outlined earlier tends to show, it could be construed as a meretriciously jejune performance. On the other hand, besides the awkward uploading of Orientalist-style 'information' about Islam through the mind of Kaukab, Aslam's choice of a woman to represent a puritanical and intolerant form of the religion is worth commenting on. In view of the ubiquitous stereotyping in literature and journalism of Muslim men as violent and authoritarian and of Muslim women as victims (see my next two chapters), it is perhaps surprising that Aslam shows both women and men to be the victims of religion in the novel. The avowedly secular, former communist Shamas, and his brother Jugnu, stand out as sensitive unbelieving males. In addition, Aslam goes out of his way to connect them with a prose of intricate and precious poetic diction directed for the most part towards description of moths and butterflies and the local flora. All the more bald in contrast is the dry reportage of the depressing incidents of violence and bigotry juxtaposed alongside and effectually in opposition to the ethereal prose-passages. This is done in a manner that is almost Hardy-esque: the harsh socio-religious code seemingly out of sync with the natural beauty of the environment. From the sociological point of view the sub-continent's *baradarism* is kept in the background in both Pakistan and Britain, but plausibly worked into the threat of violence that hangs over both men and women. There is also, as already stated, the occasional appropriation of non-authoritarian forms of Muslim culture such as Sufism (or local traditional Islam) to express individualism and intimacy in contradistinction to strict authoritarian Islam.

Perhaps only a readership that has signed up and is as committed to the view of Islam the novel represents could be as indulgent towards its crude one-sidedness as those who have praised it so fulsomely (*vide* the book-cover of the first UK paperback edition). The 'fundamentalist' turn Pakistan has taken in recent years and Aslam's connections with the Indo-Pakistani anti-religious, secular intellectual elite may partially account for the novel's sustained attack on an authoritarian version of Islam. His statements in his *Granta* essay specifically connect this form which he dislikes so intensely with political regimes in the wider Islamic world. Rather than the kindness Shamsie sees in *Maps*, the long confrontational scene verging on violence between Kaukab and Mah-Jabin during the latter's visit home displays the personal bitterness of at least some among the westernized diasporic elite who take the opportunity of the safety of their position in the West to castigate a hated strand of society in Pakistan:

'Here we have proof that Chanda was murdered by her brothers, that a family can kill one of its own [...] My god, for all of you she probably didn't die hard enough: you would like to dig her up piece by piece, put her back together, and kill her once more for going against your laws, codes, and so-called traditions that you have dragged into this country with you like shit on your shoes' (114).

Powerful as this is, its distribution of blame – directed by the westernized daughter against her Pakistan-raised mother who for most of the novel appears barely human – is disturbing and redolent of the condemnation of migrant monocultural fundamentalism already raised in my discussion of Kureishi. The oppression Muslims receive in Britain is sometimes gestured towards in *Maps*, but though it curls in the background it hardly ever comes forward, at least to mount a semblance of exoneration of Kaukab. Using Tariq Modood's work to explain more clearly the imbalance between the westernized individual's take on his/her ethnic community, and the situation of the majority of its excluded members, Rehana Ahmed states:

In his discussion of multiculturalism, Modood exposes the dialectical relationship between marginalisation and an assertion of a communal identity. He points out that the experience of marginalisation or 'exclusion' sustains 'group identity', which then enables the group in question to transmute its negative representations by mainstream society to a positive self-assertion of a collective identity. Given that Muslims experience a relatively high degree of exclusion in contemporary Britain [...], a communal identity is more likely to be important to more of them (Ahmed, R. 2009b: 33).

However, as I have argued above, such an identity is not likely to be esteemed very highly in the individualistic, pro-liberal mainstream inhabited by writers like Kureishi, Ali or Aslam.

Leila Aboulela: Muslim Faith in a Secular Culture

Individualism of a different kind to that of the 'native-informant' secular-oriented writer of Muslim origin is discernible in Aboulela's work. In an interview with Claire Chambers, the Sudanese-British writer makes the following disclosure about her writing:

> Islam isn't just part of the culture of my fiction, it's not a social norm or something like that, it's to do with the individual and their faith and their own belief and what they want to do [...] this is what makes my writing different from that of other writers, who see the *sharia* as solely part of society and part of culture, rather than belonging to the individual herself. It's highlighted in my work, because my characters are largely based in Britain, which is not a Muslim country, and yet they as individuals want to practice Islam (Chambers 2009).

As I have argued elsewhere, and as the quote above amply bares out, this could not have taken the form it has without the writer's acculturation to western forms and codes supplied by the age of globalization (Nash 2007: ch.5). My argument here will be that Aboulela, though in Arab migrant literature she represents more or less a school of one,[18] is nevertheless a significant foil to the other writers I have been discussing, not so much because her work has the 'authenticity' that some, mainly Muslim, readers have claimed for it, but because it demonstrates that given broadly the same conditions of possibility, a sympathetic 'insider's' voice is operable within the genre of 'Muslim' fiction.

It should comes as no surprise that this is so. Aboulela went so far as to report to a journalist: 'It was only in Britain, where she came [from Sudan in 1989] to study for her PhD, that she began to feel able to express her faith'. At this point 'the word "Muslim" wasn't even really used [...] you were either black or Asian' and it was in this environment that she 'felt very free to wear the hijab' for the first time (she hadn't felt able to wear it in Sudan in the 1980s).[19] In fact she explains that in the Arab intellectual circles to which she has been exposed religion 'is almost a taboo subject'.[20] Nonetheless, the secularized godless western metropolis has not only freed humans from 'metaphysical control' (Cox 1966: 182), it has also provided the space in which an individualized faith commitment can grow free from the tyranny of '*the* officially enforced world-view beside which no others are tolerated' (ibid.: 69; original italics). That can happen despite the pressures exerted by the new fundamental faith of secularism (though as they mount these supply the believer with an added frisson not unhelpful for sustaining belief), and the authoritarian Islamist regimes of the homeland which Aboulela seems to have left behind. Ironically perhaps conditions in the western city facilitate the voluntarist faith that shines through her writing – 'I have always wanted,' she has said, 'to write about what it feels like to have faith in the modern secular world.'[21] Without the secular western environment in which her work is mainly set, Aboulela would probably not have been able so effectively to inscribe the impact of faith and the tension opposing non-belief supplies. Her chief protagonists are women making statements about their faith and about themselves – statements which they presumably could not have made in the same way in Sudan or Egypt. (Though she had the inclination to express herself religiously, in her native country 'the atmosphere wasn't conducive to it growing'.)[22]

Aboulela is also sophisticated enough as a writer to know that whatever as a Muslim Arab-African woman she wants to say about faith and being a believer, this will be construed according to the paradigms entertained by her largely secular western audience. From the point of view of the cognoscenti, she realizes Islam has its place as a category within current modes of cultural theory, pre-eminently Orientalism and postcolonialism.[23] While this is unavoidable it also represents an opportunity. Rather than conform to the stale Orientalist discourse of much western writing on Islam, fictional or otherwise, Aboulela adopts a subtle transgressive discourse which engages Orientalist and postcolonial tropes in such a way as to project herself, as Waïl Hassan has argued, as a representative for Islam.[24] Hassan's reading of Aboulela's fiction alongside that of Tayeb Salih pays her the homage of a considering her a serious postcolonial writer. Broadly speaking, he sees her work as both a continuation of the dichotomy of metropolitan, colonialist north and colonized south; for him, Aboulela's fiction like Salih's defines itself against the values of the secularist, Orientalist, Islamophobic West. But where Salih's fictional representations of north/south contact are 'narratives of failure [...] hers are narratives of redemption and fulfillment though Islam' (Hassan 2008: 300). The key issue then becomes how we articulate Aboulela's engagement of postcolonial and Islamic constituents in her writing. I feel that Hassan is right when he speaks of Aboulela's development beyond Salih in terms of a 'rift between politics and spirituality' (ibid.: 303); however, in spite of the credit he gives her for using 'intertextual and translational strategies' in representing the late twentieth century north/south encounter, ultimately he is not convinced that her 'Islamic fiction' satisfactorily fills the postcolonial gap Salih's work opened, largely because he does not see the adoption of a quietist Muslim identity as the solution to the predicament of people from the so-called Third World (ibid.).[25]

We might scrutinize then the signifiers Islam and postcolonialism in Aboulela's writing in order to probe how apposite the terminology Islamic postcolonialism might be in critiquing Aboulela's work. That will mean endorsing the main thrust of Hassan's argument. Aboulela's project entails addressing the gulf between former colonizer and colonized, showing an awareness of Orientalism without setting out directly to deconstruct the West's image of Islam, but rather to Islamicize the process of 'writing back'. As a writer whose main characters are migrants she sets out to appropriate the emptiness of the western metropolis exposed by writers like Selvon, Naipaul and Salih. This entails absorbing the secular, postcolonial environment into an Islamic schema inflected by postcolonial mappings. The terminology of metropolis and periphery is maintained: the metropolitan centre which is cold and closed off to the migrant is not so much a site of conflict, and even less one of vengeance or self-destruction, but incorporated instead into the providential scheme. As for the formerly colonized periphery, this is simultaneously a place of emotional wealth and one where political instability is endemic, but it is not narrated in terms of 'national allegory'. The damage done by the colonizer to the colonized periphery is mostly perceived as the perversion of the upper middle class elite to which Najwa, the female central protagonist of *Minaret*, belongs. The Islam of the ordinary people – evocatively projected through Sammar's eyes in *The Translator* – has been left largely in tact. There is no sense in Aboulela's writings and interviews that Islamism has decisively impacted on her faith. In *The Translator* the Sudanese, presumably Islamist, regime is dismissed as incompetent in an apolitical way, whereas in *Minaret* (2005) the secularist political order in Sudan is an object of criticism.

In terms of the postcolonial chronology Hassan has in mind in probing the connection between Salih and Aboulela, the writer from the later generation has largely transferred her focus from the postcolonial margins to the centre. It might be argued, I think with some justification, that as far as Aboulela's work is concerned Sudan is a place to be left, rather like the Caribbean island is in Caryl Phillips' early fiction. There is, it is true, the inscription of the communal warmth of Salih's *Wedding of Zein* into 'The Ostrich', the short story from *Coloured Lights*; but overall a re-calibration of the postcolonial balance according to a generational shift is required. In *Season of Migration to the North*, Salih focuses the impact of colonization on a previously integrated African Islamic society, even as the novel underlines the fact that there is no road back to the pristine pre-colonial village (if such ever existed). Aboulela on the other hand does not even attempt to go there. Her Sudan is still the repository of a traditional Islam that impacts in personal terms upon both Sammar and Najwa, but a claustrophobia with strong familial/gendered overtones inhibits the development of faith there. Fathers and brothers are victims to the intrusion of western capitalism which has undermined a traditional Islamic society with its community-centred faith practice, while the predominantly male intelligentsia are absorbed in Leftist politics. From the males the females derive their engagement with the empty imported materialism and scepticism about religion, only, paradoxically, to find their enfranchisement from these more fully as migrants in the West. In her first three volumes of fiction then, the western metropolis is the site from which Aboulela draws her aliment.[26] The forces diffused from the globalizing West act so as to draw populations from the East and in the process re-birth them. Women characters especially are enabled by the metropolitan space to rediscover faith, better understand their faith commitment, and even engage in *da'wa* (mission work) among westerners.

In *The Translator*, the opportunity to teach the faith falls to Sammar, and the object is a western male who possesses a latent receptivity. During a visit with her friend to her employer Rae's flat she picks up a magazine containing maps and photographs of north-east Africa.

> She knelt and sat on her heels to look more closely. The familiar names of towns, in black type against the yellow, moved her. Kassala, Darfur, Sennar. Kadugli, Karima, Wau. Insider her was their sheer dust and meagreness. Sunshine and poverty. Voices of those who endured because they asked so little of life. On the next page of the magazine there was an advertisement for education materials. Schoolgirls in Somalia, smiling, arm in arm. Short-sleeved white shirts under a navy pinafore, white belts around their waist. She had dressed like that, been a face like that once [...]
>
> When she looked up, Rae was watching her, a look in his eyes like kindness. Encouraged she said, 'I used to wear a uniform like that in secondary school.'
>
> 'They made us wear shorts,' he said, 'even in winter. It was awful, walking to school in the cold. I was glad when I got expelled.'
>
> 'You got expelled from school?' asked Yasmin. 'What terrible thing did you get up to?'
>
> 'I wrote an essay,' he was laughing so that Sammar did not know whether he was joking or not. 'I wrote an essay entitled *Islam is better than Christianity*' (Aboulela 2001b: 17; original italics).

Here everything seems to turn on the kindness of Rae who smoothes over Sammar's sense of Third World inadequacy by teasing out commonalties between himself, the seemingly more advanced western male (in age, social position, culture), and the young African woman. He too has experienced the cold that is central to her homesickness and sense of exclusion from the wealthy but soulless northern hemisphere. At the same time, Rae goes a step further and moves into Sammar's territory by revealing his affinity for Islam in the details of his school expulsion, thereby announcing the frame which the novel will now occupy: the possibility that he will move over completely to sharing her world-view by becoming a Muslim.

In spite of their activism as carriers of faith, Aboulela's heroines are prone first of all to passivity (an Orientalist trope) on coming to the West. Galvanized into life by the deaths of loved ones – Sammar's husband Tarig in *The Translator* and Najwa's father in *Minaret* – and family breakdown or unhappy love affairs, they find in the British city, whether Aberdeen or London, encounters which, in comparison with a home which may be nurturing but is also without dynamism, activate faith and set into motion providentially ordered tests. Hassan has written perceptively of the way in which Aboulela inscribes Muslim faith extensively in her writing, especially in passages connecting individuals with community life, ritual and the moral, everyday demands of sharia. This is exemplified in the following extract from *Minaret* in which the setting is a children's Eid party at the London Regent's Park mosque:

> There are more children in new clothes to kiss and admire, the surprise – I almost squeal – of seeing a friend for the first time without hijab. This one is all peaches and cream, this one is like a model, this one is mumsy with or without hijab [...] This one looks Indian, as if the hijab had made me forget she was Indian and now she is reminding me – in the sari with her flowing hair and jewellery, she is relaxed, traditional. And the one who looks like a model confesses to me in a whisper, don't tell anyone else, Najwa, please, but she was actually Miss Djibouti long ago, before coming to Britain, before having children and covering her hair with a scarf (Aboulela 2006: 185–6).

From this one can see how in Aboulela's fiction, 'Islamic identity takes precedence over, and in fact renders irrelevant, cultural, ethnic, and national identities' (Hassan 2008: 312). The identity marker in the passage is the most obvious one of all to a western readers: the hijab, emphasized by its triple use as well as by its synonym 'scarf', is an outer cover that far from hiding oppressed women is merely the public uniform of a variety of types: feminine looking, attractive, glamorous, motherly, Somali, Indian – all united by the occasion and a further implied emphasis: living in Britain.

The Islamic identity Aboulela articulates may be conservative and quietist from the standpoint of secular Arabism (the intellectual circles that she knows but which are alien to her) and empty of the 'resistance' element espoused by postcolonial theorists (albeit, for all practical purposes, only in texts), and it certainly does not pack the activist punch of political Islamism. It nonetheless confirms the postmodern paradigm articulated by Akbar S. Ahmed: Aboulela fictionalizes 'a straight fight between two approaches to the world, two opposed philosophies [...] one [...] based in secular materialism, the other in faith.' What is peculiar to her work is the Islamic inflexion of this binary largely in terms of the western urban terrain, of the Muslim migrant experience, of a locale in which Muslims may be marginalized and to some extent oppressed, but in which they are responding in a positive way and actually winning victories for themselves and for individual westerners who become converts (unlike in the fiction of Kureishi, Ali and Aslam where the migrant reaction is almost uniformly self-destructive).[27] It is this positive image of Islam and Muslim identity which has attracted readers, and not only female Muslim ones, but others who recognize the conditions of possibility within which Aboulela writes, and out of which she translates her otherwise unfamiliar message to a wider readership.

Conclusion

This chapter has sought to demonstrate the existence and viability from a critical point of view of a category of Muslim fiction first coherently posited by Amin Malak. My discussion has embraced authors representing a range of positions, from the critical/anti-Muslim 'native informant' type – Hanif Kureishi, Monica Ali and Nadeem Aslam – the neutral – Farhana Sheikh – through to a committed Muslim point of view – Leila Aboulela. My reasons for including them all within one category, variant as they are, are the same as Malak's: each to some degree works, partially or wholly, from the inside of Muslim culture, whether or not they accept Islam in creedal terms. Hanif Kureishi, Monica Ali and Nadeem Aslam, are all writers of Muslim or semi-Muslim extraction who inscribe variations of traditional or revivalist Muslim identity in their fiction. They form a secularized critical category, in which a personal Muslim connection still exists residually; in the case of Kureishi and Ali, as a hybridity inherited from the union of Muslim and non-Muslim parents. In Aslam's, the intimacy is almost umbilical, causing a need to denounce Muslim identity as one might rebel against and repudiate an embarrassing family connection. All, including Aboulela, utilize the western secularized space to imagine Muslim identity in their own terms. This space provides in each instance an opportunity to engage with Muslim subjects and also the polemical environment in which to situate their preferred discourse. For each writer alongside the signifier Muslim the migrant experience is the other value that needs to be factored in. Their fictions are at least in part imaginatively derived from existing immigrant communities. British migrant Muslim fiction began with Rushdie in the 1980s, cohered around an emergent British Muslim identity in the 1990s, and in the first decade of the twenty-first century saw the production of richly textured novels that have proffered non-Muslim readers the opportunity of engaging imaginatively with conceptual issues surrounding a still by no means well understood religious identity that is becoming ever more deeply rooted in their midst.

Chapter 3

Fixing Muslim Masculinity, Saving Muslim Women: Azar Nafisi, Asne Seierstadt, Taslima Nasreen, Irshad Manji, Ayan Hirshi Ali

Narratives written about Islamic societies with the aim of producing representations of female subjugation by patriarchal oppression have become a common feature of western discourse.[1] The fault-line between Islam and the West is often articulated by the projection of the western discourse of rights on to Muslim societies, focusing on Muslim men's 'oppression' of Muslim women. Difference is frequently constructed according to notions of the phallo-centric, traditional/fundamentalist Muslim male who is threatened by female sexuality and incapable of grasping subtle argumentation. Alongside him are juxtaposed Muslim women who are defined by their absence from the public space, and their repressed/controlled/subservient presence within the male-dominated household. Muslim women, it is implied, can only achieve their rights by throwing off the burka/hijab, dressing as they like, achieving liberation from captivity in the home, going out to work and, above all, effecting their enfranchisement from Islam. Invariably, such narratives focus on Muslim men's control over female sexuality. However, while feeding off a notional feminism and by focusing on such issues as arranged marriage, polygamy, divorce, and sexual encounter, these narratives run the risk of defining women according to their sexuality alone, a bind first pointed out by feminists with respect to western women.[2] In addition, frequently missing in western constructions of Muslim male and female identities, beyond its function of signifying difference from western norms, is the sign 'Muslim' which in effect becomes a term emptied of other meanings. Before making readings of some prominent examples of these types of narratives,[3] it will be necessary to review the universalizing discourse(s) upon which they draw. These, as we shall see, in turn draw heavily on earlier tropes of Orientalism.

Feminist Positions and Western Universalizing Discourses on Muslim Men and Women

The debate as to whether feminism is a wholescale western importation into the Muslim world or entirely a 'local or indigenous project' (Abu-Lughod 2001: 106) is not the concern of this chapter. Neither is there space to go into the debate over the designation 'Islamic feminism'.[4] My aim here is to provide a general background to feminist issues primarily in the Middle East context in order to contextualize my discussion of discourse about Muslim women (and males) in western literary texts. Western programmes for female 'liberation' within the Muslim world inevitably put pressure upon indigenous feminist writers, scholars and activists who are in turn pressured by the strong importance given by their own societies to cultural authenticity and the need many in them feel to resist western cultural imperialism. According to Kandiyoti there are two directions open to feminists in the Muslim world: 'either denying that Islamic practices are necessarily oppressive or asserting that Islamic practices are not necessarily Islamic' (Kandiyoti 1995: 9). For such feminists the first proposition would be difficult to uphold, while the second carries implicit appeal to an 'uncorrupted original Islam against which current discriminatory practices may be denounced as falling short of truly Islamic ideals' (ibid.: 10). A prime example of this approach is to be found in Moroccan feminist Fatima Mernissi's writings which, according to miriam cooke, engage 'in the revisioning of Islamic history and the reinterpretation of Islamic texts' (cooke 1999: 94). Such a methodology, she claims, challenges 'not the sacrality of the Quran but the temporality of its interpretations' (ibid.: 95). Recognizing that in the Middle East 'religious identity at the individual communal, national and international levels has become a contested terrain' (94), cooke goes on to argue: 'To call oneself an Islamic feminist [...] does not entail the fixing of an identity but rather the creation of a new and highly contingent subject position.' This may involve challenging certain forms of western feminism 'as being implicated in anti-Islamic ideologies and practices' while still being able to form 'contingent coalitions' with feminists who have refused to take up such positions' (96).

Cooke's formulation of an Islamic feminist position perhaps somewhat belies the predicament of Muslim women in general who are caught – as other Third World women – 'in polemics about cultural authenticity' (Abu-Lughod 1998: 5). In the immediate postcolonial period nationalist regimes in the Middle East bought into the western discourse of developmentalism enthusiastically embracing the replacement of 'old sexually segregated patriarchal systems', and ostensibly allowing 'women's rights to public space' (Tucker 1993: 39–40). Their introduction of social changes favouring women were partially western-inspired. Middle Eastern modernist-nationalist regimes may have taken on 'feminist' measures such as promoting the education of girls and enfranchizing women to work in specified areas like education, health and social welfare. While emphasis was placed on the state-sponsored bourgeois nuclear family, however, there was silence on gender equality within the family – 'public liberty of women co-existed with personal forms of subordination in the family'. Middle and upper-class women emerged as the largest beneficiaries, though 'only the needs of urban women were accommodated' (ibid.: 40).

After the Iranian revolution of 1978–9, the pressure to return to, or at the very least take greater account of, perceived Islamic norms impacted on most regimes in the Muslim world, whether professedly secular or religious. Both modernist-nationalists and Islamists used defence of Islamic culture as a basis of their political legitimacy. At best women's rights were afforded a secondary priority. Nevertheless, Islamist movements have had in their ranks 'large numbers of middle-class women who [have] supported conservative political and social agenda[s]' (ibid.: 41). Middle Eastern feminists in exile excoriate Islamist regimes, while others, in Iran for instance, have engaged with and 'accept alliances with Islamist reformers' (Keddie 2002: 560; see also Moghissi: 1999). In analysing these trends, contemporary Middle East academics and feminists such as Kandiyoti and Abu-Lughod adopt the postmodernist strategy of de-emphasizing grand narratives and foregrounding local specificities. 'Women in the Middle East must be studied not in terms of an undifferentiated "Islam" or Islamic culture but rather through differing political projects of nation-states, with their distinct histories, relationships to colonialism and the West, class politics, ideological uses of Islamic idiom' (Abu-Lughod 1998: 5). Such a positioning emphasizes 'local' feminisms and avoidance of cultural binaries (Abu-Lughod 1998: 16; Kandiyoti 1995: 18).

Feminists who are sensitive to such binaries need no reminding of the role Orientalism has played in the representation of Muslim women in the West. Nikki Keddie writes of nineteenth and early twentieth-century western stereotypes of Muslim women: '[They] were seen as little better than slaves, either totally repressed or erotic objects, and as needing Western control or tutelage to gain any rights. Many Westerners saw women's bad conditions as stemming directly from Islam' (Keddie 2002: 555). In the late twentieth century, according to Deniz Kandiyoti, 'Orientalist depictions of subjugated women entrapped in the fast-frozen relations of an atemporal Islam' still persisted (Kandiyoti 1995: 9). It has been argued that such representations complied with colonialist objectives to use Oriental women 'to subvert the [indigenous] social system while pretending to liberate them from their own men' (Mabro 1991: 12). Juliet Mabro claims: '[Western] feminists [have been] as guilty of Eurocentric [...] and colonialist attitudes as anyone else' (13). For Arab feminist Leila Ahmed the term 'Colonial feminism' expresses the 'resemblances she perceives between the colonial discourses and some Western feminists of today' (Abu-Lughod 1998: 14; Ahmed 1992). Over twenty years ago, in her seminal essay 'Under Western Eyes: feminist scholarship and colonial discourses', Chandra Mohanty situated universalizing discourses about Muslim women, Islam and the veil within broader contemporary western feminist categorizations of Third World women who, she argued, were largely defined (along with western women) in terms of their victim status: '[To speak of] "women" as a group, as a stable category of analysis [...] assumes an ahistorical, universal entity among women based on a generalized notion of their subordination' (Mohanty: [1988] 1993: 204). While western feminists of the first wave may have claimed sisterhood with third world women, they retained a superiority vis-à-vis their more deprived sisters on account of the addition of 'third-world-difference' to 'sexual difference' (ibid.: 215). From these feminists indigenous valorization of specific social practices including marriage and religion received the standard de-legitimization of western 'humanistic and scientific discourse'; veiling in particular was seized upon and marked out for 'assertion of its universal significance' (215, 209). This type of feminist discourse may be situated within what Lila Abu-Lughod calls 'universalising discourses about patriarchy, Islam, and oppression' (Abu-Lughod 1998: 22) in which Third World women fail to be afforded recognition as women 'through the complex interaction between class, culture, religion and other ideological institutions and frameworks' (Mohanty: 207). For contemporary Middle Eastern feminists and scholars like Kandiyoti and Abu-Lughod the imperative is one of deconstructing 'grand narratives within feminist scholarship [...] which attempted to pinpoint universal causes for the subjection of women' (Kandiyoti 1995: 18).[5]

Middle Eastern feminists have sought to develop reasons and use various means of explaining the ways in which male patriarchy has disadvantaged Muslim women. In her autobiography, Leila Ahmed, an Egyptian feminist domiciled in the United States, differentiates between an official, text-centred Islam of the ulama, which coheres around the masculine world of the mosque and a woman's understanding of Islam, largely transmitted orally through female relatives. According to Ahmed the form of Islam privileged by literacy promoted a fixed and authoritarian interpretation identified with state power; throughout Islamic history this form was the enemy and oppressor of women. Far from having the best understanding of Islam the mullahs and ayatollahs who perpetuated this version had only 'a deeper understanding of [...] their own gloomy, medieval version of it' (Ahmed, L. 2000: 129). Evidencing to her own argument that modern women's access to education and work has resulted in 'a laying [of] siege to the places considered until then the private preserve of men and the privilege of maleness', Fatima Mernissi identifies a rear-guard action – which she associates with among other things re-veiling – by some Muslim men with the aim of putting things ' back in order' (Mernissi 1991: 23–4). In her study of Muslim traditions or hadith – previously the preserve of males – Mernissi has identified what she terms 'a tradition of misogyny' behind the historical Islamic construction of women. For her part, Algerian writer Assia Djebar, in celebrating the emancipation of her women compatriots as an interiorized unveiling in *Women of Algiers in Their Apartment*, subtly invites her readership to consider the loss sustained by an entire society through its implementation of a segregation instituted in terms of biological difference:

> *New women of Algiers, who have been allowed to move about in streets just these last few years, have been momentarily blinded by the sun as they cross the threshold, do they free themselves – do we free ourselves – altogether from the relationship with their own bodies, a relationship lived in the shadows until now, as they have done throughout the centuries?* (Djebar 1999: 2; original italics).

Perhaps the most direct attempt to deconstruct traditional Muslim maleness by a Middle Eastern feminist is to be found in both the fiction and non-fiction of Nawal El-Saadawi. Her project has consistently been to assert female identity by direct confrontation with patriarchal norms. 'Nawal al-Sa'dawi's narrative is intellectually focused against an adversary who is narratively drawn and depicted in the form of grandfathers, directors, guards and presidents' (Al-Musawi 2003: 225). Her approach appears to conform to a category of Middle Eastern women's writing which 'needs adversaries, represented by patriarchy as atemporal structure' (ibid.). An issue arising from this form of essentializing is the degree to which it feeds off western stereotypes, so reaffirming the Third World as undeveloped and backward. As one critic phrases it: El-Saadawi can appear to be pointing out progress in the achievements of American women while at the same time showing Arab women continuing to groan under Islam (Amireh 2002: 42, 48). Middle Eastern feminists' criticisms of Muslim males undoubtedly register split cultural significations. El-Saadawi, Mernissi and even Ahmed are considered by some to have ventured too far in the direction of Orientalist discourse in raising criticisms against a patriarchal Islam. On the other hand, Moghissi (1999) posits the danger that 'anti-Orientalist studies of gender and Islam' has led others in the opposite direction: 'They needed to counter anti-Muslim prejudices and neo-Orientalist representation of Muslim women, without getting caught in an apologetic or self-denying defence of Islamic gender practices or a justification of the oppressive discourses and actions of Islamist ideologues and rulers' (37).

In an article reviewing academic work done on the impact of Said's *Orientalism* in the field of Middle East Feminist studies, Lila Abu-Lughod (2001) instances the writings of Fatima Mernissi: especially her *Dreams of Trespass: Tales of a Harem Girlhood*, which for all its 'celebration of women's traditional powers of beauty' inscribes her account of twentieth-century Moroccan women's lives in familiar Orientalist terms: 'Tradition and Modernity. Harems and Freedom. Veiling and Unveiling. These are the familiar terms by which the East has long been apprehended (and devalued) and the West has constructed itself as superior. These are some of what Said calls the dogmas of Orientalism' (108). Abu-Lughod warns 'to launch feminist critiques [of Middle East countries] in a context of continuing Western hegemony is to risk playing into the hands of Orientalist discourse' (107).[6] This is an important statement which I will be using in my readings of a number of books published in the West by women from Muslim countries. If this warning appertains to the field of Middle East academic study under Abu-Lughod's purview, it is even more pertinent to the general inscription from within the West of work purporting to represent women's lives in the Muslim world with the aim of exposure of their indigenous repression. More specifically, Roksana Bahramitash has pointed out how opportunist feminism can be parasitic on Orientalism, adapting the term feminist Orientalism (as argued by Parvin Paidar (1995) in her study of women's involvement in Iranian politics) to the political environment of the first decade of the twenty-first century: the aftermath of 9/11, the invasion of Afghanistan and the so-called 'War on Terror':

> It assumes a binary opposition between the West and the Orient: the Occident is progressive and the best place for women [...] the Muslim Orient is backward, uncivilized and the worst place for women [...] feminist Orientalism [...] regards Oriental women only as victims and not as agents of social transformation [...] Therefore Muslim women need saviours, i.e., their Western sisters [...] [it] assumes that all societies in the Orient are the same and all Muslim women there live under the same conditions (Bahramitash 2005: 222).

I now intend to test the applicability of such feminist Orientalism to two popular books purporting to disclose the burden of male oppression of women within Islamic societies apparently beyond the reach of benevolent western influences.

Constructing the Muslim Male: *Azar Nafisi's Reading Lolita in Tehran* and Asne Seierstad's *The Bookseller of Kabul*

Azar Nafisi's *Reading Lolita in Tehran: A Memoir in Books* and Asne Seierstad's English version of *The Bookseller of Kabul*, are alternately insider and observant-outsider reports that fulfil the function of exposing male oppression of women in Iran and Afghanistan respectively. Nafisi's book can be approached from a variety of standpoints. And while there are definite insights to be gained in connecting it to the burgeoning publication in the United States of American-Iranian female memoirs, I have chosen to emphasize the Iranian context out of which the text was constructed. This may seem paradoxical, for one critic at least has accused the book of showing 'no awareness whatsoever of the lively and controversial literature created in Iran prior to, during, and after the revolution. In fact, it suggests a total absence of interest in literature by the local culture' (Keshavarz 2007: 7). This is most likely the case, and it may well be true that texts such as *Reading Lolita* and *The Bookseller of Kabul*, while knowledgeable about the countries they represent, lull western readers into accepting a universalizing discourse that neither troubles nor challenges them with regard to the peoples and cultures being reported on. In my readings of Nafisi and Seierstad's texts, I aim to test the proposition that both are formed around the kind of feminist Orientalism (or 'Neo-Orientalism' – the term Keshavarz employs) which Bahramitash specifically lays at the door of *Reading Lolita in Tehran.*

It has often been pointed out that in spite of the Islamic Republic of Iran's turning back of the clock in respect of obvious areas of women's presence in the public arena, writing by Iranian women has increased exponentially since 1979. In his chapter on women's literature in *The Politics of Writing in Iran*, Kamran Talattof (2000) outlines the conditions that gave rise in post-revolutionary Iran to a burgeoning of women's writing on feminist-oriented topics and themes. This occurred in spite of the dismantling of women's rights, in the areas of divorce, custody of children, right to equality in the workplace and unfettered travel, immediately pursuant to the establishment of the new Islamic regime. New laws made it possible to stone women for committing adultery and to apply up to seventy-six lashes to those appearing in public unveiled. 'The veil – or more precisely, the woman's body – has become a locus of contention and a battle ground between Western modernity and Islam' (Talattof 2000: 136). In March 1979 women's groups demonstrated against Ayatollah Khomeini's speech calling for mandatory public veiling for women. Although these demonstrations caused the Government to climb-down, the victory was short-lived. 'Members of various Islamist women's associations, violent extremist groups, and the police again began to enforce the veil' (ibid.: 138). Significantly, the feminist women's demonstrations were not supported by the leftist opposition 'because they believed that feminism was associated with bourgeois ideology' and independent women's agitation 'would jeopardise the sense of unity necessary for the struggle against imperialism' (ibid.).

Nafisi's narrative records these events and her personal debates with members of the left opposition with which she claims to have been once loosely allied. Repeatedly comparing the Iranian revolution to the Russian revolution, she brands Iranian radicals – from the secular left and religious right alike – as ideologues addicted to totalitarian absolutes. However, in spite of the conservative religious turn taken by the Iranian revolution, it has been accompanied by a spread of feminist debates that were once unheard of. Furthermore, literature written by women 'has increased dramatically'. Of particular interest to discussion of *Reading Lolita* is Talattof's affirmation that 'ordinary women who are confined to their homes spend a great deal of time reading' (Talattof 2000: 139–40). The framing narrative of *Reading Lolita* concerns the private and informal women's reading group meeting weekly in the author's Tehran apartment. A retired academic – or rather one who has decided for political reasons not to continue teaching – she has nevertheless agreed to lead a tiny class self-selected from among her former students. Both professor and students are devotees of modern literature in English, an unassuming enough fact in itself until viewed in the context of Iran's recent complex cultural history. Nafisi's avowed pro-westernism – she told an American journalist she thanked the Islamic Republic for teaching her 'to love Austen and James and ice cream and freedom' (Wasserman 2003) – is to be situated within Iranian intellectuals' love–hate relationship with western culture. Wild fluctuations in response – from adoration to execration – litter Iran's reception of western influences in the twentieth century. (In the 1960s, Jalal Al-e Ahmad coined a Persian neologism – *gharbzadigi* – loosely translated as 'westoxication' – as a term of opprobrium directed against the pro-West fashion.) Nafisi spent the 1970s, the period of mounting agitation against the Shah's regime, as a doctoral student in the United States. Though she makes an unconvincing case for her dilettante involvement in anti-regime activities while abroad, the figurative silk-chiffon scarf always worn stylishly round her neck (never over her head) attests to her love for the chic, the *recherché*, in short all that indicates privilege and class in an Iranian setting.[7]

Nafisi's narrative of Iran under the Islamic republic depicts a grim tragi-comedy in which a succession of Muslim Malvolios blindly and contemptuously espouse and erect a regime of virtuous dogmatism with no regard for persons, place or time. Provocatively re-writing Austen, she angles her satire against the mullahs: 'It is a truth universally acknowledged that a Muslim man, regardless of his fortune, must be in want of a nine-year-old-virgin wife' (Nafisi 2003: 257). Islamist values and their associated repressive anti-humanitarian practices entrench themselves within Iranian society. The Ayatollah's victory over the Left ensures the implementation of an Islamist programme that Nafisi figures as the figment of old men's (i.e. the mullahs') dreams. 'A stern ayatollah, a self-proclaimed philosopher-king, had come to rule our land' (28). This imposition of Islamist measures impacts most of all on Iranian women. Public and private spheres become hostile, contradictory nodes in a new religio-political geography. Nafisi's discussion group takes place in a private cocoon consciously woven against the harsh realities outside. The exterior world intrudes in the women's reports of daily humiliations centred on dress, appearance, and social behaviour. These humiliations range from the absurdity of having the length of one's eyelashes measured, to youth, innocently caught in mixed company when a private house is raided by religious police, being imprisoned and punished with lashes. For the women it becomes difficult to know which is real: the social space presided over by witches and hobgoblins (especially the regime's female religious police who accost their fellow-women over dress codes), or the private apartment (which is also not immune to incursions by revolutionary guards) where together they create a sustaining, feminized discourse.

The young women's response to the outside world is mediated through literary discussions of the novels of Nabokov, Fitzgerald, James and Austen. Gillian Whitlock has pointed out 'the powerful affirmation of Nafisi's reading group for Western readers, for [it] [...] present(s) a powerful defence of the Great Tradition of English in the course of its critique of the Islamic republic'

(Whitlock 2008: 11). The literary texts themselves become a means of exposing the 'false dreams' of totalitarianism and are made to disclose readings that may or may not seem attractive to western readers but should be considered Iranian in their subjection to ideological analysis. According to Talattof, Iran's modern intelligentsia have for some time had the habit of forming literary communities that read texts according to the 'dominant metaphors of their own time'. Breaking down the orientations of such twentieth-century reading communities into Persianist, Marxist, liberal, Muslim, and feminist categories, he argues these have often been formed around the ideology of the writers themselves.

> By encouraging such a mode of reading, authors promote a subjectivity in their readers, teach them the desired way of interpreting a text, and establish a set of criteria for evaluating literature. Such an enterprise shapes the readers' literary tastes and teaches them to value political meaning rather than literary form (Talattof: 15, 16).

In her classes, Nafisi adopts the creative role, forming the responses of her 'girls' around notional aesthetic, experiential, and humanist axioms. By foregrounding such literary/humanist qualities as sensitivity to moral conscience and awareness of ambiguity, the 'open spaces' of the novels are invariably set against the closed mindset of supporters of what is persistently and ironically nomenclatured 'the Islamic Republic'. Nafisi's iteration of this expression makes it an object of absurdity and contempt, disclosing the political orientation of her readings.[8] Lightly flecked as they are with Iranian cultural nationalist nostrums, with rigid religious dogmatism as the implied adversary, most importantly of all they are underscored by her self-valorization as a member of the pre-revolutionary Iranian elite. This identity is instrumental in nurturing her sense of moral and social superiority. Her family's proclaimed association with Iran's past (non-Islamic) cultural eminence; the 'insubordination' of her father as mayor of Tehran during the Shah's time; and her mother's apolitical aloofness while functioning as one of the first six women to be elected to the Iranian Parliament in 1963, are each invoked. These qualifications align Nafisi with the bourgeois-nationalist phase of Iran's political and cultural development, in addition to registering disdain for anti-hegemonic positions such as that of Said (which she contends play into the hands of the Islamists), alongside an overtly pro-western feminism:

> At the start of the twentieth century, the age of marriage in Iran – nine, according to sharia laws – was changed to thirteen and then later to eighteen. My mother had chosen whom she wanted to marry [...] When I was growing up in the 1960s, there was little difference between my rights and the rights of women in Western democracies.[9] But it was not the fashion then to think

that our culture was not compatible with modern democracy, that there were Western and Islamic versions of democracy and human rights. We all wanted opportunities and freedom. That is why we supported revolutionary change – were demanding more rights, not fewer (Nafisi: 261).

A case has been raised against Nafisi that she has been co-opted by Orientalists like Bernard Lewis and American neo-conservatives pushing for regime change in Iran – a consummation devoutly to be wished by pro-Shahi factions with whom she would be in sympathy (Bahramitash 2005: 230). More to the point as far as the book's feminist claims are concerned is its silence concerning subaltern women as opposed to 'her immediate circle of privileged women' (ibid.: 231). Bahramitash points out that Nafisi mentions her children's nanny only very briefly and makes deprecatory remarks about the women students at a non-elite engineering college where she had once taught. She also contests Nafisi's claim that Iranian universities are 'bastions of male domination', citing 'official enrolment data that over 60 per cent of Iranian students in higher education are women' (233). The burden of this criticism is that the work expresses both Islamo- and Iranophobia, and panders to a white middle class 'liberal feminism' at a time 'when the Bush administration has been preparing the American public to support its foreign policy against Iran' (234).[10] Even Moghissi, certainly no friend of the Islamic Republic, seems to pre-empt Bahramitash's criticism of Nafisi's style of discourse when she writes of: 'Self-congratulatory discussions from a Western hegemonic position about women's rights "here" as opposed to their deprivation "there" work[ing] to fuel racism, somehow softening the shame of the West as a violent, clumsy bully' (Moghissi 1999: 37).

The Iranian male is represented in the narrative in a number of guises that range from students, revolutionaries (favouring either the Islamic Republic or the secular totalitarian left), Islamic guards policing women in line with the Ayatollah's fatwas, to variously tolerant and intolerant, kind and unkind, fathers, uncles, brothers and husbands. Curiously, far from representing them as ubiquitously dominant and phallo-centric, Nafisi sees Iranian men beset by a vulnerability to which they are incapable of giving voice. An embarrassed and clumsy gate-man forced to chase after her when she attempts to enter the university unveiled; a mysterious, reclusive aesthete who engages as her mentor; and a strangely aloof student in her English class who is also a leader of the Muslim Students' Association, are all made to embody shifting ambiguities which make them anything but intimidating or oppressive. The only aggressively patriarchal male character is, ironically, the spoiled younger brother of one of Nafisi's student circle. In spite of its ideological message, then, *Reading Lolita in Tehran* is not a diatribe against men, Muslim or otherwise. If anything, the book evidences to an understanding or at least an awareness of an aspect of Muslim societies that Al-Musawi finds lacking in the confrontational El-Saadawi. 'The social dimension of sexual repression which provokes the

[male] gaze [...] The coffeehouse, the pub, the public garden and the streets are terrains of frustration and fear as much as they are sites for socialization' (Al-Musawi 2003: 223).

In spite of the, I think on the whole, pertinent criticism of feminist Orientalism raised against *Reading Lolita*, it can also be said in the book's favour that while Nafisi may well be arguing that the return to conservative values in Iran is excessively unfair on women, she also implicitly recognizes its adverse effects on men too. Where does this leave us then? It might be contended that through representing Muslim men (other than the Islamist clerics) in a sympathetic way, Nafisi is condemning Islam as deficient in so far as the arrangement of gender relations is concerned. On the other hand, the uncertainties of the men, who are mostly, after all, products of a Muslim culture, might suggest that that culture has left their humanity, at least partially, in tact. Overall, as I indicated at the start of this chapter, by constructing the sign 'Muslim' as overwhelmingly a signifier of binary gendered identities, in which male and female occupy positions very different to those prescribed by western norms, the sign itself becomes emptied of all other meanings. Despite its proclaimed aestheticism, humanism, and feminism, Nafisi's book performs precisely this operation.

The Norwegian journalist Asne Seierstad wrote *The Bookseller of Kabul* following a period of residence with the family of Sultan Khan, an Afghani businessman and bibliophile, who had suffered at the hands of both communist and Taliban regimes. At the outset the author describes Khan as 'a man who had tried to save the art and literature of his country, while a string of dictators did their best to destroy them' (Seierstad 2003: 2). Liberal in thought – 'he was a freethinker of the opinion that everyone had the right to be heard' – modern in his interpretation of Islam – 'he was a believer but a moderate Muslim' – innovative if dictatorial in his business practice, Khan appears to have characteristics that might make him attractive to a western reader (ibid.: 17–18). Seierstad's narrative is nevertheless structured in such a way as to reveal the supposed contradictions and inconsistencies in Khan's behaviour. This is achieved by juxtaposition of his 'liberal' against his 'recidivistic' side, summed up in his patriarchal treatment of his family, especially the womenfolk. At the centre of the text the author has constructed a paradox, expressed in the publisher's blurb: 'While Khan is passionate in his love of books and his hatred of censorship, he also has strict views on family life and the role of women.'

The narrative begins with Khan's second marriage to Sonya, a girl from a distantly related but much poorer family who is nearly forty years younger than himself (she is sixteen, he in his fifties). Though married for many years to an educated woman who once taught Persian and has given him three sons along with other female children, Khan decides to avail himself of a Muslim male's right to plurality of wives. Chosen for her youth and beauty, the new wife has very limited mental horizons and shows no inclination to question her husband's decisions. While Khan is seen neither to beat his wives or daughters, nor to keep them imprisoned in the house, he is pictured on a journey between Peshawar and Kabul salivating in anticipation of return to his 'delicious child-woman' (64). In fact it is his eldest son, Mansur, who is the more chauvinistic in his treatment of women. He abuses his aunt Leila – who is no more than a couple of years his senior but as the youngest daughter among Khan's siblings is the domestic drudge for the family. 'He has grown up with his three-years-older aunt, not like a brother, but like a master' (156). Mansur's humiliation of Leila recalls John Reed's chauvinistic abuse of Jane Eyre: 'You parasite [...] this is not your home, it is my home' (146). Though he is critical of his father's vengeful pursuance of a petty thief who stole some of Khan's postcards to sell to a business competitor, Mansur's sensitivities are distorted by his insatiable sexual appetite. Seierstad allies Mansur's chauvinistic treatment of women with the religious/sexual dichotomy he carries inside him. Disgusted after a friend invites him to share intercourse with a child beggar, Mansur engages in a pilgrimage to the shrine of Ali at Mazar-i Sharif in the vain hope of regaining purity and obtaining God's forgiveness. His pilgrimage is motivated as much by a need to escape from his domineering father as to obtain absolution. He exclaims to his friends: 'I love Mazar, I love Ali, I love freedom, I love you!' [...] It is the first time he has travelled alone, the first day in his whole life he has not seen a member of his family (137).

But if Seierstad, like Nafisi, is aware of the vulnerability of men within Islamic societies, the reader is not invited to pity the lot of the Muslim male for very long. Leila's victim-status is prioritized as successively she is seen failing to obtain official teacher-status, and losing an enlightened potential suitor dissuaded from making a marriage proposal by her self-interested nephew. At one point, before these hopes of escape are raised and lost, we see Leila the last to turn in to bed and the first to awake in the early hours. 'She washes the oil off her fingers and goes to bed, in the same clothes she has been using all day. She rolls out her mattress, pulls a blanket over her and falls asleep, until the mullah wakes her a few hours later. A new day begins, to the sound of "Allahu akhbar" – "God is great"'(157). The juxtaposition can hardly be missed: patriarchal Islam in the form of the mullah predestines the life of drudgery of the Muslim Cinderella ensuring that in her case no Prince Charming will arrive to take her away. Seierstad eschews detailed reportage of the kind of lurid patriarchal atrocities to be found in the books of Jean Sasson, although she manages to quote a short narrative about a woman's stoning (not in Afghanistan) from a novel by Leon Uris. There is also de rigueur material on honour killings, and extensive representation of the Afghan male as lustful, dictatorial and disrespectful to women.

For the most part, *The Bookseller of Kabul* functions at the level of a narrative of domestic life.[11] Although both President Hamid Karzai and Northern Alliance warlord General Dostum make cameo-appearances, surprisingly little reference is made in the text to the political configurations that are responsible for Afghanistan's decline. Western figures occasionally surface to purchase chocolate in Sultan Khan's 'little booth in the dark lobby of one of Kabul's hotels' (177) and one of his male relatives accompanies an American journalist to the Pashtun border areas in search of Osama Bin Laden and Mullah Omar. But no time is spent analysing the international political interests that, in the words of the UN Secretary General, created 'a new regional version of the "Great Game" [in Afghanistan] [...] A vicious cycle [...] in which the inability of the Afghan factions to agree to a political settlement is both the cause and the effect of persistent outside interference in the affairs of Afghanistan' (Amnesty 1999). Perhaps this is unsurprising. Western governments supported after all both the Afghan Mujahidin and the Taliban at particular stages in their development. 'Instead of undermining the credibility of Islam', writes Mark Huband of the West's backing for the anti-Soviet Afghan Muslim militias, 'the West sent weapons, advisors, money and support' (Huband 1998: 15). When the Taliban ousted the Mujahidin, Russia, Iran, India, Uzbekistan, and Turkmenistan continued to back them, while the United States agreed with Pakistan that only the Taliban could guarantee Afghan stability (ibid.: 22).[12] This despite the fact that under the Taliban girls and women were effectively imprisoned within their homes. As an Amnesty International report put it:

> The status of women in Afghanistan has been, and continues to be used by armed groups as a political tool in their struggles to secure and maintain power. Most armed groups have imposed restrictions on women in the name of religion and culture as a means of consolidating their power and legitimacy. At the same time, acts of violence perpetrated against women – public beatings, rape and sexual assault – appear to have been used as instruments of intimidation, humiliation and coercion of women and the wider population. The repression of women symbolises not only their vulnerability, but also the powerlessness of their male relatives to protect them (Amnesty 1999).

Western writers on the gender politics of Islamic societies may prefer not to dampen their powder by acknowledging that the political interference of their own governments may have played its part in bolstering what they might otherwise consider to be the perpetual patriarchal structures of lands like Afghanistan. Any social advances these societies might make are due to the beneficial interventions of the West; the many evils they are guilty of are solely the fault of themselves. Seierstad's narrative points out the improvements in Afghan's women's lives since the departure of the Taliban. But, she seems to imply, there is a watermark beyond which Afghan Muslim males can scarcely rise. This is probably the underlying message of the book, once the titillating extremities of child-rape, child-marriage and honour killing have been negotiated.

We return to Sultan Khan. If a figure like him cannot escape the harsh gender imbalance traditional to Afghan society, Seierstad implies, what hope for the rest? 'In many ways Sultan *was* liberal. When he was in Iran he had bought Sonya western clothes. He often referred to the burka as an oppressive cage, and he was pleased that the new Government included female ministers. In his heart he wanted Afghanistan to be a modern country, and he talked warmly about the emancipation of women. But within the family he remained the authoritarian patriarch. When it came to ruling his family, Sultan had only one model: his own father' (Seierstad 2003: 237). Sultan Khan's liberal qualities then do not prevent him from conforming to type. In Seierstad's rendition, the Muslim male is confirmed as an authoritarian patriarch. The epilogue of *The Bookseller* reports the break up of Khan's extended-family ménage. The fact that his mother and sisters split away actually adds to his status as a practitioner of liberal middle class values. In constructing her narrative around the putative contradictions in his personality, Seierstad misses or consciously sets aside the specificities of Khan's position. No less than Nafisi, who clearly inhabits the subject position of the urban, upper class beneficiary of the modernist-nationalist 'feminist' policies of the Pahlavis, is he the product of a specific political/cultural formation. But while her privileged background has enabled Nafisi to throw off the derogatory designation 'Islamic', Khan's has not.

Asne Seierstad's narrative may project a sympathy for the plight of Afghan women but it does not pass up the opportunity to rehearse the usual sexual stereotyping of the Muslim male that paradoxically condemns Muslim women to continue to be defined primarily as sexual objects, powerless to alter their fate. Azar Nafisi is not concerned with producing a text that essentializes the Muslim male per se, though she certainly does set out to satirize a particular group of Muslim men. She is equally interested, however, in using a humanist hermeneutic to project western literature as a weapon by which to expose Iran's Islamic republic. Rather than encourage the Orientalist presentation of Muslim women as slaves and erotic objects, Nafisi de-centres such issues as arranged marriage, polygamy, divorce and sexual encounter. She appears to be more aware than Seierstad of the implications of falling into the language game of sexual binaries, a game indulged in both by Islamism and colonial feminism alike. Thus while she attacks the male-mullahs' projection and imposition of their own fantasies on to a vulnerable female population, Nafisi also demonstrates an insight into the destructive effects of such thinking on men and women alike. She condemns the Islamists for using religion ideologically as an instrument of power, and calls for a re-establishment of the private and public spheres in Iran, this in order to ensure separation of the personal and the political 'to prevent the political intruding in our individual lives' (Nafisi 2003: 273). Nonetheless, in this Nafisi reveals her positioning within nationalist-bourgeois privilege: she occludes, as Bahramitash shrewdly points out, the millions of women whose lives, in both public and private spheres, are marked by the politics of social class. Both texts, however, miss out the western imperialist interpolation: Nafisi, one suspects, out of hatred of a form of Islamism which she accuses of robbing Iran of its history; and her enshrouding within an aesthetic of western modernism that, she herself acknowledges, has in the West virtually been ousted by postmodernism. Seierstad, on the other hand, is silent on western governments' interference in Afghanistan. Absent from here book is reference to western complicity in sustaining Afghan tribal fanaticism, and using Islam for purposes of power, in the process almost totally ignoring the plight of Afghan women when protesting against this did not suit the political agenda. Both these narratives therefore remain markedly partial in their foregrounding of issues relating to male and female Muslim identities. Seierstad is too uncritical in her indulgent utilization of religio-cultural sexual binaries, and Nafisi too fixated with class politics and a self-consciously elite positioning with respect to Iranian cultural history to be able to envisage new pathways for men and women within Afghan and Iranian society.

Migrant Women and the 'Flight' from Islam

In an essay on immigrant Muslim writers in Germany, Georg Stoll points out that a desire 'to distance oneself' from Islam is 'a constantly recurring theme for female characters, who are often treated by women immigrant writers' (Stroll 1998: 273). Such characters usually do not desire a complete break from Islam; they may not wish to relinquish its spiritual and moral dimensions, or vacate it when it requires defending as part of their identity. But they reject its 'instrumentalization [...] to serve patriarchal or political interests' and commonly 'the first-person female narrator tries to escape, through rebellion and flight, from the religiously grounded claims to male power and control' (274–6). Women suffering this sort of dilemma do not inhabit works of fiction only: the real, living woman in flight from her ancestral religion, witnessing to its incorrigible oppression of her sex, has become an archetypal figure in the western discourse of rights directed specifically against Islam. Moving through the roles of communal victim to liberated individuals and tapping into the western discourses of feminism and the individual's right to freedom, a handful of Third World women escapees have accumulated the necessary symbolic capital to become iconic native converts to western liberalism. In their struggle for the enfranchisement of Muslim women (starting usually with themselves), they denounce forced, arranged marriage, assert the right of homosexuals to transgress Islamic codes, and produce generally provocative assaults against Muslim 'patriarchal chauvinism'. Eagerly promoted by both the western publishing industry and the electronic and print media, as examplars and writers they have made high-profile contributions to the *Kulturkampf* against Islamic belief and practice.

A pioneer in this mode is the Bangladeshi writer Taslima Nasreen, who first came to prominence in the West when she apparently fled Dhaka in the summer of 1994, flying on to Stockholm under the protection of officials from the Swedish Foreign Ministry. Her offence was to have given an interview to the *Times* of India, for which she was subsequently charged under the Bangladeshi penal code, of 'deliberately hurting religious sentiment' (Deen 2006: 2). In Sweden she gave more controversial interviews to the Indian press and was fêted by Swedish PEN who awarded her a prize which the previous year they had given to Salman Rushdie. For journalist Hanifa Deen, and apparently quite a few of the people she interviewed who knew or had met her in Bangladesh, India and Sweden, Taslima Nasreen was consciously playing a role. In Europe she was embraced as an *ersatz* Rushdie figure who it was possible to laud without running the danger of incurring the wrath of Iran. But she also alienated a string of individuals and organizations (from the Swedish Defence of Rushdie Committee to liberal Muslims and feminist activists in Bangladesh) that had previously supported her. According to Deen, they later recognized Nasreen as a publicity seeker who partly faked her 'flight' from Bangladesh and who was more a celebrity than a writer. 'When the West looked at Taslima they saw a victim, but in Bangladesh, even human rights activists conceded that she was a woman complicit in her own downfall. Her ambition, her self–involvement came at a price: she gave no thought to the consequences of her writing, nor to the expectations her community had of its writers' (ibid.: 90).

However, in comparison with self-proclaimed feminist, lesbian 'Muslim' controversialist Irshad Manji, a case might possibly be made for Taslima Nasreen as a serious writer.[13] Daughter of Egyptian-Gujarati parents who brought her to Canada from Uganda at the age of four, self-confessed 'Muslim refusenik' and 'Muslim Zionist' Irshad Manji, if her work *The Trouble With Islam Today* is anything to go by, has since her teenage years been in flight from 'mainstream Islam'.[14] Admittedly, the young Manji's preference for the horizons on offer in suburban Vancouver at 'my school and Rose of Sharon Baptist Church' as opposed to 'the confines of Muslim Uganda' (Manji 2005: 20–1) seems natural enough. Were this an evangelical paperback, however, for which its folksy, rhetorical North American patter supplies the necessary stylistic qualifications, and not the 'wake-up call for Muslims' claimed by its subtitle, we would hardly expect to read an enthusiastic quote from *The Independent* on its jacket nor, perhaps, to find inside the Canadian *Globe and Mail* describing its author as 'a blazingly articulate young Canadian Muslim'. Laying the hype aside, we might hesitate to trust Manji's judgment on the place and significance in Islamic history of the Mu'tazila, the role of muftis ('why do we need these guys at all?'), or her convictions about Israel's unequivocally generous biculturalism. But we could well applaud the note of self-deprecation in: 'It might appear ridiculous that someone who's not a theologian, a politician, or a diplomat […] has the chutzpah to comment on what could be done to reform Islam. On occasion, I've felt presumptuous just thinking about it'. Until we arrive at the rejoinder: 'but only on occasion. Change has to come from somewhere. Why not from a young Muslim woman who's got no investment, emotional or otherwise, in defending the status quo?' (ibid.: 177). Bearing in mind the role she and the media have constructed for Manji, the last statement is disingenuous to say the least.

No doubt the ideas Manji holds forth on are worthy of consideration: Muslims thinking for themselves, distrusting their mullahs, reading the Qur'an and saying their prayers in English, disabusing themselves of their belief in Jewish plots, making mention of Abraham as the inventor of monotheism, and so on. Inevitably that must also mean scrutinizing 'Islam's' treatment of women and Muslim homosexuals. By now it will not surprise us that both these causes should be presented in the most lurid light: 'Girl coerced into sex [in Nigeria] to receive 180 lashes'; homosexuals (presented by Manji herself on *Queer TV*) denounced by Toronto Muslims as 'dogs' and Jews. There is even room for exposure of Muhammad Ata 'and the boys['] expect[ation of] unfettered access to dozens of virgins in heaven' (57) as vainly based on a mistranslated Syriac expression into Arabic.[15] In spite of the disavowal quoted above, all of these charges are proposed in the context of Manji's self-proclaimed, self-vaunting expert status. 'It wasn't just the modern Muslim in me who had to wrestle with these issues. My career as a TV journalist and commentator placed me on the front line of the public's own questions about Islam' (33). But if she is qualified to expatiate on Islam by virtue of first hand experience as a young Muslim growing up in North America, why does Manji's writing tell us so much about herself, and next to nothing about the community to which she once belonged? She makes no reference, for example, to the existence of large numbers of North American converts to Islam, black or white. She appears ignorant of how ubiquitous institutionalized white racism encouraged Afro-American women to adopt Muslim dress as a marker of self-esteem.[16] Dismissing Said for giving Muslims the ammunition to condemn any type of criticism of Islam as Orientalism, she defends Rushdie over *The Satanic Verses*, but omits to mention Said's support for him (31). All of which merely confirms how determined, if ostentatiously partisan, is Manji's intervention into the polemics against Islam. This migrant woman whose flight from Islam was accomplished relatively painlessly has become a more effective campaigner than Taslima Nasreen, who suffering from the imprint of the sub-continent, is now reduced as a propaganda tool to the domain of India.

Completing a trio of migrant women whose opposition either to Islam or to traditional Muslim practice has brought them celebrity, but arguably more plausible than either Irshad Manji or Taslima Nasreen, is the Somali human rights campaigner Ayaan Hirsi Ali. She became well-known after collaborating with the Dutch filmmaker Theo van Gogh on a ten-minute film entitled *Submission* for which she as the scriptwriter was responsible for the scene in which the opening verses of the Qur'an were displayed over a woman's body. This highly provocative act was intended to demonstrate that a woman might obey the injunctions of the Qur'an yet be forced to submit sexually to a man she hated but who she was forced to marry; or she might be flogged for falling in love. Hirsi Ali explains in her autobiography, *Infidel*: 'I saw this as the first in a series of films that would tackle the master-slave relationship of God and the individual. My message was that the Quran is an act of man, not of God. We should be free to interpret it; we should be permitted to apply it to the modern era in a different way, instead of performing painful contortions to try to recreate the circumstances of a horrible distant past' (Ali, A.H. 2008: 314). However the subsequent murder of Theo van Gogh by a religious extremist took the struggle into realms neither he nor Hirsi Ali had envisaged. Malise Ruthven writes: 'As a Dutch MP, Hirsi Ali mounted a successful campaign to expose honor killings of young women in Muslim families for alleged sexual misdemeanours, and the scandal of circumcisions performed on little girls on Dutch kitchen tables.' However, 'Unlike Muslim feminists such as Fatima Mernissi or Leila Ahmed who challenge the misogynistic and patriarchal interpretation of the holy texts, she confronts, and rejects, the canon in toto. This is not a position from which she is likely to have much impact on Muslims with a deeper knowledge of their religious traditions' (Ruthven 2007).

Hirsi Ali's youthful reading experiences, especially in exile from Somalia in Kenya, are not greatly dissimilar to Egyptian and Sudanese writers Ahdaf Soueif and Leila Aboulela in that she, like them, is stirred by Mills and Boon-style romance stories (and later 'sexy books' by Barbara Cartland and Danielle Steele!). Through reading in translation novels like *Wuthering Heights*, *The Thirty-Nine Steps* and *Cry the Beloved Country* an 'entire world of Western ideas began to take shape' (Ali, A.H. 2008: 69). Significantly, traditional Somali poetry with its disdain for the 'low' topos of sexual desire 'lacked the seductive power of the stories our classmates lent us' (ibid.). Here – and quite often elsewhere in her autobiography – Hirsi Ali consciously takes traditional religio-cultural axioms and turns them on their head. Those 'decadent' aspects of western culture condemned by traditional societies, be they Muslim, Hindu or Sikh, are precisely those to be embraced. Ruthven, however, takes seriously the designation 'Enlightenment fundamentalist' that has been applied to Hirsi Ali. She articulates her life struggle in terms of a showdown between, on the one hand, modernity and its encasement within western freedoms and scientific rationality, and on the other, restrictive traditional customs and behaviours as much sanctioned by tribal and folkloric patterns as by Islam. An eclipse of the moon in Saudi Arabia received by the locals as a sign of the Day of Judgement and dismissed by her father as 'barbaric, all Arab desert culture' (51); the inconsistency between the supposedly 'different but equal' status of Muslim men and women ('the Quran said "Men rule over women"' (102)), are each presented as data that can be rationally discoursed: 'I needed my belief system to be logical and consistent' (ibid.). Having escaped from an arranged intra-Somali marriage, on her first stop in Germany, Hirsi Ali tots up almost at a glance the benefits western modernity offers over her traditional native Muslim society. The shackles of frustrated sexuality (no threatening harassment by 'lecherous' men – 'I felt safe'), mental confinement ('I could follow my curiosity'), and material degradation (no 'potmarked streets', 'beggars' or 'orphans') are each of them thrown off (185).

Hirsi Ali emerges a genuinely articulate, if simplistically naïve, Third World woman migrant in flight – a kind of Candide in reverse, who finds in traditional society the worst of all possible worlds, and in the West the best. Genuine and moving as her story often is (particularly in its representation of the parlous condition of her fellow Somalis trapped in East Africa), there is a more seamy side to the trajectory it has taken. Joining first of all the Dutch Labour and then moving to the more ideological Liberal party, she ends up in the embrace of the US neo-Cons – moving in effect from reckless but idealistic campaigning in Holland on to the payroll of big time anti-Islamism. To support his argument that in Europe 'anti-Islamism is currently providing a useful foil for the political mobilization of anti-immigration sentiments', Graham Huggan adopts Theo van Gogh's and Hirsi Ali's anti-fundamentalist film as a case study. He sees in it:

> a polarizing rhetoric – Huntingdonian in its simplicity – revolving around the much-vaunted 'clash of civilizations' and the apparent threat to national security by a growing number of anti-western militants perceived as both hostile to the dominant national ideology and to its primary religious creed [...] both van Gogh [...] and [...] Ayan Hirsi Ali, have been constructed as heroes for the cause of free speech in the face of fundamentalist oppression, conferring on the former's death the kind of retrospective martyrdom that reads almost as a twisted parody of the Islamist liberation cause (Huggan 2008: 245).

Conclusion

Clearly, there are human rights issues in the sort of treatment meted out to women in the contexts surveyed above. These however have been absorbed into an anti-Islamic discourse fronted by 'Muslim' women, privileged as 'experts' and first-hand reporters, who lay open Muslim men's mistreatment and abuse of their sex. In the process these voices instruct us on the enemy's apparent weaknesses: 'But Muhammad [...] married a nine year old girl. Don't you think that's awful?' They also ventriloquize words some in the western world would most like to hear Muslims speak: 'Why do you not condemn human rights in Islamic countries, when you regularly speak out against such atrocities in the United States and Israel?' They dismiss a crucial moment in the history of human development by ignorant, crude, ahistorical cliché: 'Before A.D. 610, when a man in a cave suddenly had a few ideas, Islam didn't exist' (Ali, A.H. 2007: 90–1). They repeat platitudes about western democracy and human rights without speculating too deeply on the negative aspects of life in the West (such as its racism or anti-immigrant behaviours). They ignore how western states' foreign policies impact on Muslim nations, such as their double-standards of supporting or ignoring ugly regimes, then suddenly turning volte-face and fortuitously discovering and condemning human rights abuses in them, especially ill-treatment of women. They dismiss criticism of such inconsistencies as joining the ranks of 'Muslim sympathisers' and fellow travellers like Said. Not all of these voices are mere stooges of western anti-Muslim propaganda; but taken together they clearly demonstrate a discourse nurtured and disseminated by an ideology much more powerful than the individual units I have been discussing.

At the beginning of this chapter I set out to test a number of propositions. The issue of the construction of that abstract entity, the oppressive, patriarchal 'Muslim male', alongside its corollary the oppressed 'Muslim woman', has been my chief concern. I have traced in my discussion how this operates through an intersection of memoir and journalism with, in Seierstadt's case, the further dimension of travel writing. All of the writers I have reviewed are women. Where, one might ask, is the native male voice in this discursive field? One way to respond to this question is to answer that the Muslim woman in flight is a more potent tool in the *Kulturkampf* against Islam than, say, a 'reformed' Muslim male. Another answer is that the former has become a commodity, a signifier that may or may not connect to an original signified, but which has taken on a life of its own in the ubiquitous book cover image of the veiled woman. A still further explanation might lie in the fact that the native male has been utilized elsewhere in the (more serious?) project of uncovering the Islamic terrorist.[17] I will be examining the fictive branch of this enterprise in Chapter 5.

Chapter 4

Discoursing Muslim Modernities and Eschatologies: V. S. Naipaul, Naguib Mahfouz, Jamal Mahjoub, Shahrnush Parsipur

In his battle with *taqlid* (imitation and decay) in late nineteenth-century Muslim society, the Egyptian reformer Shaykh Muhammad Abdu frequently iterated that the Qur'an and indeed the example of the scientists and thinkers who had reared the great medieval civilization presided over by Islam 'enjoin[ed] rational procedure and intellectual inquiry [...] It forbids us to be slavishly credulous.' He then went on to argue: 'If Islam was the first religion to address the rational mind, summoning it to look into the whole material universe, giving it free rein to range at will through all its secrets, saving only the maintenance of faith, how is it that Muslims are content with so little and many indeed have closed and barred the door of knowledge altogether, supposing thereby God is pleased with ignorance and a neglect of His marvelous handiwork?' (Kurzman 2002: 59). Abdu's questions were raised during the period in which the Muslim intelligentsia, some of whom had visited Europe, understood that 'the challenges of modernity appeared to threaten the very existence of Islam' (ibid.: 7). The response with which Muhammad Abdu is associated – Islamic modernism – has since the early 1900s gone through a series of mutations.[1] Since that time the notion of reform has been entangled in Muslims' resistance to western imperialism, and recourse to nativism with its associated search for re-instatement of a distinct Muslim identity.

In this chapter I shall be looking at some recent literary articulations of the possibilities (and impossibilities, if some are to be believed) of combinations of Islam and modernity. In addition, I shall also consider some responses to the trauma brought about by the impact of modernity which have been framed in non-rational terms. Discourse concerned with messianism, or eschatologies of the 'end times', has always been a feature, if mostly a largely peripheral one, of Muslim societies.[2] 'The clear disjunction between public life and the messianic ideal contributed to the popular expectation of a future messianic figure, the mahdi (guided one), who would come to deliver the community from oppression by the forces of evil and restore true Islam and the reign of justice on earth' (Esposito 2003: 44). In part a response to the decline of

Islam in particular periods of history, in recent times eschatological motifs have been incorporated by some Muslims into their own narratives of the end times. Always liable to be labelled 'extremist' by mainstream exponents of the faith, the messianic movements also ran the danger of moving into heretical territory, either in the form of setting up new structures of faith or practice, or adopting mystical or other interpretative methods that went beyond the limits of orthodoxy.

Islam and Modernity: Discourses on Islamic Revivalism, Reform and Authenticity

Arguments that Muslims individually and collectively have failed to accommodate themselves to modernity, along with the corollary that Islam dooms them to be out of step with the present and imprisons them in the past have, as suggested in the opening chapter, featured prominently in and constitute a major plank of what I have termed the *Kulturkampf* against Islam. When a renewed Muslim consciousness emerged (to the world outside Islam) at the end of the 1970s in the form of the Iranian Islamic revolution a host of 'experts' turned to thinkers previously considered arcane or unknown in an effort to account for this unexpected and for some unfathomable manifestation, which was widely associated with reaction or reversion to the past. The most prominent of these thinkers, 'pious educated men with traditional Islamic religious backgrounds and a knowledge of Western thought' (Esposito 2003: 51) were: Hassan al-Banna, founder of the Egyptian Muslim Brotherhood; Indian journalist Mawlana Abul Ala Mawdudi; and quondam member of Egypt's literati Sayyid Qutb.[3]

Sensitive handlers of this trend, now usually classified as Muslim revivalist thought, reject the simplistic notion that these 'resurgent voices' were just reactionary. For Robert D. Lee 'they describe a world so deeply marked by Westernization that the restoration of the status quo ante is unthinkable' (Lee 1998: 4). It is true, 'all are critical of the West and advocate a return to Islam as an alternative to Western capitalism and communism [...] each reflects the belief that rectification of the plight of modern Islam requires the recognition and reappropriation of Islam as a total way of life' (Esposito 1983: 63). They place 'the primary blame for the ills of their society and the decline of the Muslim world upon European imperialism and westernized Muslim elites. Like revivalists of old, they initially called for moral and social reform but soon also became embroiled in political activism and opposition' (Esposito 2003: 51). Lee places Sayyid Qutb in the ranks of western and non-western thinkers who reject both tradition and modernity, seeking instead 'to discover a mode of truthfulness beyond accepted truth'. This he identifies with the trend in western thought originating from Rousseau, and including Nietzsche and Gramsci, which 'challenges modernization theory from within as well from without and, by doing so, establishes a link between Western thought and the reemergent phenomenon of authenticity movements in the Third World' (Lee 1998: 52). Qutb 'writes against modernity in a modern way', and though he 'deplored many aspects of modern society and modern thought', and indeed 'can be called anti-modern for these reasons, he appears more modern in his attachment to the idea of change, if not progress' (ibid.: 100–1).

Yvonne Haddad emphasizes Sayyid Qutb's worldwide influence among Muslims. She attributes this to the clear style of his writings and their revivalist message (Esposito 1983: 68). His revolutionary articulation of Islam has helped further the trend in which the importance of 'the traditionally educated rabbical class of *ulama*' has been replaced by 'autodidacts emerging from secondary schools and universities [...] [a] newly enfranchised class of intellectuals, who usually come from rural backwaters' (Ruthven 2004: 72). Undoubtedly these Muslim radicals, who Ruthven includes within the category of fundamentalism, have to be seen within the context of other movements and trends hostile to modernity. While religious fundamentalists are by no means limited to the Islamic world, Muslim fundamentalism has been disproportionately emphasized (in comparison with Christian, Jewish and Hindu varieties) due to the political threat it is held to represent. To the charge that Islam requires a Reformation we might reply: it is happening now, but not in a way that is convenient for the West. The emergence of the Muslim radicals, Ruthven contends, 'has parallels with the Reformation in Europe' (ibid.).

There are of course other voices, which for a variety of reasons are more modulated and less urgent than those of the radicals. They may have come from figures embedded in western culture, such as the late Moroccan academic Mohammed Arkoun, or within secular national cultures, like novelists Naguib Mahfouz and Orhan Pamuk. That is not to say these are any the less 'authentic'. The catholicity of a Seyyid Hossein Nasr or the widely engaged concern of a Ziauddin Sardar deserve admiration. But the answers – or in Sardar's case the questions – they provide in response to the issues thrown up by modernity are too complex to find a place in the hearts or minds of Muslim activists, as Qutb or Mawdudi do. Sardar's memoir, *Desperately Seeking Paradise: Journeys of a Sceptical Muslim*, proclaims the search for a revitalized, spiritually renovated Islam, and he moves through a range of modern Islamic movements and groups, testing them intellectually, empirically, and experientially, without selecting a definitive winner from any of them. The faith of Sayyid Qutb's Muslim Brotherhood, which he articulates as 'stored in the concept of belief and martyrdom', he dismisses as 'blind [...], devoid of all rationality' (Sardar 2004: 38). Sardar's intellect and insistence on praxis remain unsatisfied by proselytizing groups such as the pietist Tablighi Jamaat or the politically oriented Jamaat-i Islami (founded by Mawdudi). Organizations sponsored and funded by Muslim states such as Iran and Saudi Arabia eventually demand too high a political price of him. Sufi groups are inward-looking and run by autocratic leaders. In Peshawar, a young Taliban-style Muslim who challenges Sardar for not wearing a beard gets his faith rattled (at least in the re-telling) when Sardar argues: 'if blades had been available in his time, I'm sure the Prophet would have used them' (ibid.: 222). In spite of Sardar's scepticism (beloved by western editors), overall the motif underwriting all his journeys is the commitment of a sincere Muslim confused by the magnitude of the task of finding a form of Islam that is at once true to the faith which inspired a great civilization, and still effective within a world in which secular, anti-religious forces have gained the upper hand.[4]

Naguib Mahfouz and V. S. Naipaul: Travelling Through the *Dar al-Harb* and Beyond

Journeys and search are also motifs within the texts I will now proceed to discuss. These have as the centre of their discursivity the question as to whether Muslims can or cannot progress beyond memories of their illustrious past and effectively re-orientate themselves with respect to modernity. Naguib Mahfouz's *Journey of Ibn Fattouma* is an articulation of the problem from within the frame of an imagined journey. V. S. Naipaul's two pieces of travel writing – *Among the Believers: An Islamic Journey* and *Beyond Belief: Islamic Excursions Among Converted Peoples* – adopt a similar strategy. Both Mahfouz and Naipaul's journeys are read here against the paradigm of Islamic pilgrimage (*haj*), and according to whether the traveller can be seen as a pious or impious pilgrim (*haji, kafir*). Mahfouz's fictional Muslim traveller conducts a pilgrimage in search of wisdom, which because it is carried out in the domains of infidelity involves him in much painful soul-searching. The writings of V. S. Naipaul are overtly hostile and use colonial discourse to fix various Islamic states (Iran, Indonesia and Pakistan) according to a common Islamic identity that is historically frozen and which robs Muslims of agency in the modern world. Naipaul's narratives represent consciously impious pilgrimages performed with the purpose of unmasking the lack of civility/alienated Muslim identities of non-Arab Islamic countries. By performing a *haj* to important centres of contemporary Muslim consciousness, be they ones associated with religious revivalism (Qum) or with a combination of religion and developmentalism (Jakata), his aim is to uncover nullity or delusion. He re-inscribes western Christendom's image of the Islamic domain as the abode of imposture and self-deceit. The domain of infidelity (*dar al-kufr*) thus acquires a doubleness depending on from which terrain it is viewed: western Christendom or the abode of Islam (*dar al-islam*). The discursive field is constructed around key religio-political-cultural-semantic categories raised in recent and current debates between the West and the Muslim world, which have engaged both modern and medieval imperialisms. These may be translated into subversive travel theory, but may (and I argue *should*) themselves equally be subverted.

Regarding the Islamic notion of *dar al-islam* and *dar al-harb*. Seyyed Hossein Nasr writes:

> In traditional Islamic language the world is divided into *dar al-islam*, the 'abode of Islam' or where Islam rules as a majority religion, that is, where the Islamic Scared Law or *Shari'ah* governs human life; *dar al-sulh* the 'abode of peace' where Muslims live as a minority but where they are at peace and can practice their religion freely; and finally *dar al-harb*, the 'abode of conflict or war', where Muslims are not only in a minority but where they are in a state of conflict with and struggle against the external social and political environment in order to be able to practice their religion' (Nasr 1990: 76–7).

While this encoding has remained more or less constant throughout the course of the inception and development of the Islamic community or *umma*, the weighting of *dar al-islam* and *dar al-harb* has changed according to historical conditions. To elucidate this point I shall refer to Wilfred Cantwell Smith's articulation of what he termed the two 'great crises' of Islamic history. The first resulted from the Mongol invasions of *dar al-islam*, culminating in the sack of Baghdad and destruction of the Abbassid Caliphate in 1258; while the 'modern period constitutes the second' (Smith 1957: 40–1). From the inception of Islam to 1258, Smith argued, the 'Muslim could look out upon a world in which the essence and the existence of Islam more nearly converged. The religious reality in which his faith taught him to believe, and the historical reality by which he saw himself surrounded, seemed in reasonable equilibrium' (ibid.: 35). This period could be classified as the age of Islam triumphant; one in which, again to use Smith's phrase, the 'salient characteristic of success' (ibid.) could be observed in the supremacy of the Islamic political, economic and cultural achievement. Clearly, in such circumstances, where the *umma*, for all of the efforts of the infidel crusader, was well consolidated and able to withstand attack, the *dar al-islam* appeared vigorous and confident in relation to the *dar al-harb*. Post 1258, in spite of the conversion of the Mongols and emergence of the powerful Ottoman empire, the *umma* would not again possess the same sense of assurance. 'The Muslim world seemed to have lost the capacity to order its life effectively; Muslim society was losing its once firm, proud grip on the world' (46). By the late eighteenth century, the puritanical Wahhabi movement arose in an attempt to smash the accretions that had perverted the *umma* and return it to its pristine purity. At the same historical moment, an expanding Europe reset the balance of *dar al-islam* and *dar al-harb* to its own advantage. And so to Smith's crucial point: 'The fundamental spiritual crisis of Islam in the twentieth century stems from an awareness that something is awry between the religion which God has appointed and the historical development of the world which He controls' (47–8). The *dar al-islam* comes under siege and is invaded first by European and later by American imperialisms.

The greatest traveller of the Medieval Islamic world was Ibn Battuta. The early fourteenth century *dar al-islam* in which he began his travels had coped with the great Mongol invasions of the previous century to the extent that converted Mongol rulers imbibed Arabo-Persian civilization and embarked upon its embellishment in Iran and Central Asia. The Muslim traveller sets out from the western boundaries of the *dar al-islam* (poorer no doubt for the loss of all but a corner of the once Muslim lands of Andalusia) but still confident in its superiority over the infidels of the *dar al-harb*. He may rely on the hospitality afforded to pilgrims and traders throughout the *umma*. Scion of a clerical family, eventually to establish himself as a *kadi*, a judge of Islamic law, Ibn Battuta wherever he goes takes his place in the cosmopolitan society of the Muslim *ulama* or educated elite, mixing with and receiving largesse from noblemen and princes along the way. The 'universalist standards of the law' (Dunn 1986: 7) mean Ibn Battuta is never a total stranger in the Islamic lands he visits, even when, in Asia minor, he encounters Turks who cannot speak Arabic. 'It was marvellous to see the joy and gladness with which they received us, though they were ignorant of our language and we of theirs' (Ibn Battuta 1926: 127). On the frontline between the *dar al-islam* and the *dar al-harb*, where Byzantine Greeks clash with Ottoman Turks, Ibn Battuta reports the first signs of an emerging Ottoman polity that eventually will drive the border between believer and infidel as far west as the outskirts of Vienna. In the lands of the Mongol Horde, around the Black Sea, he enters an area where Christians predominate, but Muslims can freely practise their faith. Nevertheless, he finds the experience of the ringing of church-bells devilish and frightening.

In literal terms, Ibn Battuta's journey is a *haj*: he performs the pilgrimage to Mecca twice over, as well as visiting the farthest flung domains of the *dar al-islam* and beyond. (Whether he did, as he claims, get as far as China, is still a matter for conjecture.) But he did accomplish the desire, as he put it, 'to travel through the earth'. He reports the infidel Other, be they pagan Africans, Hindus, Buddhists, or the traditional enemy from Christendom, secure in the knowledge of a strong and expanding *dar al-islam*, even if it is one that might be said to have passed its zenith, and to retain scars of the Mongol destruction. Ibn Battuta, then, is not an impious *haji* – he is the complete antimony of one. Other than in the occasional falling out between traveller and princely patron Islamic order is confirmed and facilitated in most of the journey's stages. All this, because the traveller travels without any sense of disjunction between the divine provenance of the Islamic *umma* and its embedding within the historical moment.

The contemporary travellers I shall be discussing belong to another order. They either inhabit or engage with the modern crisis of Islam in which the *umma* has come under the dominance of an advanced industrial, politico-economic, cultural and military complex. The superiority of the latter lies, as Bassam Tibi puts it, 'in its scientific-technological development and its high degree of mastery over nature' (Tibi 1988: 2). In *The Journey of Ibn Fattouma* (rihlat ibn fattuma; published in Arabic in 1983), Mahfouz re-writes and updates the wanderings of the medieval Muslim traveller. The classical Muslim travelogue of the likes of Ibn Battuta and his predecessor Ibn Jubayr of Granada provides a likely analogue, together with accounts of Arab travellers to Europe which date from the second quarter of the nineteenth century onwards.[5] Mahfouz's fictional traveller engages in an imagined *hijra* (emigration) to the lands of impiety beyond *dar al-islam*. This in itself is a potentially impious act, for it assumes that in leaving the *dar al-islam*, the believing Muslim's faith may be endangered or compromised by the alien practices he encounters. In fact, it represents a complete reversal of the meaning of *hijra* entertained 'in the classical period [when it] meant the obligation to migrate from non-Muslim lands (*dar al-kufr*) to Muslim ones (*dar al-Islam*)' (Eickelman and Piscatori 1990: 11). As a necessary corollary of making such a journey Ibn Fattouma must overcome an initial trepidation of 'the trials that lay in wait for my faith and my piety' (Mahfouz 1992: 32). Although the tension supplied by a fear of corruption by non-Islamic practices never entirely dissipates, the journey becames a *rihla* or 'religiously inspired travel' (Eickelman and Piscatori 1990: 5) on which there is occasion to broaden the mind, to awake on the traveller's part to his own cultural limitations sutured to the realization that cultural difference is a condition of modern life. In the process of this engagement the fictional Ibn Fattouma demonstrates a willingness to negotiate with and learn from certain aspects of the culture and behaviour of non-Islamic societies which at least some of his fellow Muslims might be considered *haram*, prohibited. As far as Ibn Fattouma is concerned, the journey he undertakes in the *dar al-harb* not only evidences to the superiority in many instances of other societies compared with his own. It also causes him to interrogate the divergences of his own Islamic society from the standards laid down in the Qur'an and *sunna*.

From another perspective, however, Ibn Fattouma's credentials are inscribed within an older Muslim eclecticism that incorporated non-Muslim domains of learning and culture within a civilizing Islamic framework. He might lay claim to a *hadith*, a reported saying of the Prophet: 'seek knowledge even as far as China'. A Sufi strain is also attached to Ibn Fattouma's declared intention to 'acquire knowledge' and 'seek wisdom'. The goal of his journey is the land of Gebel ('mountain') from which no traveller has returned to report. This may signify a this-world Utopia (whether Mahfouz had read More's *Utopia* or Morris's *News from Nowhere* I am not aware). Alternatively, it may stand for the seeker's attainment to a state of perfect wisdom and spirituality in a world beyond this. The narrative proceeds through Ibn Fattouma's visits to five separate lands, each with their own discrete political and religious orderings of state. The fifth and penultimate stage of his journey is in fact a preparation for the land of Gebel; here people communicate telepathically, and an aged sage informs the traveller he must 'open the doors to hidden treasures' before he can cross to Gebel.

An iterated self-criticism runs through the text: one which argues, from a position of injured faith rather than impiety, the failings and corruptions of Ibn

Fattouma's own Islamic society. In so doing, the domain of infidelity is doubled with the abode of Islam. Muslims are seen to have fallen short of the divine commands of their religion and are in their behaviour in certain respects no better than the infidel. In fact as recipients of divine revelation they are afforded less excuse than pagans and atheists. Here Mahfouz is operating in a sensitive terrain, one adopted by rationalizing modernists like the nineteenth century Egyptian chief mufti Muhammad Abdu,[6] and shared with (so-called 'fundamentalist') Salafi/neo-Wahhabis, including movements like the Muslim Brotherhood (*ikhwan al-muslimin*) and other even more recent 'radical' Muslim groupings. Where Mahfouz departs from the fundamentalists is in the openness with which he invests Ibn Fattouma: he is ready, if not to compromise his core Muslim beliefs, then at least to contextualize them according to the new set of conditions with which he is presented.[7] An example is his encounter with a liberal Muslim cleric in Halba, the land of freedom (a place bearing no slight resemblance to the United States). He finds the cleric drinks alcohol in moderation and invites the traveller to his home where he is directed to sit down to dinner with the man's wife and attractive daughter.

> The sheikh removed his turban and rubbed his hand across his head then put it back and said, 'Freedom is the sacred value accepted by everyone.'
> I protested. 'This freedom has overstepped the boundaries of Islam.'
> 'But it is also sacred in the Islam of Halba.'
> Frustrated, I said, 'If our Prophet were to be resurrected today he would reject this side of your Islam.'
> 'And were he, may the peace and blessings of God be upon him, to be resurrected,' he in turn inquired, 'would he not reject the whole of your Islam?'
> Ah, the man had spoken the truth and had humbled me by his question (86).

Ibn Fattouma, it is clear, both admires the value set on freedom while at the same time censoring its excesses. The principle of independence of thought is brought home to him by the sheikh's daughter when she says: 'The difference between our Islam and yours [...] is that ours has not closed the door of independent judgement, and Islam without [that] means Islam without reason' (103). The Arabic term *ijtihad*, or independent reasoning, is one that has been much debated by Muslim scholars (and some western writers).[8] Mahfouz appears to side with those modernists who reject the axiom 'the gate of *ijtihad* is closed', in practice arguing that Islamic law and codes of personal conduct are not fixed, but are capable of re-interpretation according to the social exigencies of the time. As one Albanian-Turkish reformer[9] stated towards the end of the nineteenth century: 'It is a regrettable circumstance that, because today civilization seems to belong exclusively to the Christian nations, ignorant masses of our own nation take it to be a symbol or prerequisite of Christianity, and thus deem distancing themselves from it and guarding themselves against it to be a religious duty. We can affirm that it is not the religion of Islam which prevents Muslim nations from becoming civilized' (Kurzman 2002:7).

As regards the five different societies through which Ibn Fattouma journeys, and on occasion settles and marries in, each embodies a salient principle of political order and belief that either resembles or contests facets of his own society. The first, a pastoral society set in a tropical land, where the populace is effectively slaves of a warrior overlord, is evidently feudal. No religion sustains it other than a sensual paganism whose polyandry threatens the Islamic marriage code. In the second, a ruler is worshipped as a god – another profanity, until the traveller recalls that in his homeland rulers also act as gods, 'Who is worse [...] he who claims divinity through ignorance or he who exploits the Quran for his own ends?' (Mahfouz 1992: 62). The sexual licentiousness of both societies insult Ibn Fattouma's Muslim sensibilities, but in the third land, Halba, the land of freedom, he is perplexed to observe a public demonstration on behalf of legal rights for homosexuals. If the poverty and tyranny of lands one and two remind him of his own country, the democratic constitution of Halba receives his open admiration. But his friend, the sheikh, comments: 'It would have been more appropriate for the Muslims to have propagated it before others' (87). The strongest contrast in Ibn Fattouma's response to diversity of belief is encountered in the fourth land, which resembles a Soviet-style socialist society. Here, his admiration is 'aroused to the highest degree' by the civic order, but so is his disgust at its atheism (125).

Ibn Fattouma becomes cognisant of one universal that unites humanity whatever social constitutions people live under: the reality of war, entered into for the most hypocritical of reasons. The *dar al-harb* lives up to its name not only on account of its frequent hostility towards Islam, but because of the conflicts that break out between each of the states that it comprises. War deprives him of his families on two occasions, and the threat of war forces him to depart prematurely from the benevolent forestland presided over by the aged mystic. His account ends on a note of indeterminacy: does he reach the land of Gebel or not? An editor announces: 'No history book makes any mention further of this traveller.' Such open-ended closure accords with the traditions of mystic storytelling that, it might be argued, form the core of a traditional Islamic world-view. The abodes of Islam and infidelity are dissolved; each of the respective systems of belief and social practice are superseded. In Sufi terms, the different stages or cities of knowledge have been traversed. Only the determination of the traveller to attain to the ultimate destination of wisdom remains. For all the probing of his own society and its failings, Mahfouz does not in the end stray that far from its deepest aspiration.

The publishers of a paperback edition of *A Bend in the River* once saw fit to inscribe Bernard Levin's encomium on the rear cover: 'Mr Naipaul is our greatest reporter from the frontline of the modern world's *Kulturkampf*.' I shall now interrogate Naipaul's journeys in the *dar al-islam* as another stage in his Manichean battle with the dark forces affronting western civilization. In this application, the dark forces embody the threat of Islamic faith towards secularism. It hardly matters that seventeen years separate the publication of *Among the Believers: An Islamic Journey* in 1981, from *Beyond Belief: Islamic Excursions Among the Converted Peoples*, in 1998. Though the first text pre-dates it, taken together Naipaul's journeys through Muslim lands sit perfectly alongside of Huntingdon's clash of civilizations theory. Both of Naipaul's books assume the modern crisis of Islam, which is related in turn to the triumphalism of Islam's imperial past, when borders of the *dar al-islam* were extended and comprised, at different historical moments, lands such as Persia, India, and latterly Malaysia and Indonesia. Given this framing, it may be argued that Naipaul's 'Islamic Journeys' carry distinct overtones of impiety: they are pilgrimages conducted with the aim of subverting the Islamic beliefs or ideology of the countries and peoples through which and among whom he is travelling. From this traveller's point of view, they are travels in the *dar al-harb* rather than in the *dar al-islam*. The *dar al-harb* is tacitly understood to be the lands where Islam's imperial trajectory swallowed up more ancient cultures; the implication is that these lands are still *dar al-harb*, since Iranians, Indians and Indonesians have never been properly accommodated within the *dar al-islam*. In Naipaul's travel writings, we may argue the domains of faith and infidelity have been reversed. *Among the Believers* and *Beyond Belief* narrate impious pilgrimages performed with the purpose of unmasking the lack of civility/alienated Muslim identities of non-Arab Islamic countries. Naipaul re-inscribes western Christendom's image of the Islamic domain as the abode of imposture and self-deceit, reviving the West's 'old theme of the Satanism of Islam' (Keane 1999).

Sumal Gupta has argued that in his Islamic journeys, especially in *Beyond Belief*, Naipaul is interested to bring 'his analysis of Islam [...] in line with the modes of cultural evaluation he had evolved in other social, usually colonial/postcolonial contexts' (Gupta 1999: 76). The new area of discourse thus performs a similar task to his earlier *Kulturkampf*s against narratives of liberation in colonial and postcolonial societies – 'this akinness of socialist revolution and Islamic revolution' (ibid.: 70). Both incorporate Naipaul's project of exposing the delusions and fallacies of revolutionary movements. All that has happened is that Islamic movements with goals of revolutionary change have replaced Marxist and Third World nationalist ones. This shift represents a judicious resetting of the West's *Kulturkampf* in terms of a new enemy for the post-Cold War era. Naipaul's emphasis is now on the irration-ality of Muslim fundamentalism: 'the fundamentalist rage against the past, against history, and the impossible dream of the true faith growing out of a spiritual vacuum' (Naipaul 1998: 59). On both his visits to Iran, Naipaul was concerned to stress the similarities of Khomeini's revolution, enjoying full communist support, with earlier totalitarian upheavals in the West. The difference between the two texts may, as Gupta proposes, be that the earlier possesses 'an exploratory air', while 'the latter is more statemental' (71). The observations in *Beyond Belief* are 'more hard nosed' (ibid.), and the writer's claim that the stories fitted into their own order is even more disingenuous the second time round. Many of the persons interviewed and places visited on the first journey re-appear on the second. Nevertheless, it is true to say that Naipaul's personal alienation from the Islamic Other on both occasions belies the sympathy he is capable of extending to individuals. 'Nothing,' he writes in 1981, 'of the intellectual life that I valued was of account; the convergences of sentiment or reason that occurred from time to time were coincidental' (Naipaul 1981: 333).

By and large the object of Naipaul's antagonism is the 'fundamentalism' of what Hossein Nasr terms 'counter-traditional' Islamic movements. According to Nasr, these movements, 'possess a violent and revolutionary political nature and in some [...] the most fanatical and volcanic elements of Western repub-licanism and Marxist revolutionary theory and practice have been set in what the followers of these groups consider to be an Islamic context' (Nasr 1990: 85). For Naipaul, the 'dangerous fantasy' of such formulations resides in their attempt to recover the 'ancient dream' of a revived, purified Islamic community that is believed to have existed in seventh century Arabia (Naipaul 1998: 55, 163). As applied in twentieth-century Iran and Pakistan, this fantasy accomplishes a double alienation, because the convert is not merely doing violence to the times in which he lives, he rejects his own authentic cultural identity: 'His holy places are in Arab lands; his sacred language Arabic. His idea of history alters. He rejects his own; he becomes, whether he likes it or not, part of the Arab story' (ibid.: 1).

What forms, then, incorporate this residual identity? Not only does *Beyond Belief* assimilate a western hostility towards Islam, the text is also aligned with another historic enmity. Naipaul projects negative formulations of past Islamic conquests as the swallowing up of ancient cultures by an aggressive 'imperi-alist power with a strong sense of mission and a knowledge of the world' (Naipaul 1981: 126). The oft re-iterated 'destruction' of India, and subsequent expansion into Indonesia – 'this part of greater India' (ibid.: 31) – attests to Naipaul's renewed sympathies towards his own Hindu heritage.[10] He has, as Gupta emphasizes, fastened on to a form of cultural essentialism that he seeks to excavate and set up as an antithesis to medieval Islamic imperialism. In India and the East Indies, it is 'the long Buddhist-Hindu' past that is more authentic, and on the arrival of the new imperialisms of Europe, better equipped to accul-turate to the modern world.

Such a view may recycle some of the observations on the modern crisis of Islam made by W. Cantwell Smith, but this is performed in a distorted way. Perhaps more significantly, it closes off the possibilities of shared re-alignment of both Islamic and non-Islamic cultures in recognition of their commonalities. Naipaul, whose grasp of Islamic history and culture may not be comprehensive enough to support the assertions he makes, ignores the trend in both western and eastern scholarship of Islamic societies that stresses their connection with their non-Muslim eastern neighbours separate from occidental intrusion. Another criticism I would wish to make of Naipaul's position is its failure to valorize the spiritual dimension in a society ordered on religious principles, what might be termed the affirmation of the sacred in a secular age. Naipaul embraces the dogmas of secularism in his rejection of 'the rigidities of a revealed faith'. His subversive theorization of Islamic fundamentalism includes the charge that the fundamentalist frame of mind disavows historical complexities and movements of peoples. But this criticism could equally be made against Naipaul himself. His account elides the accomplishment of the various historical Islamic societies, and disqualifies modern Muslim nations' embrace of the developmentalist discourse of western modernity as well as the continuing evidence of civility and tolerance the *umma* has to offer. Naipaul's stance, so fixed and uncritical of the limitations of western secularism, invariably occludes opportunities to draw parallels across cultures, and, perhaps most seriously of all, is silent on the violence the imposition of secularism has visited upon Islamic societies in the East.

Naipaul's travelling theory, which 'puts European scholarship, "discovery" and power at the centre of human affairs' (Griffith 1993: 90) in its evaluation of a crucial formation in a unified world history, lapses into the modalities of an old demonology. He embodies Said's charge (1996) that 'Western Orientalists are re-writing the history of Islam as a tale of anger and irrationality'. Discursive fields constructed around categories such as the abodes of peace and infidelity, the clash of civilizations, us versus them, are revived by Naipaul à la Huntingdon, and are in turn repeated by sections of the western intelligentsia who have endorsed Naipaul's narrative of travel in Islamic lands. Naipaul's writings are, as I have argued, basically subversive in intent, their declared aim being to unmask Islamic fundamentalism and, we might add, to impoverish the achievement of Islamic civilizations and deconstruct Islamic modernism in almost any form. But they can themselves be subverted on a number of grounds. To start with Naipaul has an imperfect knowledge of Islamic history and displays a lack of self-criticism with regard to the West's recent history, in particular the absolutist tendencies of secularism. In addition, by inscribing the Iranian revolution as an exercise in reactionary authoritarianism; Naipaul both condemns the backward-looking Islam of Iran and Pakistan and deconstructs narratives of developmentalism in modernizing Islamic nations such as Indonesia and Malaysia, in the process denying the possibility of Islamic accommodation to modernity in either guise. Naipaul barely understands the voices of Muslim authenticity who oppose both tradition and modernity, such as Muhammad Iqbal or Sayyid Qutb, since his argument is trapped in a crude historicism focused on Islam as a recidivistic product of seventh- century Arabia.

Muslim Eschatologies: Jamal Mahjoub's *In the Hour of Signs*, and Shahrnush Parsipur's *Touba and the Meaning of Night*

In his novel *In the Hour of Signs*, Jamal Mahjoub revisits the Mahdi episode, inserted into popular British imperial history almost entirely on account of the death of Gordon at Khartoum and the revenge of Kitchener at Omdurman, and rewrites it from a postcolonial perspective. On the eve of Kitchener's massacre of tribal Sudanese warriors, a British officer presents a Sudanese prisoner with a stark choice: "'You can stay in the stone age [...] or you can be in at the start'" (Mahjoub 1996: 232). 'Part of Mahjoub's achievement [in the novel] is to split the apocalypse of 'Signs' between those religious ones pertaining to the Last Days, and the signs of the age of imperialism, of the European later nineteenth century. This splitting is carried on through to the clash of civilizations constituted by the West's invasion of the *dar al-Islam*, and the staging of Islamist resistance' (Nash 2007: 95). The 'choice' proffered by the English officer – which is in reality a bully's threat – announces the end of one of the century's last Islamic movements of protest,[11] and the commencement of the intrusion of global western modernity into another Muslim land.

In western restagings of the his story, the Mahdi himself is an exotic barbarian.[12] Jamal Mahjoub, in contrast, has written a serious novel which is anything but an exercise in cliché of the kind to be found in popular fiction.[13] *In the Hour of Signs* forms part of the author's Sudanese trilogy in which geography and the land of Sudan is a prominent character (see Mohsen 2000). It is an exploration of the power of faith written in the wake of the Islamist seizure of power in Sudan in 1989. Mahjoub's sources are the usual English ones starting from Wingate and Slatin's *Fire and Sword in the Sudan*; on the Sudanese side they include the memoirs of an eyewitness, Babikr Badri, and professor of history, Mohammed al Gaddal. The novel embodies a cyclical sense of history in which spiritual ideas are later reborn in a modern mode: the work is overshadowed by the showdown between the fundamentalist political Islam of the new regime represented by Hassan Turabi and the spiritual ideals of the Mahdi which Mahjoub conceives to have been renewed and updated by Mahmud Muhammad Taha.[14]

Mahjoub moves through a chronological, episodic narrative structured around the historical events of the Mahdist revolution and the creation of the Mahdist state. He begins with a prologue which imagines the moment when Muhammad Ahmad ibn Abdullah is recognized as mahdi by Abdullahi, later Khalifa. Then follows the clash at Aba island in August 1881 between the Mahdi's forces and those of the governor-general commanded by Muhammad Bey Abu Saud in which the latter is defeated. Having declared himself the promised one in June 1881, the Mahdi moves into Kordofan and takes El-Obeid. Next he defeats an expeditionary force sent from Cairo and led by Colonel William Hicks. General Gordon arrives in January 1884 and the siege of Khartoum ensues, culminating in the death of Gordon in January 1885. The

Mahdi's transformation of spiritual leadership into theocratic rule is abruptly terminated by his death in June 1885. His successor Khalifa Abdullahi rules over a tense, troubled, and divided kingdom, initially supported by the ascetic pietists, the *awlad al-bilad*. His government turns into an 'autocracy' of the Ta'aishi tribe until the defeat by Kitchener at Omdurman in 1898 (Shaked 2008: 1–9). Alongside the Mahdi and the Khalifa, other historical protagonists, such as the prominent general of Mahdist forces Abdul-Rahman al-Nejumi, feature in the novel. A key fictional character is the peripatetic scholar and truth-seeker Sheikh Al Hawi, called back from his travels by the fame of the Mahdi. Others are Medani the cook, Ellesworth, an English officer, Kadaro, a soldier from a small troop of *bash-buzuq* (irregular soldiers in the pay of the Egyptian Khedive), and an unnamed Sudanese girl.

As already suggested earlier, Mahjoub makes the eschatological elements 'The hour' and 'signs' (Arabic: *ashrat al-sa'a*, lit. signs of the hour) double for the Islamic belief in the coming of the mahdi, and the western assertion of the miracles of the age of progress. Given that he is writing about a historically grounded manifestation of mahdism, Mahjoub does his best to remain true to the spirit of the time in which the novel is set. The eschatological motifs are embedded in the politics of the Sudan of the 1880s, in which the Khedival government of Sudan (in practice Egyptian but still nominally under Ottoman suzerainty) is hated for its corruption. This sense of aggrievement can be said to fuel support for the Mahdi and in a sense prepares his appearance.[15] However, Mahjoub's concern is not simply to write an historical novel; the dimension of his own times is not merely an added extra, it is a vital point of reference. As David Cook (2005) establishes in his study of contemporary Muslim apocalyptic literature: Muslim writers of recent times 'write at the margin' and use traditional apocalyptic strands in a new way, to account for the preoccupations and concerns of their own age, be they Arab defeat at the hands of Zionism, Jewish conspiracy, or the clash of civilizations. Mahjoub, however, writes about an apocalyptic subject not only from outside orthodoxy but from a secular postcolonial perspective. He does not underwrite a traditionally Islamic view of the hour of signs, associated as this is with the Day of Resurrection.[16] Nonetheless, a spiritual or idealist dimension is integral to the vision of his novel. It should be stressed Mahjoub neither belittles nor patronises traditional belief as Aslam does in *Maps for Lost Lovers*; but like Aslam he turns to Sufism as a foil to scriptural literalism. The hour of signs is accorded a Sufi breadth and inwardness that gestures towards the specific ideas of the reformer and mystic Mahmud Muhammad Taha.

The first and major context of Mahjoub's probing of the meaning of the hour of signs is Muhammad Ahmad ibn Abdullah's claim to be the Mahdi in 1881; the second embedded one is the career and execution in January 1985 of Mahmud Muhammad Taha. Both the Mahdi and Taha were products of Sudan's complex and fissiparous array of Sufi organizations according to Mohamed A. Mahmoud. Muhammad Ahmad arose to head one of the

divisions of the Sammaniya order before responding to the messianic temper
of the times. Whereas the Sufi orders were indigenous to Sudan, the *ulamas'*
scholastic *madhabs* (schools of jurisprudence) were an import that was central
to the religious policy of the ruling Turco-Egyptians (Mahmoud 2007: 4–5).
In both Muhammad Ahmad and Taha's cases, the juridical Islam of the
ulama was set against the arguments of Sufi-inclined revivalist leaders. 'The
internecine conflict within the contest of Sudanese Islam resonated with
echoes of centuries-old conflicts of orthodox scholars and Sufis and what
they considered "deviant" Sufis' (ibid.: 26). However, while it is unmistakably
the case that Muhammad Ahmad's 1881 'Mahdist claim and his call for jihad
[...] against the "infidel Turk" struck a timely chord with a great number of
people throughout the country' (6), the circumstances surrounding Taha's
career were substantially different. Taha was a revivalist and an Islamist in
the sense that he accepted the temper of the times constituted a world crisis
to which Islam was the only solution. He called for a revival of the Prophet's
model and sharia, but he differed from mainstream Islamism, with the Muslim
Brotherhood at its core: 'Although Taha shared these principles with other
Islamists [...] what is significant in his case is his degree of willingness to open
Islam to change, a willingness that led him to develop a distinct and separate
revivalist project and discourse' (18–19). This project had a decidedly political
dimension which probably accounted for Taha's eventual fate. At its heart
was his 'messianic zeal' which led to his creation of a neo-Sufi style *tariqa* with
a political name 'The Republican Brotherhood' (*al-ikhwan al-jumhuriyun*).
However, as Mahmoud makes clear, 'the movement was politico-religious, with
the emphasis placed on its religious aspect'. At the heart of the brotherhood
was Taha's claim of an unmediated, direct spiritual relationship with God (31).

Taha's notion of modernity made his movement distinctive in the manner
in which it incorporated tendencies towards accepting the political tenets of
socialism and democracy and, notably, emphasized the equality of men and
women. This last principle became bound up with his schema of a modernized,
second Islam. As the translator of Taha's most influential work, *The Second
Message of Islam*, puts it: Taha's ideas on 'the evolution of Islamic law may be
summarized as follows. Islam, being the final and universal religion according
to Muslim belief, was offered first in tolerant and egalitarian terms in Mecca,
where the Prophet preached equality and individual responsibility between
all men and women without distinction on grounds of race, sex, or social
origin. As the message was rejected in practice, and the Prophet and his few
followers were persecuted and forced to migrate to Medina, some aspects of
the message changed in response to the socioeconomic and political realities
of the time. Migration to Medina (*hijrah*) was not merely a tactical step, but
also signified a shift in the content of the message itself' (An-Naim, in Taha
1987: 21, 23).[17] The problem in modern times is that the sharia 'does not treat
women and non-Muslims equally with male Muslims' (ibid.: 22). Rather than
revert to the piecemeal reform of modernists such as Muhammad Abdu, or

to the demotion of sharia from the public to a private space, Taha advocates an evolutionary approach to Muslim law: 'Explicit and definitive texts of the Qur'an and Sunnah that were the basis of discrimination against women and non-Muslims under historical Sharia are set aside as having served their transitional purpose. Other texts of the Qur'an and Sunnah are made legally binding in order to achieve full equality for all human beings, regardless of sex or religion' (23). Thus through 'the rationale of abrogation' which removes what is historical but now outdated, a modern Islam is able to emerge with truly universal jurisdiction. However, such a bold proposal – which took a practical form when Taha's Republican Brothers opposed the implementation of sharia by President Jaffar Numeiri – sealed the reformer's fate.

Mahjoub's response to Mahmud Muhammad Taha's teaching is not to incorporate it substantially into *In the Hour of Signs*. Without a section updated to modern times, which Mahjoub does not adopt, this would obviously have been anachronistic. Instead, through the figure of Hawi, Mahjoub seems to endorse Taha's views on 'a second Islam'. Indeed, even before the Mahdi's appearance Hawi has been moving in the direction of heterodoxy. 'He began to question the very ideas he was supposed to defend, to talk of a second, hidden message concealed within the holy scriptures' (Mahjoub: 17). In an early scene involving the returning Hawi and Sheikh Rahman, a religious scholar associate from former days who holds to literalist interpretation of the sharia, the pair clash over Hawi's interest in the newly declared Mahdi. Rahman, a Hassan Turabi-type figure, says: 'They should hang this man as an apostate a blasphemer, for making such claims' (23). (The same charge and punishment that Turabi and the Muslim Brotherhood demanded for Taha.)[18] He condemns Hawi for abandoning the teaching of his former teacher: 'all your talk of hidden meanings in the holy scriptures'. A shudder went through Rahman [...] 'He never forgave you for that' (ibid.). Later, hearing again about the Mahdi's claim from a merchant, Hawi registers an inner awakening: 'This, thought Hawi, this is where it begins [...] he felt what it must have been like at the beginning, in the moment of transition when religion was born, when the words of God were revealed to man' (56–7). Another view of the Mahdi, from someone in the Khedive's party but still a Muslim, is focalized through an ageing Circassian officer, Ala'adin Pasha, sitting in the governor's palace in Khartoum:

> Those in Cairo had no idea what they were dealing with up here. This land took time to learn, time to love, but it had its beauty: the raw charm of nature itself, something rare and unfouled by the ways of men. No wonder the people were given to mystical flights of fancy; no wonder there were seers and madmen, dervishes and prophets. If a Mahdi was to make an appearance in the world, he could hardly pick a better place. [...]
>
> The signs were obscure; with the rise of tribal conflicts and superstition, there was something unsettling about this Mahdi and his call for a return to the golden age of Islam [...]

And what were the signs so far? A comet crossing the sky; a gap in the front teeth and a mole on the right cheek of a soft-spoken man given to smiling (40–1).

The Circassian's thoughts connect with a revivalist note and utilize a collocation of messianic vocabulary. Hawi, however, is more intimately attuned to the apocalypse of revelation: 'the moment of transition when religion was born, when the words of God were revealed to man.' The part of him that pursues 'a second Islam' and 'hidden meanings in the holy scriptures' is still more occult and inward. In his character Mahjoub has joined the messianism of the mahdi ideal and the mystical soul-searching of the Sufi.

Concerning Muhammad Ahmad's claims, his sudden death and the eventual erasure of his state by the forces of British imperialism, history is fully aware. As for the fictional Hawi, he dies at the end of the novel in a squalid way. Condemned as a false prophet and apostate he is hanged at the orders of the former *bash-buzuq*, now turned station-master, Kadaro. Hawi's final message is a poetic formulation of Taha's recognition of the impulse of change, and the cycle of prophetic revelation:

History repeats itself, but never in the same manner. Place is not spherical and nor is time [...] The end of the cycle resembles the beginning ... but is distinctly different [...] 'Everyday He has a fresh concern.' People say that only that which is imperfect evolves and develops. This is not so. Perfect men aspire towards something more. Perfection is a fluid state of renewal and progression, not stagnation (245).

Hawi, as I have argued elsewhere, is one of a group of individuals in Mahjoub's fiction who are 'struggling to move beyond the boundaries of their own societies' (Nash 2007: 100). At the same time, *In the Hour of Signs*, along with the two other novels Mahjoub wrote about Sudan, produces a vivid Sudanese historical-geography, which asks the reader to extrapolate meanings across different terrains and times. The specific Sudanese conflict between messianism and scriptural literalism, Islamist revivalism and visionary Sufi radicalism, plays out across generations and becomes firmly lodged within wider contexts and debates concerning alternative Muslim modernities. Indeed, as much as the ideas Hawi expresses here are Mahmud Taha's, they could equally have been inspired by the Indian poet and reformer Muhammad Iqbal who was in his turn influenced by the Victorian Indian modernist Muslims Sayyid Ahmad Khan and Sayyid Amir Ali. Each of these thinkers made it their mission to connect Islamic thought with current European philosophy. Javed Majeed (2009: 97) states: 'Iqbal [...] conveys a sense of the ongoing nature of questions as motivating intellectual history and lived experience in his preface to The *Reconstruction of Religious Thought in Islam*, when he stresses that "there is no such thing as finality in philosophical thinking" [...]' While he considers that

Iqbal patronized modern European philosophy as inferior to the Qur'an and Sufism, Allawi (2009: 52) agrees his was 'probably the first modern attempt by a committed Muslim to rediscover the vitality of Islam in the light of the evolution of western philosophical thought and the realities of the new, West-dominated world'. The problem nevertheless remained as to how eclectic one could be, as Allawi puts it in his discussion of the contemporary Iranian thinker Abdul Karim Soroush, without moving beyond the 'inherited legacy' of Islam (ibid.: 128) and so jettisoning the creed altogether.

Born in 1946 in Tehran, Shahrnush Parsipur is one of the most important Iranian writers to emerge in the period of the Islamic revolution.[19] Her novel *Touba and the Meaning of Night*, first published in 1989 and subsequently banned in Iran, spans almost a century of Iranian history. Like Naguib Mahfouz in his *Cairo Trilogy*, she sets out in her novel to imagine her country's recent history by focusing on one family. The narrative begins towards the close of the nineteenth century, when Iran is ruled by the Qajar dynasty and the country has barely begun to modernize. It ends when the second Iranian revolution breaks out in 1977–9. During the supervening period Iran has experienced the Constitutional Revolution, or *mushrutih* (1905 to 1911), passed through two world wars, changed its ruling dynasty, and become an oil rich state ruled by a modernizing autocracy. Throughout Parsipur probes the effects of modernity and the testing political and social changes it brings, along with its uprooting of tradition. She develops the key thematics of modernization and feminism by combining feminist perspectives and a magical realist narrative technique to promote a picture of Iranian society in which traditional, mystically oriented religious and modernizing secular ideas are juxtaposed alongside one another. Characters, crossing three generations, range from members of the Qajar royal family to the children of a poor mason. Socially and politically the novel takes in aristocrats, traditional religious scholars, revolutionary preachers, secular politicians, communists, and Islamists. Important stages of Iran's modern history and specific incidents and events correlate with aspects of Touba's own development as an individual and as a woman. According to Houra Yavari, the novel 'meticulously captures the expansive breadth of the social and political events of this hundred-year period of Iran's history, and delicately incorporates them into the imaginary account of the different stages of Touba's life and the tale of her house' (Yavari 2007: 387).

In order to understand the development of Touba and the other characters it is important to have an overall idea of these main events, all of which are integrated into the novel. In the last decades of nineteenth century the restriction placed on women's lives is highlighted when Touba's father Haji Adib, who is a religious scholar, becomes obliquely aware that women have minds:

> The women were laughing behind the cellar window. Haji thought disparag-
> ingly that they were behaving with typical women's foolishness. One pushed

and the others burst out laughing; one tickled while the other tried to get away. If there had not been a man in the house, their laughter would probably have been heard all over. Undoubtedly some of them were going crazy for not having a husband, but it was not possible to find husbands for them. They were dependent on Haji Adib, and there was not a man available at the moment who was rich enough to take one of them. Besides, if they did get married, who would then weave the carpets? For that, he couldn't bring strange women into the house. They might then participate in some perverse activities with one another.

Haji Adib pressed his lips together in anger. He decided, 'Yes, the earth is round. Women think. And soon they shall have no shame.' A small cloud covered the sun, a gust picked some dust and twigs off the ground. 'That is the way it is. As soon as they discover they are able to think, they shall raise the dust. The poet Hafez of Shiraz was right: "This witch was the bride of a thousand grooms."' He suddenly realized why the earth had to be square, why it had been considered unmoving, and why every man had a right to build a fence around his land. If they left this prostitute to her own devices, she would constantly spin around and throw everyone off balance. Everything would then be chaos (Parsipur 2007: 24–5).

The passage is replete with a dubious irony: the termination of the static, traditional patriarchal world of Haji Adib governed by the misogynistic need to exert control over women has been irrevocably announced by a recent incident in which he had been humiliated at the hands of a westerner. He determines on educating his daughter, Touba, as a means of deflecting the impact of the foreigners – 'then even if [they] did tell her their own version [of the modern world], it would not have the same effect. His daughter, with all her intelligence and her clever questions, needed to know' (ibid.).[20] Here Parsipur's symbolism transparently joins modernity, the Iranian encounter with a triumphalist West, and the forces moving women's emancipation.

On her father's death, and while only fourteen, to save her family Touba instigates her own marriage to Haji Mahmud who is many years her senior. However, she is irked by the restrictions this brings; her resolve to break free from the marriage coincides with the *mushrutih* and is strengthened by the image of the revolutionary cleric, Shaykh ('Mr') Khiabani.[21] She idolizes Khiabani at the same moment as debate over women's emancipation enters the political arena. While offstage some of her sex are appearing on the streets and otherwise involving themselves in the revolution, Touba achieves her freedom by engineering her own divorce.[22] Married again, this time to a member of the Qajar royal family, Prince Fereydun, Touba enters the harim only to discover her husband is serially unfaithful to her. Owing to her marriage she is personally affected by the fall of the Qajars in 1925, her brother-in-law Prince Manouchehr Mirza reacting in a frenzied outburst to the collapse of his family's dynasty (162–4). That same year Reza Shah founds the Pahlavi dynasty and inaugurates a policy of top–down modernization including compulsory unveiling. Though she is slow to embrace the transformation of the lives of upper and middle class women in the early 1930s, Touba goes to the movies and she and her sister-in-law Turan O-Saltaneh nevertheless respond to Reza Shah's banning of the chador by going out together in a carriage unveiled.[23] In the later 1930s, Touba shares the pro-Hitler sympathies of the upper classes. Then her daughter Moones clandestinely marries Ismael, her childhood sweet-heart but social inferior, who is imprisoned for his pro-Tudeh (communist party) sympathies. Reza Shah's deposition at the hands of invading British and Soviet troops in 1941 is not regretted by Touba's family who in the early years of the 1950s support Nationalist premier Mosaddeq's nationalization of Iran's oil. In the meantime they have taken in the three orphaned children of a poor mason, Kamal, Maryam and Karim. Each of these grows up to support the different factions – Leftist and Islamist – whose opposition to the Shah results in his departure from Iran in 1979.

The novel sets out the divisions between the sexes and the patriarchal oppression of women in Iran in both the private and public spheres. Feminism does not feature in an open, obvious way. None of the female characters identify with or become involved in an overtly feminist political agenda. Instead, Parsipur shows her main women protagonists reacting to rapid and acute social change at another level: the mythic and mystical. Touba is named after the tree of divine light and wisdom in Persian legend. As Persis M. Karim explains, 'Parsipur's writing style in this novel was a departure from previous prerevolutionary writing, which either deployed a straightforward social-realist style or an allegorical and often political message. Two of the characters [i.e. Prince Gill & Layla] come from ancient times to the present, and Parsipur uses the fantastic as well as a shifting sense of narrative time' (Karim 2007: 411). The postmodern writing techniques of magical realism and interrupted narrative, in which chronological progression is disrupted, is employed in order to project the specifically female consciousness of the women characters. The use of interrupted narrative also operates in such a way as to contest and break up master/metanarratives associated with the public world.

At the outset Touba enters powerless into the male-controlled public worlds of politics and religion. Parsipur articulates absence of female agency through Touba's early fixation on male figures Mr Khiabani and Master Geda Alishah, who are symbols respectively of the male-centred worlds of modernizing revolution and Sufi mysticism. The orientations of her consciousness towards these figures are subtly revised through the novel as Touba is progressively enabled in exercising her own occult powers. For instance, one of her earliest dark epiphanies occurs when she envisions a starved boy sitting upright but dead in a cart. On visiting the cemetery where he is being buried in a mass grave she sees that the undertakers are unable to straighten his corpse from the sitting position (35–6). There she encounters for the first time the cleric Khiabani who delivers a modernist speech to her, blaming the people's fatalism for the poverty and hunger which are still killing them even in the twentieth century. The starving boy and Touba's visit to the graveyard are dream-like events, her visionary faculty registering change in Iranian society in an apocalyptic fashion, into which Khiabani's speech is inserted as an epitome of the social message of the *mushrutih*.

Touba and the Meaning of Night proffers a subtle, diffused feminism which is tied to the three generations of women characters: Touba, her daughter Moones, and her adopted daughter Maryam. Neither Touba nor Moones feel able or inclined to break into the discourse of modernity, which belongs to the public world (the implication being that in spite of its adoption of a programme of modernization ostensibly including rights for women, patriarchal structures remained intact in the Pahlavi state). On a domestic level, however, Touba's increasing self-sufficiency is displayed in her carpet weaving and her control over the house. Moones enters employment as a secretary but scarred by her abortion of Ismael's child retreats again into her mother's world of domestic seclusion and mysticism. It is left to the youngest generation in the person of Maryam to embrace the apparent promise of modernity by, at Ismael's instigation, studying to be a doctor. But ideological issues cause divisions between herself and her brothers, Karim and Kamal (342). These come to a climax after she is converted to the revolutionary cause by the Marxist Kamal only to die as a result of the struggles on the streets. In contrast Touba and Moones' recourse to psychic powers intensifies. From a self-conscious position of male superiority Ismael rationalizes this as a continuing, indeed perennial indicator of a female's awareness of herself as powerless (279).

> Ishmael also listened to Moones talking about her supernatural experiments. She could foretell events and amazingly, her predictions often came true, just as his mother-in-law's did. Ismael grew curious about the source of this desire that women seemed to have to predict the future. Women were frightened about their current situations. Thus they were weak, and needed to be surrounded by other weak people [...] Ismael had no doubt that it was a woman who invented the concepts of storing food, weaving carpets, and knitting clothes [...] Because they are worried about storing food and keeping their homes and children safe, they are only concerned with predicting bad things (279).

Touba's consciousness, it is true, registers change in increasingly apocalyptic terms. For years her mind is presided over by the corpse of a female child, Setareh, killed by the girl's uncle after having been raped by soldiers, and buried under the tree in Touba's courtyard. Towards the end of the novel the opening up of Touba's buried secret accompanies cataclysmic revolutionary upheavals building to the violence that results in the death of her adopted granddaughter Maryam once more in Touba's house.

The image of feminized mystic knowledge embracing but at the same dispersing the memory (and historical crime) of the oppressed sacrificed female symbolized by Setareh, typifies Parsipur's message in *Touba*. The reader is invited into the separate, interior world of her female protagonists with the intention of enlarging this in such a way as to draw in the dominant consciousness of the males as well. Touba's lifelong relationship with Master Geda Alishah can be seen as the activation of a space in which women can acquire agency. Sufism is an area of the Iranian religious heritage that has operated independently from the scripturalism of the male-dominated clergy: 'Esoteric Shiism believed in a direct relationship between the individual and his or her God [and] considered intermediaries such as the clergy redundant and attempted to reach an inner meaning (*baten*) of things [...] Sufism [...] an extreme form of esoteric Shiism allowed women to participate in religious activities and many women reached the status of sainthood within it' (Paidar 1995: 35). Master Geda Alishah, the exponent of mystical knowledge Touba seems forever in need of, is connected to 'Touba's usual habit of believing men' (Parsipur 2007: 136). But eventually he abdicates his authority. Disclaiming his capacity to interpret truth alone, now she is an old woman, he invites her to sit in his place and piece together truth for herself: 'He wanted her to sit in his place because he thought that for many long years he had acted in her place on the stage of life. Now he was tired' (ibid.: 351). The Master reveals he has known of Setareh's haunting of Touba's house for a while, but pronounces its imminent collapse. He then makes the strange call for people to come to him 'and each one spread pollen of the memory of Setareh on him. Then he could become pregnant' with her, or with the idea of her (ibid.). By choosing to emphasize Touba's inner life in psychic/mystical fashion rather than tracing her development in terms of the more mainstream clash between the secular modernizing state and protesting Shiism, Parsipur has avoided the problem of having to commit to one or other of the dominant discourses of recent Iranian history. But the corollary, as the voluntary dethronement of male authority in the form of Master Geda Alishah implies, is that Sufi Gnosticism has the capacity to facilitate the mergence of male–female qualities whereas the dominant religious scripturalism has not.

Nonetheless, *Touba and the Meaning of Night* does not present a resolution of the gender imbalance that the novel implies underpins the upheavals of modern Iran. By adopting the anti- or suprarealist strategy of magical realism, tying occult, mystical and eschatological motifs to developments in twentieth-century Iranian history, Parsipur focuses on change in the treatment of women and the development of female consciousness in inward rather than outward social realist terms. To demonstrate the oppression of women throughout Iranian history she employs magic realism in the form of Prince Gill and Layla who stand respectively for the male and female principles, and appear recurrently to embody the dichotomization of gender roles across millennia. In a sense Layla is Gill's creation, since she always incarnates in one way or another the desires and fixations men impose upon women. In the 1930s she embodies the modern 'liberated woman' of the West for whom Reza Shah's reforms have apparently opened up the way. Two generations later at the close of the novel, she has to flee for her life from the now vengeful Gill (his misogynistic hatred re-ignited by the Islamic revolution?). Finally, Layla reveals to Touba her own death and transformation. But the outcome of the revolution/gender issue remains undecided: 'It is up to [people] to become liberated or not liberated' (381). In *Touba and the Meaning of Night* the conflicts, famines, revolutions and wars that play a prominent role in modern Iranian history collectively take on the characteristics of an apocalypse. Its manifestations include visions of the dead (the boy in the cemetery), corpses festering in and finally being disgorged from graves (Setareh), prophecy (Touba and Moones' powers of seeing into the future), and the disintegration of the world (the decay and progressive collapse of Touba's house). The mythical recurrence of the male–female imbalance played out across the ages draws on the ancient division of Iranian history into cycles, and adds to the novel's eschatological framing (Yavari 2007: 397–400). In this way Parsipur disengages the advent of modernity in Iran from its secular, western encoding, but also distances it from its indigenous Islamist Other. Instead she utilizes an older Iranian discourse which enables her to embue her narrative with cosmic dimensions in which her female characters appear to play a dominant role.

Conclusion

If we were looking for key texts in what Salman Rushdie once called 'the dialogue of the deaf', between the self-appointed spokesmen for a triumphalist West and for a resistant Islam respectively, where would we look? For the former perhaps, to the *Kulturkampf*-style of writing epitomised by the work of writers like Kureishi and Naipaul; and for the latter, works such as Qutb's *Milestones*, or Khomeini's *Islam and Revolution*. The writings of Mahfouz, Mahjoub and Parsipur discussed in this chapter clearly belong to an alternative body of writing about Muslim identity in the modern world. Each, in their different ways, has employed modernist, messianic or eschatological motifs to articulate variegated responses to the crisis of modernity from within the constituency of Muslim culture(s). They have not only succeeded in illuminating indigenous perspectives in which the West is de-centred, but have also attached to the topic of modern Muslim identity spiritual dimensions almost wholly lacking in the representations of Muslims projected in the *Kulturkampf* writers reviewed so far.

Chapter 5

Fixing the 'Islamic Terrorist': Ian McEwan, Don DeLillo, John Updike, Mohsin Hamid, Laila Halaby

'The crisis unleashed by the events of September 11 [2001] is one that is global and all-encompassing' wrote the late Fred Halliday in his study of the Twin Towers attack, *Two Hours that Shook the World* (Halliday 2002: 31). Consulting Halliday's book, brain surgeon Henry Perowne (a fictitious character in Ian McEwan's novel *Saturday*) is struck by the author's prognostication that the global crisis the attacks inaugurated would take 'a hundred years to resolve' (McEwan 2005: 32; Halliday: 24). Whether or not he understood his analysis of the causes of 9/11, McEwan, as well as the other novelists I shall discuss in this chapter (if they also read *Two Hours*), might have especially taken to heart Halliday's laconic statement that: 'an insecurity of the economy and market is compounded by a personal one [...] For [those] living in or visiting any city or country that had hitherto avoided such violence, *the sound of an overflying aircraft causes anxiety. A sense of assumed security in much of modern life has, for some time at least, been significantly eroded*' (Halliday 2002: 32–3; my italics). This suddenly acquired anxiety no doubt contributed to a surge of interest in books such as *Two Hours*; *A Fury for God: The Islamist Attack on America* (Malise Ruthven); *Why Do People Hate America?* (Ziauddin Sardar and Merryl Wyn Davies); and translations of the Qur'an, among westerners up until then not unduly phased by Islam, the Middle East, or the so-called 'Islamic' terrorist.

But what of those caught on the other side – those at risk of being identified as 'Islamic' terrorists? In his work on Palestinian identity, Rashid Khalidi describes how that identity was especially susceptible to alteration in times of unusual contingencies, particularly after momentous events (Khalidi 1997: ix). In several key aspects, the experience of the Palestinians can be said to have been extended after September 11 to all the peoples of what Halliday termed West Asia (the Middle East, Iran, Afghanistan and Pakistan). The dispiriting experience at border crossings which Khalidi describes as the inheritance of every Palestinian has now been extended to incorporate potentially anybody with a Muslim name – even non-Muslims who on account of their nationality, or simply a non-Northern European appearance, are taken to be Muslims.[1]

Such treatment most likely has the effect, as it has had with Palestinians, of reinforcing the very identity its interrogators find suspect. A westernized Pakistani working for an elite American company like Changez in Mohsin Hamid's *The Reluctant Fundamentalist* discovers his primary identity is Muslim when confronted by a violent white man in a car park who insists upon it.

If the focus of this chapter falls largely upon Anglo-American writers' exploration of the fear and anxiety unleashed in them and their characters by the September 11 attacks, this is because, unsurprisingly, theirs has been the response most favoured by publishers and most discussed in the media. Anglo-American fiction and journalism that attempts to probe the events of September 11 and their ramifications frequently projects an incomprehension as regards the 'enemy' that is not so much mutual, as heavily weighted on the Anglo-American side. The main reason for this may well be ignorance on the part of authors (and hence their protagonists) of other cultures beyond the American/Western European. Perowne's blurred ideas about the invasion of Iraq and the way he views Saddam Hussein are crystallized in his memory of treating an Iraqi patient, formerly a professor of ancient history at the University of Baghdad, who has been tortured by the Ba'athists. We are not told whether he is a migrant, refugee or asylum seeker. Miri Taleb's attitude to the impending invasion of his country is ambivalent: 'Now the Americans are coming – perhaps for bad reasons' (McEwan 2005: 64). In the aftermath of the invasion (which McEwan does not write about) identities became clearer. The doctor 'NHS terrorists', who might have been Taleb's sons, and who having experienced at first hand the American bombing of Baghdad subsequently made a bungled explosives attack on Glasgow airport in the summer of 2007, were unmistakeably Muslims.[2]

Deranged fanatics and traumatized victims: Anglo-American literary responses to 9/11

In an article which he begins by quoting writers' personal statements concerning the impact 9/11 had upon them, Pankaj Mishra implies that celebrated Anglo-American authors like Martin Amis, Don DeLillo, and John Updike failed to do justice to the magnitude of their topic. This was due to the clichéd way in which they represented the terrorists. In *Falling Man*, Mishra claims, DeLillo 'remains strangely incurious about [the hijackers'] pasts and their societies, and he makes little attempt to analyse, in the light of the biggest ever atrocity, the origin and appeal of political violence [...] Not surprisingly, [he] ends up relying on received notions about Muslim "rage"' (Mishra 2007). Robert Eaglestone lays a similar charge against some post-9/11 writers' 'inability to address the terror that is their proclaimed subject' (Eaglestone 2007: 21). McEwan, DeLillo and Amis instead create terrains inhabited by terrorists who are fetishized in terms of rituals of fanaticism and violence, explicable to the rational mind only as disorder/disease and a mutant incivility.

According to Martin Amis: 'Terror always has its roots in hysteria and psychotic insecurity; still, we should know our enemy' (Amis 2008: 7). Amis's real-life 9/11 terrorist Muhammad Ata is chronically constipated and motivated solely by a lust for killing ('the core reason was of course all the killing – all the putting to death'), but he possesses the ultimate qualification for the 'Islamic' terrorist: 'he was prepared to die' (ibid: 122, 98). In fact, Amis writes, the 9/11 attacks would have failed ridiculously like other al-Qaeda missions had it not been for 'The "Hamburg contingent" (Ata et al.): these men were superficially Westernized, and superficially rational; they were possessed by just the right kind of functioning insanity' (Amis: 146). These horrible mutants flew planes and read airline timetables. They were effective because they aped the exteriorities of western civilization, but they remained, we must presume, internally unaffected by its true values, even though in their operational rationality and recidivistic violence and barbarism they recall Kurtz and the Nazis. As a foil to the terrorists' core irrationality and fanaticism, and in confirmation of the Yeatsian diagnosis of modernity, it is the 'sane' rational western mind, which is vulnerable to bouts of introspection, loss of meaning and breakdown of memory, that may coalesce with and even expand beyond fixation on terrorist attack.

Where the post-9/11 fictions I shall be discussing do score is, again unsurprisingly, in the area of their Anglo-American characters' personal responses to terror. To convey these DeLillo, Updike, and McEwan use tropes which attempt not only to convey the impact of the terrorist violence and traumas of recurrence on the part of those directly affected, but also to invoke in others (including readers) 'the sound of an overflying aircraft [that] causes anxiety', and their sense that the 'assumed security in much of modern life has, for some time at least, been significantly eroded'. Beyond this, other tropes also seep into post-9/11 fiction to broaden the sense of anxiety. It is almost as if the deranged terrorist mind infects laterally the already vulnerable psychological state of western individuals; or it may be that western civilization itself has created simultaneously the susceptibility for its destruction from without and its disintegration from within.

The major trope that accompanies the panic about terrorist attack from outside in the novels I shall be discussing, is that of loss of memory and/or mental disintegration. This may be connected to the effects of the 9/11 attacks, or exist in its own space. Post-traumatic amnesia has been called a form of forgetting in which the mind shuts itself off as a means of self-protection. It may be seen as a mechanism that files away the memory of painful experiences thus allowing humans to continue living their lives. Mohsin Hamid's *The Reluctant Fundamentalist* includes a case of mental illness, a sort of post-traumatic amnesia in reverse, in which the patient inhabits a moment in the past and progressively loses contact with the present. Don DeLillo's *Falling Man* and Ian McEwan's *Saturday* incorporate narratives of Alzheimer's patients whose minds are disintegrating. Each fictional treatment of mental impairment can be taken as synecdoche for wider processes in which the threat of individual memory erasure can be extended to embrace an entire culture's fear of the present, future, and/or the desire for escape through solipsism or collective rites of nostalgia. Treatment of memory loss among the older generation characters may be an indicator of fear of individual and collective dissolution: erasure of the individual memories of earlier twentieth century lives entails a failure to transmit their record of remembrance to succeeding generations. Alternatively, the young can be subject to mental breakdown as well, as seen in a young woman's absorption in a relationship with a dead lover, a disconnect that eventually results in her suicide. The woman's regression has been seen by critics and reviewers as a metaphor for American cultural myopia and withdrawal from post-9/11 realities.

Besides memory loss, a further dimension related to the crisis of meaning in these novels is the relationship of children and parents. Parents display heightened anxiety towards their offspring owing to their perceived inability to protect them from a world of potential terrors. In Don DeLillo's *Falling Man* and Laila Halaby's *Once in a Promised Land* this anxiety is intensified by placing parents and children in separate mental spaces; parents are unable to communicate with their children who inhabit isolated, sealed off worlds. In DeLillo's novel the fear of terror exercising parents is passed on subliminally to their children who respond by staging atavistic re-enactments of it. In Halaby's, the teenage boy whose erratic behaviour results in a fatal road accident has developed an obsessive hatred of Arabs. Aberrant behaviours among the young and dissolution of memory among the old can also be connected to wholesale breakdown of community, and with it the collapse of societal meanings. So while these behaviours may accompany the effects of 9/11 and be linked to the perceived ongoing threat of terrorism, they can also be considered as symptomatic of a world in which change is taking place too rapidly. In a number of respects then, I shall be probing in this chapter a complex of which the constituent parts are not easily separable. A critical condition for this emphasis on crises of meaning and loss or impairment of memory is their occurrence within a society unable or unwilling to comprehend the sources of and reasons for the terror attacks.

The texts I shall be scrutinizing first of all, the Anglo-American, are able to achieve precious little critical purchase on the events they represent beyond a vague focalization on the West in peril. As Robert Appelbaum and Alexis Paknadel point out: 'So much media attention is paid to terrorism, and so little direct experience is possessed by the people writing the novels about it, that the novels may be accurately said to *re-narrate* the subject, basing themselves on previous narrations as likely to be discovered in the media as in previous literature' (Appelbaum and Paknadel 2008: 400; original italics).[3] Each of the Anglo-American novels I discuss is univocal: in DeLillo's *Falling Man* and Ian McEwan's *Saturday* the terrorists and their land(s) and culture(s) of origin are exterior and remain shadowy and unrealized. Only Updike's *The Terrorist* directly situates the terrorist threat from within. In these representations of the events of 9/11 and their aftermath, anxieties about the precariousness and/or meaninglessness of life in postmodern western cities predominate over attempts at understanding the motivation of the attackers. There is either unwillingness or wilful refusal to link the so-called 'Islamic terror' to wider currents within western and global societies. Instead, the novels appear to cordon this off as a 'threat from outside' while, subliminally, it is woven into their probing of the neuroses of the times.

Meaning and Forgetfulness in time of Terror: Ian McEwan's *Saturday* and Don DeLillo's *Falling Man*

In this section I shall scrutinize the crises of meaning and the trope of memory loss inscribed within two fictional works concerning 9/11. One is an evocation and the other a direct representation of the events and their aftermath. Set in London over a period of twenty hours on the day of mass demonstration against the approaching invasion of Iraq in 2003, McEwan's *Saturday* makes play of thrusting both the terrorist threat and the prospect of personal mental disintegration to the centre of his main protagonist's life. Of the two, however, fear of terrorism appears by far the more importunate. It impacts on brain surgeon Henry Perowne's consciousness when he wakes at 4 a.m. and from the window of his central London house observes an aeroplane with one of its engines on fire. His fixation with terrorism at once causes him to assume that the aircraft trailing flames is a terrorist atrocity in the making. He spends the next few hours scanning the television news in the morbid hope of confirmation. As one theorist of terrorism puts it: '[W]hat we know as terrorism is actually a media creation: mass media define, delimit, de-legitimize, and discredit events that we have not actually seen' (Farnen 1990 in Houen 2002: 11). Even though Perowne *has* seen the plane, and has attributed its distress to a terrorist attack, terrorism must receive its imprimatur of facticity through a media that is itself the origin of his obsession.[4] Apparently never having met a 'Muslim' terrorist, McEwan's main protagonist forms his diagnosis of the 'war on terror' from news reports he processes addictively with a contradictory mix of scepticism about his worst fears and desire for their affirmation:

Despite the troops mustering in the Gulf, or the tanks out at Heathrow, on Thursday, the storming of the Finsbury Park mosque, the reports of terror cells around the country, and Bin Laden's promise on tape of 'martyrdom attacks' on London, Perowne held for a while to the idea that it was all an aberration, that the world would surely calm down and soon be otherwise, that reason, being a powerful tool, was irresistible, the only way out; or that like any other crisis, this one would fade soon, and make way for the next, going the way of the Falklands and Bosnia, Biafra and Chernobyl (McEwan 2005: 32).

McEwan's decision to stage an assault by homegrown thugs on the Perowne London family house gives the novel an off-centre feel. The entry of Baxter, the young thug and replacement terrorist figure, into Perowne's house is a synecdoche for the terrorist threat that hangs over the novel as a whole without directly impacting on the lives of its characters. Baxter, with whose car Perowne is in collision on the day of the demonstration, suffers from the first signs of a chronic debilitating nervous disease. In the ensuing confrontation Perowne initially deflects the threat of violence by presenting Baxter with a diagnosis of his condition and a fake upbeat prognosis for a cure. This misuse of his expertise leads to the later showdown in which Baxter and his sidekick break into Perowne's house and his family are implausibly saved from rape/murder when his daughter recites Arnold's 'Dover Beach'. (The recitation has a comparable effect on Baxter to Prospero's magic upon his enemies.) However, an onslaught led by Perowne's son leads to the intruder being thrown down the stairs, giving Perowne the opportunity to play God on a diminished scale by operating on Baxter's injured skull, even though he knows his disease to be incurable. 'And here is one area where Henry can exercise authority and shape events. He knows how the system works – the difference between good and bad care is near infinite' (278).

Enlightenment science, rationality and order are the organizing factors of Perowne's (and McEwan's?) world-view ('*reason*, being a powerful tool, was irresistible, the only way out'). They are Perowne's professional raison d'être: his faith in scientific explanation and his expertise as a surgeon is exemplified in the long – some have said meretricious – descriptions of the pathology of the brain and Perowne's surgical operations that abound throughout *Saturday* and which are represented as heroic interventions on behalf of life and sanity. Seemingly oppositional, the 'Radical Islamists' Perowne imagines are constructed in Popperian terms as enemies of the West's piecemeal, rationally engineered society: '[not] really nihilists – they want the perfect society on earth, which is Islam. They belong to a doomed tradition [...] the pursuit of utopia' (34). Baxter's sickness makes him, like the crazed terrorist, 'a special case – a man who believes he has no future and is therefore free of consequences' (210). The implied message here could be that it would be better to surgically operate on the malign influence, though in Baxter's case Perowne knows that would be futile.[5] Perowne's focalization of the *ersatz* terrorist belongs to what Eaglestone terms 'a western discourse that brands him as evil, and as psychologically (and so bodily) sick' (Eaglestone: 22). For Perowne 'Islamic' terrorism can only spring from 'primitive thinking of the super-naturally inclined [...] excess of the subjective [...] an inability to contemplate your own unimportance [...] psychosis' (McEwan: 17). Islam and terrorism are conflated, Othered, and turned into enemies of the western Enlightenment world-view. They exist at the back of Perowne's consciousness making periodic intrusion over the twenty-four hour period covered by the narrative.

For him mental disintegration and terror are both terminal threats to reason. But terror, perhaps because it is the product of conscious agency, however deluded, is for him a threat that can and should be faced. He sees it as connected to a range of utopian fantasies, one among others being belief in an ideal Islamic community:

> Out in the real world there exist detailed plans, visionary projects for peaceable realms, all conflicts resolved, happiness for everyone, for ever – mirages for which people are prepared to die and kill. Christ's kingdom on earth, the workers' paradise, the ideal Islamic state. But only in music, and only on rare occasions, does the curtain actually lift on this dream community, and it's tantalisingly conjured, before fading away with the last notes (ibid.: 171–2).

Retreat into the momentary epiphany – and the equally transient gratification of sexual pleasure, status and ownership of things – does not however suggest that McEwan has given up on the paraphernalia of enlightenment, only that he would most probably endorse the apocalyptic quotation from Rushdie's *Shalimar the Clown* which Eaglestone uses as a heading for his essay: 'The Age of Reason is over ... an Age of Fury was Dawning'. Perowne is thus firmly located within the contemporary western 'community of anxiety', his beloved London metonymically standing for civilization on the edge, as it did in Edwardian England in *Heartbreak House*. Alternatively, like Orwell's 1930s suburbs, it lies directly in the path of future wars: 'Perhaps a bomb in the cause of jihad will drive them out with all the other faint-hearts into the suburbs' (276). (At least one part of Perowne's prognostications would come to pass: McEwan wrote his novel only a few years before the London bombings of 7 July 2005)

Besides the terrorist menace a second front is opened against Perowne's enlightenment faith and frankly hedonistic lifestyle. His mother suffers from dementia, 'a terror of our time – either in ourselves or those close to us' (Harvey-Wood and Byatt 2008: 34). After his morning encounter with Baxter and a competitive squash match with a colleague, Perowne fulfils two family duties: a drop in on his guitarist son's jam session, and before that a visit to his mother in her old people's home:

> Being with her isn't so difficult. The hard part is when he comes away [...] when the woman she once was haunts him [...] when he feels he's betraying her, leaving her behind in her shrunken life, sneaking away to the riches, the secret hoard of his own existence. Despite the guilt, he can't deny the little lift he feels [...] when he turns his back and walks away from the old people's place and takes his car keys from his pocket and embraces the freedoms that can't be hers (153).

A reconstruction of his mother's life prefaces Perowne's narrative of the visit, as he struggles against an outcome that is not only personally distressing but also irreconcilable to his reason. The mother's residence is 'a few minutes away from the old Perivale family home' (158) and can therefore be included in a history invested with order and meaning. Once a competitive swimmer 'in 1954 she swam for Middlesex in the county championships' (156). Perowne believes he has inherited aspects of her character: equating her once tidy house with his feeling of belonging in the operating theatre. Her former domesticity – testimony to a bygone construction of the female – is valorized through the nineteenth-century novels his daughter reads. In these disorderly reality is overcome by artful completion: the teleology of the omniscient novelist's ordered world: 'Unlike in Daisy's novels, moments of precise reckoning are rare in real life; questions of misinterpretation are not often resolved [as they are in Austen or Eliot's novels]. Nor do they remain pressingly unresolved. They simply fade. People don't remember clearly, or they die, or the questions die and new ones take their place' (156). The phrase 'people don't remember clearly' has immediate connection to the muddled mind of Mrs Perowne who still doesn't understand her own mother died in 1970. Her son can at least account for her dementia by rehearsing the causes behind it, and the stages of its development, thus re-inscribing disorderly reality in the rational codes of scientific explanation. Nevertheless, the progress of the disease re-arranges everyday realities and consequences irreversibly, making life disorderly, ridiculous, ultimately empty of meaning. For this aporia on the periphery of his personal life Perowne's one recourse, apart from escape to his still sexy and attractive forty-something wife and accomplished children, appears equally self-centred. He must stay healthy for as long as he can. 'Elevated levels of lictoprotein-a are said to have a robust association with multifarct dementia [...] He isn't ready to die, and nor is he ready to half die. He wants his prodigiously connected myelin-rich white matter intact, like an unsullied snowfield. No cheese then. He'll be ruthless with himself in pursuit of boundless health to avoid his mother's fate. Mental death' (165). But even Perowne knows this struggle with the disorder he perhaps fears most (because it is personally known and close to him unlike the terrorist) is self-defeating, that his present orderly existence will ultimately unravel. *Saturday* concludes with a return to the self-satisfied life of comfort and controlled, moderate stimulation McEwan has constructed for his hero. As he prepares for sleep having just made love to his wife (as he had earlier that morning) Perowne contemplates. 'There's always this [...] And then: there's only this. And at last, faintly, falling: this day's over' (279).

In spite of its obvious gestures towards the London novel (*Mrs Dalloway* and *Howard's End* come to mind), with its uncritical representation of an individualistic, high-achieving central protagonist and his equally talented and attractive wife and children, *Saturday* more resembles up-market soap opera than canonical fiction. Noting the enthusiastic reception the novel has received from critics and reviewers, John Banville asked: 'Are we in the West so shaken in our sense of ourselves and our culture, are we so disablingly terrified in the face of the various fanaticisms which threaten us, that we can allow ourselves to be persuaded and comforted by such a self-satisfied and, in many ways, ridiculous novel as this?' (Banville 2005)

Don DeLillo wrote in *Harpers* a few months after the attacks:

> In the past decade [...] multinational corporations have come to seem more vital and influential than governments [...] All this changed on September 11. Today, again, the world narrative belongs to terrorists. But the primary target of the men who attacked the Pentagon and the World Trade Center was not the global economy. It was America that drew their fury. It was the high gloss of our modernity. It was the thrust of our technology. It was our perceived godlessness. It was the blunt force of our foreign policy. It was the power of American culture to penetrate every wall, home, life and mind (DeLillo 2001: 33–4).[6]

In comparison with McEwan's platitudinous, off-centre terror novel manqué, DeLillo's *Falling Man* sets out to treat the subject head on, re-enacting the events of 9/11 and their aftermath through the lives of a series of introverted, self-absorbed, sometimes paranoiac New Yorkers. Where McEwan's writing works towards the re-establishment of order, DeLillo constructs his in broken, detached blocks that mediate the thoughts and experiences of his central characters. He writes in an intense fragmentary style that is more contemporary, more mimetic and abstruse than McEwan's, whose traditional, linear mode of narrative hardly diverges from normative twentieth-century British fiction. When it comes to moving outside the familiar cultural terrain of New York or London, DeLillo attempts to understand the motivation of the terrorists by extending the meaninglessness implicit in the lives of the New York characters to encompass their life-experience too. They find their solution in a creed of death which, however exterior it may appear to westerners, remains connected to their world. Though probably less fatuous and dismissive of the Arabs as human beings than McEwan or Amis, DeLillo's version of the terrorist story is only marginally more convincing and like them reinforces the view of Islam as a religion of fanatics.

The unifying factor in *Falling Man* is its presentation of diverse individual responses to the events of 9/11, but unlike *Saturday*, it proceeds on the premise that you cannot defray the inevitable, be it a terrorist attack or mental death; it might be just round the corner waiting for you. Both terror and mental introversion and dissolution are woven together into the fabric of the text. On the day of the disaster Keith's first port of call after escaping his office in the Towers is the flat where his wife Lianne, a freelance copy-editor, lives with their young son. 9/11 changes Keith in a number of ways: his life afterward supplies temporary, often banal meanings that help deflect the trauma of memory. Previously estranged from his wife, he gives up womanizing and returns to his marriage, but now engages in sexual intimacy with her in public places; 'at traffic lights people watched, a few, and the driver watched, lights or not, eyes gliding across the rearview mirror' (105). He also conducts an unlikely relationship with Florence, an Afro-American and fellow survivor of the Towers who he tracks down as a result of picking up her attaché case in the mêlée of escape. Their compulsive relationship is at first centred solely on shared experience of the attack: 'the only words that meant anything to him were the ones she'd spoken and would speak' (92). But when it becomes sexual Keith ends it abruptly. He finds a way both of blocking out memory but also of retaining a subliminal connection with those members of his old poker group who died in the Towers by retreating into the twenty-four hour casinos in different locations of the world.

Lianne also finds herself confronted by problems of remembering and forgetting; first of all through her father, who committed suicide before a degenerative disease took hold of him. His death robbed her not only of a father, it also brought the realization that without his memories her roots are irrecoverable. In addition she holds the fear that the illness may be congenital. Her sense of loss leads her to engage in voluntary work with a class of first-stage Alzheimer patients who are writing down their memories while they still can: 'The truth was mapped in slow and certain decline. Each member of the group lived in this knowledge' (125). The same preoccupation with ageing and mental deterioration also exercises Lianne's concern for her mother, Nina, a retired academic fine arts specialist. At the end of the novel, Lianne's night-mares about her mother are realized when fears of imminent terror attack have partially receded: 'Her mother had a mane of white hair at the end, the body slowly broken, haunted by strokes, blood in the eyes' (234). Disjunction, isolation and introversion spread outwards as *Falling Man* progresses. DeLillo's characters retreat more and more into private inner worlds, Keith to the gaming table, his wife with almost practised intent to her sealed-off self: 'She was continuing to withdraw, but calmly, in control. He was self-sequestered, as always, but with a spatial measure now [...]' (212)

A further privatization of meaning is discovered in the behaviour of Lianne and Keith's son and his young friends during the days immediately after the attack. Their parents find them 'searching the skies' (71) for aeroplanes: withdrawn into a world of fantasy presided over by a mythical Bill Lawton (the children's Bin Laden). Among themselves they originate a system of monosyllabic communication, a code excluding the adults. Lianne's response – 'Damn kids with their goddam twisted powers of imagination' (72) – reveals the children's atavistic response to 9/11 has opened a deeper level of anxiety within herself. Their behaviour extends the confusion, confirming the fragmentation of meaning; as Lianne tells Keith towards the end of the novel: 'I know that most lives make no sense. I mean in this country, what makes sense?' (215). What 9/11 does is to force New Yorkers to address the question proposed in the second sentence. From Lianne's Alzheimer's class it elicits a unified response: 'The one subject the members want to write about [...][was] the planes' (31). (Although understandably one named Omar is initially reluctant to do so.) Otherwise DeLillo makes few clear-cut connections between fear of terror and clinical memory loss beyond integrating both topics fully into his novel.

Interestingly, the comparatively few passages that include the plane hijackers work in connection with this common link. The Arabs operate in the same meaningless world as the Americans: the main variant is that their version of Islamic jihad supplies them with a totalizing if closed set of meanings which the Americans lack. The 'terrorist' parts of the narrative are focalized through the eyes of Hammad, a less repellent figure than Amis's Muhammad Ata who appears in DeLillo's novel under the name of Amir. DeLillo tries to give depth to the character of Hammad by connecting his dedication to the jihadist cause with the memories of a former soldier in the Iran-Iraq war who he meets in Germany. The memory the man transmits to Hammad is of the Iranian boy soldiers who were sent to the front to be martyred. When Hammad relates the story to his jihadist acquaintances: 'They stared him down, they talked him down. That was a long time ago and those were only boys, they said, not worth the time it would take to be sorry for a single one' (80). DeLillo's attempt to humanize Hammad extends to showing him lusting after girls and secretly wanting to trim his beard: 'But there were rules now and he was determined to follow them. His life had structure. Things were clearly defined. He was becoming one of them now, learning to look like them and think like them. This was inseparable from jihad. He prayed with them to be with them. They were becoming brothers' (83).

That is probably the extent of DeLillo's sympathy for Hammad. The more he integrates with the jihadi group, the more formulaic his inner life becomes. In a training camp in Afghanistan he begins to 'understand that death is stronger than life [...] There was no feeling like this ever in his life. He was a bomb vest and knew he was a man now, finally, ready to close the distance to God' (172). On board the plane in the Hudson Corridor, in the seconds before his desire for the martyr-ideal is consummated, Hammad's conversion is complete: 'The pious ancestors had pulled their clothes tightly about them before battle. They were the ones who named the way. How could any death be better?' (239). Emptied of personality, Hammad, however, has also closed the interior emptiness felt by the Americans.

A religious creed intoxicated with death is a topic that resurfaces in the discussions Lianne listens to between her mother and her long-term lover Martin, a German art collector and dealer. Nina begins:

'Dead wars, holy wars. God could appear in the sky tomorrow.'
    'Whose God would it be?' Martin said.
    'God used to be an urban Jew. He's back in the desert now.'

[...] [Nina continues] 'It's sheer panic. They attack out of panic.'

'This much, yes, it may be true. Because they think the world is a disease. This world, this society, ours. A disease that's spreading [...] One side has the capital, the labor, the technology, the armies, the cities, the laws, the police and the passions. The other side has a few men willing to die' (46–7)

Jihad is a response to meaningless, diseased modernity, but they are polarities that ultimately join in one common nihilism. In *Falling Man* DeLillo sets out to narrativize the pessimistic perception that modern civilization is a disease. But he is disinclined to privilege argumentation in what remains a predominantly mimetic narrative. This can be seen immediately after the attack in Lianne's aggressive reaction to the woman in the downstairs apartment who insists on playing loud Arabic music. The woman contends the music gives her peace and 'has nothing to do with now or then or any other time'. Lianne responds: 'The whole city is ultrasensitive right now. Where have you been hiding?' At one level a typical New York encounter in which neither party gives quarter, the outcome – Lianne 'mashed the hand into the eye and the woman took a swing' – is visceral: 'Lianne knew she was going crazy even as she turned and walked out' (119–20).

Typically, DeLillo makes sure the incident's ideological content is blurred – the woman whose name is Elena is probably not an Arab but Greek. Another emotion grips Lianne when later on she takes her son to an anti-war march. The boy collects a leaflet on Islam and she finds herself helping him pronounce Arabic words. As he recites the words she grows uneasy, at the same time remembering an experience she had in Cairo twenty years before, when in an end of Ramadan celebration she had felt isolated as a white face in the crowd. These events, past and present, and 'the public discourse' of the leaflet ('Islam with an 800 number') engender in Lianne a desire for escape: 'she needed to flee from both crowds' (185). By this internalization of mass conflict in terms of personal withdrawal DeLillo inscribes the so-called clash of civilizations in an idiolect of anxiety and alienation that is nonetheless identifiably western.

The novel's abiding image is perhaps not the beginning and end framing sections that describe the catastrophe inside the towers. It is rather the sign of the falling man of the title: the performance artist figure who mimics the suffering of 9/11 in such a way as to render it anonymous, enigmatic, and emptied of meaning. Lianne, who personally witnesses the falling man's act, so much identifies with him that she researches his history and the different locations from which he had dangled and the disputes over whether or not the position he assumed during the fall was intended to mimic the photograph of the man falling from the tower head first. While the newspapers describe him variously as a 'heartless exhibitionist', 'moronic', and 'brave chronicler of the Age of Terror', Lianne sees him as a falling angel, possessed of an horrific beauty, empathizing with his withdrawnness. His random appearances around the city are, paradoxically, belied by his refusal to enter the public realm: 'He had no comments to make to the media on any subject' (222). Yet, significantly, her memory of seeing his fall becomes clouded as time passes: 'the man eluded her' (224). If memory is so imperfect – and DeLillo's message seems almost nihilistic here – how can any event, even one on the magnitude of 9/11 – hold any lasting meaning?

Constructing the homegrown fanatic: Updike's The Terrorist

Compared to McEwan's and DeLillo's always peripheral representations of terrorists and their putative mindset, John Updike takes the risk of focalizing precisely on this in his novel *The Terrorist* (2006). Child of a cross-cultural marriage between an Irish American woman and an absent Egyptian father, Ahmad the youthful would-be suicide bomber is home grown. Racially hybrid though he is, he can hardly be considered so in cultural terms. The forgetting in his case is a function of Updike's decision to effectively erase Ahmed's American childhood. The author seems intent on imposing an exclusively religious identity on the *tabula rasa* mind of his young proto-terrorist, a convert to Islam from the age of eleven. Apart from a subtle physical feature or an unconsciously displayed mannerism linking him with his American mother, Ahmad is born again to Muslim faith in a more radical manner than any American Christian, excising in the process all sense of connection with his motherland. His hatred of America and acceptance of a mission to blow up the Lincoln tunnel with a lorry-load of explosives is fired almost solely by ingestion of passages from the Qur'an taught him by a suave Mephistophelean Yemeni imam at the local mosque. Ahmad's 'self-elected religious affiliation' (Updike 2006: 83) is certainly strongly linked to his sense of identity, although not fed by standard alienation factors such as race prejudice or some other form of social humiliation. His distancing of himself from his schoolmates at New Prospect Central High New Jersey is sui generis, distilled out of his desire to remain set-apart from the corruption and uncleanness of his contemporaries and the immediate environment. As a Muslim convert he is uncomfortable with 'the lazy manner of ethnic [Muslim] identity' and when he passes through ethnically Muslim areas of New Jersey he feels himself to be 'an outsider among outsiders' (177, 244).

Ahmad isn't allowed to struggle with the American side of himself; it barely exerts an influence. Unrooted in his native soil, but also unconnected with and mainly disinterested in the standard Middle Eastern political hatreds, his fundamentalist religiosity is strangely uninflected by the religious history of America. Updike's character has been almost universally dismissed as monomaniacal, and his stilted, totally unidiomatic speech condemned as robotic and highly implausible. Such an unlikely central protagonist appears to undermine the novel's credibility. Updike, however, seems to have as his foremost concern a desire to explore the purely religious dimension to his

Muslim character's near fanatical hatred of America. In a notional sense by privileging the spiritual dispute and toning down the familiar ideological binaries of the West v Islam particularly at their political level, much of the repertoire of cultural chauvinism implicit in the writing of Amis and McEwan is deflected. Ahmad's faith may be sectarian but it is constructed as the polar opposite of America's godless materialism more than of its Judeo-Christian heritage. The fundamentalist Islam encoded in *The Terrorist* is engaged in mortal combat with the spiritual anomie of postmodern capitalist America more than it is with US imperialist policies in the Middle East or the old enemy, Christianity. The novel begins and ends with Ahmad's central fear: what he feels but does not say to his high school guidance counsellor: 'America wants to take away my God' (39). This positionality is structured into the novel by the further insertion of two characters who fight for Ahmad's soul. The sinister imam may be his religious tutor, but his school counsellor the atheist Jew Levy, who also becomes his mother's lover, is in fact his true spiritual mentor. Both Levy and Ahmad stand as postmodern America's condemners: Ahmad through his possession of 'a shallow and starkly innocent faith' (107); Levy through his alienation from a postmodern present that disturbs and erases layer by layer his accumulated memories of America, so confirming the ugliness and meaning-lessness of his and his country's way of life.

Like Perowne, Levy wakes up at four in the morning but there the comparison ends. His wife is obese and in her sixties and he no longer loves her; his mind at this hour is not so much shaped by fear of terrorism as by terror of ageing and death.

> He stands at a window curtained in sun-yellowed lace and contemplates his neighbourhood by the gray light of its mercury-vapor street lamps [...]
>
> As Jack Levy sees it, America is paved solid with fat and tar, a coast-to-coast tarbaby where we're all stuck [...]
>
> He stands there no longer seeing but pressing with his consciousness back against the certainty that all this will some day cease for him. The screen in his head will go totally blank, and yet it will all go on without him, dawn breaking and cars starting up and wild creatures continuing to feed in a terrain poisoned by Man (26, 27, 29).

The American dream is scarcely mentioned, but its erasure is registered throughout the neighbourhood of New Prospect. The 'lake of rubble' outside the High School signifies simultaneously the demolition of the civic landscape that had together embodied the immigrants' high aspirations and the social and ethical markers that once ordered American society. Levy's disillusionment with present-day America is inscribed in terms of its abandonment of its nineteenth and earlier twentieth-century ideals. 'His old-fashioned sense of the reason-versus-faith divide' (27) paradoxically makes him open, in spite of his contempt for religion, to Ahmad's vulnerable will to faith.

Updike's fascination with the persistence of religious ideology in a functionally materialist society and epoch unfolds dialectically by his setting the humane atheist Levy opposite the darkly sardonic, ultimately unbelieving imam beneath whose sleekly impressive oriental accoutring resides a balding, ageing coward. In this unlikely figure Updike's research into Islam produces an incongruous mix of elements: an erudite, narrowly orthodox Muslim scholar who is viscerally anti-American yet not above quoting Shakespeare, and who is also willing and able to disclose deconstructive western interpretations of the Qur'anic text to Ahmad.[7] The imam's sessions with Ahmad are intended to represent an authentic scaffolding that bears the weight of the potential Muslim terrorist. But in spite of the author's use of a system of transliteration that indicates the range of Arabic vowels, accompanied by English glossing for passages from the Qur'an, the effect overall is a confusion of idioms. It is not just Ahmad's stiff wooden responses that undermine our confidence in the novel, but the Lacanian slippages of the imam and the superficial skein of affability which evokes a Harvard professor from the past rather than a mullah from Sana'a:

'Perfect! What a beautiful tutee you are, Ahmad! I could not have put it better myself. '*ta'fu wa tasfahu wa taghfiru* – *'afa* and *safaha*, abstain and turn away! Do without these women of non-Heavenly flesh, this earthly baggage, these unclean hostages to fortune! Travel light, straight into paradise! Tell me, dear Ahmad, are you afraid of entering paradise?'

'Oh, no, sir. Why would I be? I look forward to it, as do all good Muslims.'

'Yes. Of course they do. We do. You gladden my heart. For next session kindly prepare "The Merciful" and "The Event"' (108).

The novel's generous colouring of incident and detail is, however, barely successful in embedding its otherwise unlikely central premise. Updike tries hard to supply plausibility to his two main characters, Ahmad and Levy. There is his signature staging of Levy's infidelity with Ahmad's mother, Terry; Levy's wife's telephone chats with her sister who coincidently is undersecretary to the Secretary for Homeland Security in Washington; Ahmad's love for a coffee-coloured girl from school with whom, because of his general fear of contaminating his faith through sex, he has his one and only sexual encounter; his period as truckdriver for a Lebanese family furniture firm where he is recruited, unbeknownst to him, by a CIA agent, and the suspenseful build-up to the botched attempt to blow up the tunnel in peak time traffic. In the culminating section of the narrative, when Levy manoeuvres himself inside Ahmad's driving-cab as he moves his truck towards the consummation of martyrdom, Updike seals the union of his two soul companions and completes the novel's dialectic. Humane unbelief confronts inhumane belief, but only in order for both to be cancelled out. Ahmad responds to what is human in his belief system – an untainted border of greenery approaching the tunnel (which reminds him of the Qur'anic paradise) and an innocent black child's smile. However his withdrawal from his mission entails the collapse of the system in its entirety. The skyscrapers of Manhattan face down the pure faith of the believer, both in its fanaticism and its humanity; it expires, blotted out by the atheistical surrounds. Meaning and memory are subsumed in the mindless amnesia of twenty-first century American capitalism.

In thus co-joining alienated Muslim faith and atheist scepticism, Updike eschews the nihilism of DeLillo and the fatuous complacency of McEwan. But in spite of all his efforts he is scarcely more successful than them in fixing the 'Islamic' terrorist. All three writers operate within a horizon of discourse that does not have the semantic tools to penetrate the mysteries of Muslim identity. Whether this is constructed in terms of mental pathology, nihilism or cultural alienation, it bares the imprint of western neuroses rather than it does Arab or Muslim ones. The conclusion is unavoidable: representations of the 'Islamic terrorist' in both Anglo-American fiction and journalism only demonstrate how pervasive is the failure to engage with non-western cultures and identities.

Writing back to America: Mohsin Hamid's *The Reluctant Fundamentalist* and Laila Halaby's *Once in a Promised Land*

On the other hand diasporic Muslim writers have de-centred the Islamic terrorist threat and attempted instead to account for the events of 9/11 in terms of US activities in the Third World and the Muslim migrant's experience of racist othering in America. Mohsin Hamid's *The Reluctant Fundamentalist* (2007) both affirms and subverts America's centrality to the generation of terrorism in the contemporary world; while Halaby's *Once in a Promised Land* (2007) arraigns white America's ignorance and petty-minded isolationism with respect to non-white immigrants. Some crucial elements missing from Amis, McEwan, DeLillo and Updike's writings on 'Islamic' terror are supplied by Mohsin Hamid's *The Reluctant Fundamentalist*. These are: a non-western migrant's view of what it is like to live in the West; a 'Third World' perspective on America's global activities; and an insider's view of how it feels to belong to a Muslim nation. Changez, the narrator, is a Pakistani migrant who has penetrated into the elite of America by majoring from Harvard and obtaining a position with a small but coveted valuation firm in New York. This makes his fall from grace post-9/11 all the more spectacular. As a Muslim he now belongs to a group that has suddenly replaced Afro-Americans at the bottom of America's pile of esteem (Hartnell 2007). His eventual decision to leave the United States may be his own, but it fits an emergent pattern for Muslims who, though accul-turated to America, feel obliged to leave. What needs emphasis however is the manner in which Hamid switches from the Anglo-American novelists' routine concentration on the impact of terror in America/the West.

In contradistinction to DeLillo's novel, in which the strategy is to extend the crisis of meaning of American-led modernity into the hearts of the Arab hijackers, Hamid represents an eastern society, Pakistan, in which Changez is situated throughout his narration. This is implied early on when at his company job interview Changez, attempting to invest his past with historical depth and meaning, describes his native Lahore as 'the second largest city of Pakistan, ancient capital of the Punjab, home to nearly as many people as New York, layered like a sedimentary plain with the accreted history of invaders from Aryans to the Mongols and the British.' This history is summarily erased by the interrogator's question: 'And are you on financial aid?' (Hamid 2007: 7). But when the ambitious Changez goes on holiday to Greece with several of his classmates including the beautiful Erica, she observes that his background has made him 'feel solid'; significantly, when he asks her if she feels the same she replies 'with a trace of sadness in her voice, "Sometimes, but no, not really"'(ibid.: 20).

Hamid equips Changez with dual spheres of reference: he comes from an elite eastern family now living in reduced circumstances, but while a Muslim country may be reduced to financial aid, it is implied, it hardly has an impoverished self-image. On the contrary, Changez's embrace of American culture ultimately does not uproot his sense of who he is. It is the 9/11 attack, which he learns about while on business in Manila, that makes an incision through Changez's 'treasured American self' (Chaudhuri 2007) to reveal his buried native one: 'I was in my room, packing my things. I turned on the television and saw what I at first took to be a film. But as I continued to watch, I realized that it was not fiction but news. I stared as one – and then the other – of the twin towers of New York's World Trade Center collapse. And then I *smiled.* Yes, despicable as it may sound, my initial reaction was to be remarkably pleased' (Hamid: 72; original italics). Up to this point Changez's loyalty to America could be compared to a janissary's – 'Christian boys [...] captured by the Ottomans and trained to be soldiers in a Muslim army [...] They were ferocious and utterly loyal' having 'fought to erase their own civilizations, so they had nothing else to turn to' (151). Now this starts to unravel, awakening him to the threat America poses to the world and to his own society.

Sent to Chile to value a publishing concern, Changez's newly awakened sense of the destructive effects of American business methods on Third World countries causes him to resign from his company and return to Pakistan thus lending his actions an international, anti-globalization flavour. Back home in Lahore, Changez 'seemingly through force of will, [has] compel[led] a sinister American visitor, perhaps a CIA agent with a concealed weapon, to listen to an extended and vaguely threatening monologue that catalogues the events that led him to decide that "America had to be stopped in the interest not only of the rest of humanity, but also in your own"' (Scanlan 2007). By this time Changez has come to reject his narrow absorption in the American dream, refined in his case to the uncritical belief that he could succeed as an executive as well as pursue his self-negating love for the young, blond, and narcissistic Erica. Erica's mental collapse – 'disappearing into a powerful *nostalgia*' (Hamid 2007: 113; original italics) for her dead high-school lover – causes Changez to mimic the young man briefly, before he realizes the American woman cannot be wooed. At a symbolic level, Erica's relationship with Changez, the one-way street up which her lover is forced to go, suggests the demands America makes upon the migrant: to forget his past and become totally immersed in Americanness. Erica's inaccessibility doubles for US isolationism, her impenetrability for America's uninterest in foreigners, her coyness as its refusal to be penetrated by other narratives (Hartnell 2007). But although Changez has superficially accomplished this, the new circumstances post-9/11 awaken him to the falsity of such a position. America's refusal to be penetrated by other narratives, its total lack of interest in foreign cultures, causes him to reject its unyielding terms. Nevertheless it would be a mistake to undervalue the traumatic nature of Changez's relationship with Erica. The search he conducts for his lost love when she disappears from the sanatorium to which her mental illness has taken her is a sad compulsive one. However, her likely suicide underscores an emptiness already identified by Erica herself in her earlier admission of personal insecurity. Her situation can be connected with the individual reactions to 9/11 which we have also met in *Falling Man*, and with the general paranoia of America itself.

If we are to accept the sincerity of Changez's attachment to America, what are we to make of his playful ambiguity and his narrative posturing? A dialogic dimension is attached to Changez's narrative which, while it is apparently directed at his anonymous American auditor, simultaneously addresses the larger western audience whose anger Changez deflects by his ambiguous interplay: 'But you are at war, you say? Yes, you have a point. I was not at war with America. Far from it: I was the product of an American university; I was earning a lucrative American salary; I was infatuated with an American woman. So why did part of me desire to see America harmed? I did not know, then; I knew merely that my feelings would not be acceptable to my colleagues, and I undertook to hide them as well as I could' (73). At the phrase, 'I did not know, *then*', images of Afghan training camps and terrorist videotapes, the standard offstage paraphernalia of 'Islamic' terror we meet with in Amis, DeLillo, et al., can easily supervene. Changez probably intends them to do so. Nevertheless, he has not reverted – as a superficial reading might lead us to expect – to a violent creed that hates and wills harm to America. Hamid's title is designedly ambiguous; the main protagonist is not a reluctant convert to Islamic fundamentalism. The terms 'fundamentalism' and 'fundamentalist' are applied in the novel neither to Pakistan, Islam, nor any Muslim individual or group (the phrase 'religious literalists' is the closest it gets to 'Islamic fundamentalist'). Instead, Changez associates fundamentalism with the most astringent form of American business practice, embodied in the ideals and practice he picks up working for Underwood Sampson (referred to a number of times as 'the fundamentals'). The demands these place on him to excise his buried non-American self turn Changez against America. Around his rejection accretes a discourse of opposition to the American 'empire' and its foreign policy 'aggression' that is the stuff more of liberal, or leftist, or anti-capitalist groups than fundamentalist jihadists:

> As a society, you were unwilling to reflect upon the shared pain that united you with those who attacked you. You retreated into myths of your own difference, assumptions of your own superiority. And you acted out these beliefs on the stage of the world, so that the entire planet was rocked by the repercussions of your tantrums, not least my family, now facing war thousands of miles away (168).

These are Changez's words: throughout the novel the focalization is through him. In spite of the ambiguity of its closure, the truth and authenticity of his response is never questioned. Still, here and there suggestions of a violent culmination are trailed: for instance, the waiter who the American becomes nervous about is (Changez agrees) 'an intimidating chap' who comes from the Afghan border where 'his tribe [...] has suffered offensives conducted by your countrymen' (108). The novel 'seems to end seconds before a gunshot, an-artistic-sleight of hand that creates a fragile reprieve from the inexorable logic of action and reprisal' (Scanlan 2007). Some have seen in Hamid's narrative a dialogic discourse of considered ambiguity imitating Camus, or in Changez's pursuit of Erica a resemblance to Gatsby's infatuation with Daisy. Such intertexual traces may divert us from the central message of *The Reluctant Fundamentalist* – if there is one. For Changez seems to do his best both to call down a curse on America, and in the same breath to obfuscate, here and there hinting that parts of his story may in fact be a fabrication: 'Did this conversation really happen, you ask?' (151–2). The migrant – and especially the Muslim migrant writer – might feel he can never be too careful. Hamid's work retains a purposive ambiguity in keeping with its site of enunciation: operating entirely within a western discourse it mounts a guarded resistance on behalf of the precariously placed stranger while still making overtures of reason to an audience he perhaps wishes to placate.[8]

Like Hamid's novel, Laila Halaby's *Once in a Promised Land* gives the reader an insight into the minds of people innocently branded with the stigma of the 9/11 attacks on account of their race and religion. The novel responds to a climate in which 'in the aftermath of the terrorist attacks, a national rhetoric fuelled by misconstrued patriotism rushed to vilify and marginalize persons of an allegedly suspicious racial makeup' (Banita 2010: 243). The chief protagonists are Jassim and Salwa Haddad, a Jordanian professional couple attracted by wealth and the easy living America can provide for the young and talented: 'He a hydrologist, she a banker and trainee real estate broker: this is a couple of upwardly mobile over-achievers living the American Dream who are suddenly branded as outcasts and thus advisedly selected by Halaby to suffer a long and spectacular downfall' (ibid.: 246). Completely innocent of any form of identification with the ideology of the perpetrators of 9/11, the couple are in no way terrorist material. In fact Halaby goes to some lengths to equate their aspirations with those of the standard immigrant, carefully inserting them into a larger pattern of US immigration. Salwa's love of luxury and her family's endorsement of her destiny to live out her birthright – she was born in America and therefore has citizenship – sit alongside a Palestinian refugee background and the unquestioned upholding of demands for justice and restitution for their nation that go with it. Jassim, on the other hand, is a Jordanian without Palestinian connections and no commitment to the Palestinian narrative. Unmoved by politics, he sublimates his Middle East identity into a 'purist' solution to the region's water problem, making this a marker of his commitment to homeland. Naturally enough both feel ties to Jordan, but they have reasons for being in America: Jassim because his education and career path have made him feel he has a stake in the country, and Salwa because she gave up marrying a childhood sweetheart in order to accompany Jassim there. At the start of the novel they have for the last nine years deferred returning home – 'Jordan pumps through the blood but America stays in the mouth' (Halaby 2007: 64). Nonetheless, they are an 'Arab American couple not quite at home in either their Jordanian or their American contexts' (Banita 2010: 246). While fluent in English and practised in its phatic usage, Jassim continually probes the meanings of American idioms, playing games of mental scrabble in which he re-arranges words to make other ones, so proving for himself, without the help of Derrida, that meanings are unstable and liable to slippage. In itself this habit is an indicator of Jassim's own underlying sense of the contingency of his presence in America. Like Willy Loman he still feels temporary about himself, but not because of his exposure to hostile economic forces, rather due to his realisation of his cultural otherness. Even his probing of American idioms betrays a foreigners', perhaps a specifically Arab, literalness.

Halaby wants the reader to construe the series of disasters that befall her Arab characters after 9/11 as written into their *chi* or personal destinies. The novel focalizes the thoughts and experiences of the Jordanians far more than its American characters. The couple become willy nilly emblems of the fissured hyphenation, Arab-American. Jassim and Salwa's repressed fears are too close to subliminal fixations entertained by Arabs about America and Americans to be theirs alone. They are sensitive to American obsessions about freedom and individualism translating into superficial public self-disclosure and sexual indulgence. After 9/11 they can hardly avoid picking up the new notes: paranoiac grasping after security and the concomitant knee jerk patri-otism. Their concerns are relayed to the reader in a voice whose provenance is unsure: it might be Jassim's, Salwa's or the narrator's thoughts to which we are listening, but we tend not to distinguish between them. In the last analysis, Halaby has plugged into a normative Arab narrative about America which her inscription of folk-tale sections at the beginning and end of the novel signposts rather gratuitously.

As Banita points out, Halaby prefaces the novel with the statement, 'Salwa and Jassim are both Arabs. Both Muslims. But of course they have nothing to do with what happened to the World Trade Center. Nothing and every-thing' (Halaby 2007: viii). Though entirely innocent of blame, the couple on account of their Arab and Muslim origins cannot escape inculpation. This proposition forms the didactic centre of the novel, and is underpinned by a diegetic narrative technique that implicates America in everything that goes wrong in the couple's lives, beginning with their growing estrangement from one another, what Salwa to herself calls the 'Big Lie'. Jassim has developed, for an Arab male, an almost unnatural aversion to having children. This can only be explained by his absence from home, culture, and family. Vestiges of these make Salwa feel guilty for deceiving her husband by reducing her contra-ceptive pills and getting pregnant, while at the same time, according to the same criteria, she knows his attitude to be wrong. For her own part, Salwa also stands arraigned, even though she does not at first know it, of selling herself to America. As the narrator informs us:

> What Jassim didn't know and what Salwa hadn't fully realized yet was that in breathing her first breath on American soil, she had been cursed [...] America pulled and yanked on her from a very young age, forever trying to reel her in. Only the America that pulled at her was not the America of her birth, it was the exported America of Disneyland and hamburgers, Hollywood and the Marlboro man, and therefore impossible to find. Once in America Salwa still searched and tripped and bought smaller and sexier pajamas in the hope that she would one day wake up in the Promised Land (49).

Salwa and Jassim, this appears to suggest, both set into motion their individual nemeses before American patriotism gets to work, from the moment they set foot in America almost, we might say, from the moment they first knew about America. The root of their destruction is their attraction to a false American other. Salwa's curse is her engagement (for which her sexy pajamas are a synecdoche) with an endlessly deferred image of a hedonistic fulfilment that does not exist. Jassim's is no less insidious: he is enthralled by American ways of doing things, of the diurnal routine he establishes for himself and which lends to his life a delusory sense of order and fixity. His world begins to fall apart when his early morning swim at the exercise club has to be cancelled because 'someone pooped in the pool'. This, and Salwa's disclosure of her miscarriage the same morning, complicate a road accident in which Jassim's car kills a teenage boy. His feelings of guilt prevent him from telling his wife of the boy's death. This results in Jassim compounding Salwa's lie – the withheld truth of her aborted pregnancy – with a big lie of his own. In their self-accusatory isolation, each becomes engrossed with individuals who incarnate aspects of an Arab desire for the American other. Jassim's tendencies to untrammelled idealization find an object in Penny, a 'forties-something' divorcee, possessing a direct and earthed, physical nature. Salwa's dormant sexuality is awakened by a younger man, Jake, a sexaholic drugtaking fellow employee at the bank, whose implausible attractions are enhanced by his insertion of simple Arabic expressions into his indecent insinuations. The resultant affair and its violent conclusion are redolent of other fictional Arab-westerner sexual encounters.[9] For all of this America is to blame: America has fed false images of itself to the Jordanian immigrants, supplanting the norms inculcated by their Arab culture. 'The kiss [in the office car park with Jake] had lifted from her eyes the last threads of the remaining tidy veil of name brands and small talk, the cellophane promise, the two-ply vow that anything you wanted could be yours. Anything. From a Mercedes to a house in the foothills to sex with your coworker' (189).

Along this slippery slope Halaby sets up a trail of incidents and events tangentially connected to 9/11 which accelerate towards the eventual erasure of the Arab couple's life in America. An ex-serviceman with a grudge against Jordan who tips off the FBI, and a narrow-minded racist secretary at the firm where Jassim works are the fabricators of a shallow case against him that nonetheless leads to destructive consequences in which even his liberal-minded employer eventually becomes complicit. Halaby convincingly lays before us the apparatus of American anti-Arab bigotry that ultimately brings about Jassim's investigation by the FBI as a potential terrorist, and his dismissal from his job. But all this is adds up to no more than the corollary to the Jordanians' greater corruption by America:

> [B]oth Jassim and Salwa come under personal scrutiny by citizens galvanized by Bush's call to act as the eyes and ears of the government – or what Judith Butler would call 'petty sovereigns' – a responsibility initially reserved for members of bureaucratic institutions but now extended to the entire nation. Salwa is verbally assaulted by a bank client, 'a native Tucsonan, American born and raised,' who prefers to discuss her bank account with someone she can 'understand better'. With astounding presence of spirit, Salwa offers her the option of a Mexican man, an American lesbian, or their Chinese director. Yet the point Halaby makes is that after September 11, Arab Americans have fallen one step behind other social outsiders, being branded not only as second-rate citizens but also as social hazards – 'Mahzlims who are just waiting to attack us' (56) and whose goals must be foiled at any price (Banita 2010: 246).

Banita is, however, perhaps too inclined to treat Halaby's novel as documentary evidence of American racism and paranoia post-9/11. Instead, I argue that *Once in a Promised Land* is a fairly conventional inscription of a dualistic attraction-repulsion complex many Arabs entertain about America, wrapped more persuasively on account of Halaby's intimate knowledge of the American culture she de-familiarizes through the eyes of the Jordanian couple. However seriously Halaby means us to take American racism and cultural myopia, the actual focus of her novel is not so much the events of 9/11 and their aftermath, as America's contamination of the simpler, more morally centred life of the Arab Muslim psyche stretching well beforehand.

This is not to say that the novel fails to point out some of the illusions entertained by Arab thought and culture. By living in America the Jordanian characters are able to re-form some of the impossible ideals they hold of each other. Jassim's exalted image of his wife (and of himself) stops him from disclosing his killing of the boy to Salwa. But he does come to realize she is no longer the same young girl he wooed in Jordan: now she is 'tainted with American soil [...] soiled by American dye [...] drowned by American ignorance' (300). His image of Salwa the princess, formed at the start of their relationship and which he partly derived from her parents, his conviction of 'her righteousness, her intrinsic need to fight for what was just' (301), cannot possibly withstand the revelation of her unfaithfulness at the end. But Salwa's sweetheart Hassan, the same young man who as a young woman she had idealized as 'a symbol of Palestine' (240), continues to think of her as pure, his wrappered life in Jordan preventing him from knowing 'she was no longer a perfect beauty, nor was she in any way pure' (328). As for Salwa's view of Jassim – this was from the start filtered through her ambition for wealth, position, and above all, her desire to be in America. For his own part, though Jassim felt he could go nowhere else after America, at bottom his cynical side equates his adopted home as the land of the dollar: his nine-year sojourn there being nothing more than 'a rich man's sabbatical' (218). Though he is morally devastated by his killing of the boy, Penny brings him to see it as an 'American problem' which can be solved in the American way, by paying off the family (179).

Halaby has written a logocentric narrative of American corruption and Arab naïveté. She ensures the fallout from the attacks on the World Centre teases out the threads not only of Jassim and Salwa's lives in America, but of the conditions of possibility of a larger Arab-American identity. In staging a showdown between ordinary Americans and the Arab aliens they suspect of being terrorists, Halaby appears intentionally to endorse the paradox that it is the Arabs who have most to fear. To the Haddads, what happens to them in America confirms their subliminal cultural anxieties about a land that is rootless, momentary, corrosive of morality – and dangerous.

Conclusion

Putting aesthetic matters aside (and I agree with Mishra that the topic of 'Islamic' terror has up until now appeared in more or less flawed pieces of fictional representation) it has to be conceded that Halaby's access to first hand knowledge of two discrete cultures – the American and the Arab Muslim – invests her writing with an obvious superiority to those Anglo-American authors whose tone-deafness to the latter significantly disables the value of their work. This is an exercise in which the hybrid author, conversant with the multi-facetted nature of the subject in focus, is bound to score more highly, at least in so far as cross-cultural exchange is concerned. On the other hand, for all its merits in producing an accurate representation of social reality, in aesthetic terms Halaby's *Once in a Promised Land* lacks the studied ambiguity of Hamid's novel, and thus its literary sophistication. *The Reluctant Fundamentalist* succeeds because it is able to construct a Muslim identity that is porous to the values of both East and West even as it inverts the stereotypical image of the 'Islamic' terrorist. The novel leaves open a space for the western reader to envisage Muslims as his/her equals, and this might be partly because Hamid has been emollient enough not to entirely scare such a reader away. At the same time he asserts the intelligence and resourcefulness of Changez, while keeping in the background that threat of violence necessary to keep on his toes the self-absorbed westerner who still has hegemonic intentions on his mind.

Conclusion

Are Muslims an embattled species? The reader who has advanced thus far might be forgiven for thinking so. While the constructions of Muslim identity that have emerged may not be surprising, they confirm, if not a *Kulturkampf* against Islam as proposed in my introduction, then at the very least, as far as writing is concerned, a pervasive reproduction of stereotypes that are actually quite few in number. Charges of fanaticism, obscurantism and violence (operating in private as well as in public life) are laid at the feet of Islam the religion and the Muslims who are its followers. In the family Muslim male chauvinism visits violence upon Muslim women and prohibits individuation; in public, religiously endorsed violence destabilizes Muslim communities and nations and threatens the security of everyone. The truth claims Muslims embrace are inured in a pre-modern credulity which the secular majority have long left behind. Islam itself is stuck in the past, moribund and incapable of accommodation to modernity. Repressed sexuality, in general and undefined ways, impacts upon the authoritarian politics of Muslim states, the social practice of Muslim communities, and the fanatical mindsets that engage in terror against non-Muslims. The only hope for Muslims is migration from the Muslim world (wherever that might be) to the West, and complete conversion to the freedoms on offer there.

How did the writers I have been discussing acquire these negative stereotypes? More often than not these have been filtered through a deep-seated, persistent Orientalism which, though the past creation of western Orientalists, artists, travellers and journalists, has been absorbed into wider circulation where it can be accessed by anyone who cares to – westerner, easterner, indigenous citizen, migrant or exile. Orientalism was always connected to powerful political interests, and this has continued to be the case in the time frame covered in my study – circa the late eighties to 2010, above all during the period of the so-called 'War on Terror'. The ideology of enlightenment modernism and developmentalism may have given way to postmodern late capitalism in this period, but authors have largely remained faithful to the dominant discourse on Islam. Both Anglo-Americans and writers of eastern extraction/ethnicity choose to identify with and follow a route that is the necessary prerequisite for publication and career success. (Additionally, they might actually believe what they write).

Orientalism is, however, only an available discourse which may or may not be utilized in order to promote the socio-cultural notions of superiority that attend political power. The conditions under which Orientalist modes of representation are adopted do not entirely necessitate its use. To give an example, the events of 9/11 did not predicate or determine the creation and employment of the 'War on Terror' narrative. Many in the West wanted to explore other avenues towards better cross-cultural understanding and healing. Indeed a specious secondary discourse was promoted encouraging Islamic modernism and envisaging the enabling of 'moderate' Muslim voices. Such a discourse, however, fathered as it was by advisors of western politicians (a sort of soft glove to the iron fist of military interventionism) could hardly have had as its aim the revival of Islam as envisioned by a Muhammad Iqbal or Mahmud Taha. Nonetheless, the strident, anti-Islamist tone adopted by a writer such as Kureishi in the mid-nineties looks prophetic from the vantage point of the early 2000s when draconian security agendas became the order of the day. More usually, the case was, as suggested in my chapter on terrorism, that writers needed to play a game of catch-up, their work to various degrees becoming parasitic upon narratives already established elsewhere, such as in the news media.

That said, it is not my intention to argue that the constructions of Muslim identity I have discussed in this study constitute a homogenous discourse uninflected by other topics and concerns beyond putative Muslim chauvinism and violence, or unchallenged by alternative discourses. The presence in DeLillo, McEwan and Updike's novels of other anxieties, partially deflecting the fear of 'Islamic' terror, and the presence of counter-hegemonic voices in the work of Aboulela, Hamid, and Halaby, all attest otherwise. Granted that Muslim identity is an embattled category in almost all of the texts I have scrutinized, we must also concede that its binary opposite – that is, the notionally advanced societies of the western hemisphere – do not escape entirely unblemished (except in the Never-Never-Land representations of Irshad Manji and Ayaan Hirsi Ali, and the more nuanced, because self-consciously anachronistic, humanist paradise of canonical Anglo-American literature imagined by Azar Nafisi). Still, we might ask, where in literature are the positive, upbeat, or at least neutrally observant representations of the experience of what it is really like being a Muslim in the West (and Muslim lands) today? Where as well are the theoretical expositions of Islamic culture; the accounts analytic and synthetic of the spiritual practice and theological dimensions of modern Islam, especially in Europe and America? Though largely absent from the age in which classic Orientalism flourished, in a postcolonial period such as ours, why should these be so palpably lacking in literature? Where attempts have been made in these areas, at least in so far as the main European languages are concerned, they have not unsurprisingly had to work out of the spaces supplied by the dominant discourse. Even a potentially revisionist discourse such as postmodernism, or an oppositionist one (if such we accept it to be) like postcolonialism, are problematic in relation to these enterprises, as we have seen in our discussion of the work of Anouar Majid and Leila Aboulela. While Wäil Hassan has pronounced Aboulela's fiction postcolonial in its scope, this is only for him to commit it to the ghetto of a minority Muslim literature.

If we agree that it is difficult to conceive of a Muslim literature that does not bare the imprint of western-led globalization and all the anxieties and dislocating forces that accompany it, does that necessary mean that such a literature cannot exist in some positive form or other i.e. in a form untainted by western bias? Presumably it would have to embody a dimension or aspect of resistance. How would it be mediated to a contemporary audience except, like other species of postcolonial literature, in a hybrid form? Here one thinks of the work of Shahrnush Parsipur, which is translated for a western readership into English from its original Farsi, and which inhabits simultaneously mixed Iranian (ancient pre-Islamic, Islamic and Sufi) and partially western (postmodern, feminist) thought-worlds. *Touba and the Meaning of Night* in particular is doctrinally without a pro-Islamic bias (of the kind present in Aboulela's fiction), but in the terms of Amin Malak's categorization of Muslim narrative, affirmatively about a contemporary Muslim society (if at times mordantly critical of its mores), while oppositional in terms of its refusal to embrace western modes as the antidote to indigenous repression. Parsipur's novel has as its subject an historic Muslim society undergoing extreme pressure; she articulates its concerns in her own language and in her own voice while borrowing magical realist strategies from world literature. Her fiction, which struggles with Muslim identity according to her own national-religious society, evidences to Anouar Majid's vision of Islam as a model for the world's re-discovery of spiritual/traditional values in a mix of local cultures, alongside other cultural traditions, free from liberal capitalism, in a polycentric world.

Notes

Introduction

1 Writing of his study *The Rhetoric of Empire: Colonial Discourse in Journalism, Travel Writing, and Imperial Administration*, Spurr argues the most important thing 'is, finally, not how one literary form differs from another, but how writing works, in whatever form, to produce knowledge about other cultures' (11).

2 'Nevertheless I believe that even if we do not blame everything that is unhealthy about the Islamic world on the West, we must be able to see the connection between what the West has been saying about Islam and what, reactively, various Muslim societies have done. The dialectic between the two [...] has produced a species of what Thomas Franck and Edward Weisband have called "word politics," which it is the purpose of this book [*Covering Islam*] to analyze and explain' (Said 1981: xvi).

3 For example, *India: Love on the Run* (24 mins), Friday 19 November 2010, Channel 4. 'As more young couples reject arranged marriages in modern India, *Unreported World* investigates a wave of violence that's left hundreds dead across the country's north-west states. Reporter Annie Kelly and director Katherine Churcher reveal that, despite Indian law giving everyone the right to marry who they want, increasing numbers of young couples are facing death at the hands of their own families for defying centuries of tradition.'

4 See for example my discussion of Lord Curzon's Orientalism (Nash 2005: Chapter 5).

5 Said's *Orientalism* – which anyway is not a history as such – was of course written in the late 1970s.

6 I am grateful to Hasan Majed for pointing this quotation out to me.

7 Akram's criticism builds on that of western theorists of civilizations and culture such as the Hungarian Victor Segesvary, author of *Inter-civilizational Relations and the Destiny of the West: Dialogue or Confrontation* (2000), and also the writings of proponents of 'Traditional' Islam such as René Guénon, Seyyed Hossein Nasr and Gai Eaton.

8 For the way this debate has played itself out on the Left in France see Roy (2007) and Žižek, Chapter 1 (2010).

9 Leila Aboulela said in an interview (2007): 'in a secular climate, faith is seen as either part of culture/tradition or it is seen as political [...] Muslims need, for practical purposes, to talk in this [...] language.'

10 In this, for opportunist reasons, we might include states not historically allied to the West such as Russia, India, and possibly even China.

11 Postcolonial theory's co-option of the Muslim as 'a resistant subject' has yet to be thought through, and may in fact raise difficult theoretical problems.

12 Malak includes within his category of writers involved in constructive critical engagement with their own cultures authors like Naguib Mahfouz, Yashar Kemal and Faiz Ahmad Faiz. A further distinction he seeks to make is between the terms 'Muslim', a follower or person shaped culturally by Islam, and 'Islamic', referring to the faith of Islam (5–7). His broad interpretation of the former makes possible the inclusion of Salman Rushdie, and on the other seeks to ring-fence the religion from accusations raised against 'what one author produces in a single work of literature'. However in the white heat of polemical discourse such distinctions are frequently difficult to uphold.

Chapter 1

1 It should however be noted that other Muslim scholars continue to see the situation of Muslims living outside the *dar al-salaam* in traditional terms, arguing that Muslims should consider this as only temporary and have the duty to return to Muslim lands. Shafi'i states: 'Any Muslim in the "Land of Disbelief" must emigrate to the "Land of Islam".' He can remain there only if he lives according to Islamic religious norms or if he is not able to emigrate owing to illness, weakness, or constraint' (quoted in McPhee, S. 2005: 8). However Sayyid Mutawalli ad-Darsh, a prominent imam at the London Regent's Park Mosque (d. 1997), pointed out that Muslims 'enjoy innumerable freedoms in many western non-Muslim countries [...] Freedoms which many people in Muslim countries only dream about' (Wiegers 2011: 187).

2 Tariq Modood suggests that while liberals might prefer 'that minority groups should not identify themselves so closely with religion, that religion should not be a form of group self-definition,' this may be out of 'antireligion prejudice'. Nonetheless, Jews, Catholics, Sikhs and Hindus have done the same as Muslims in holding on to their identification with their religious faith (Modood 2005: 123).

3 Malik is quoting: Sam Harris, *The End of Faith: Religion, Terror, and the Future of Reason* (2005).

4 In the last few years a plethora of titles have appeared which are addressed to the practice of Islamophobia. See, for example, the Runnymede Trust's report (Muir 2004), and Gottschalk and Greenburg (2008) who, among other things, discuss the controversy over the Danish cartoons of the Prophet.

5 Esposito's formulation can be sourced back to the classic Orientalism of Victorian imperialists such as Cromer, Curzon and Balfour, first and conclusively demonstrated by Said (1978: 31–9).

6 'Storm over Berlusconi "inferior Muslims" remarks', *The Independent*, 27 September 2001.

7 Žižek (2010), in my opinion, adroitly lays bare the double-standards of western liberal attitudes towards Muslim women choosing to wear or not to wear the veil:

> [I]t is deemed acceptable if it is their free choice and not an option imposed on them by their husbands or family. However, the moment a woman wears a veil as the result of her free choice, the meaning of her act changes completely: it is no longer a sign of her direct substantial belonging to the Muslim community, but an expression of her idiosyncratic individuality, of her spiritual quest and her protest against the vulgarity of the commodification of her sexuality, or else a political gesture against the West [...] it is one thing to wear a veil because of one's immediate immersion in a tradition; it is quite another to refuse to wear a veil; and yet another to wear one not out of a sense of belonging, but as an ethico-political choice. This is why, in our secular societies based on 'choice,' people who maintain a substantial religious belonging are in a subordinate position: even if they are allowed to practise their beliefs, these beliefs are 'tolerated' as their idiosyncratic personal choice or opinion; the moment they present them publicly as what they really are for them, they are accused of 'fundamentalism.' What this means is that the 'subject of free choice' (in the Western 'tolerant' multicultural sense) can only emerge as the result of an extremely *violent* process of being torn away from one's particular life-world, of being cut off from one's roots (52; original italics).

8 Nationalism can be militantly secular or extremist 'Christian'. Stuart Sim (2004) includes in 'Nationalist Fundamentalism' figures such as Jean-Marie Le Pen and Pim Fortuyn. The extreme strand of anti-Mulim, anti-multiculturalism produced the Norwegian mass murderer Anders Behring Breivik, responsible for the Utoeya shootings and Oslo bombing of July 2011. At first, these atrocities were taken as the work of Muslim or Arab terrorists.

9 A view that, at the time of writing, looks in need of reconstruction with the wave of popular protests and demonstrations against autocratic, western-supported regimes in North Africa and the Arab world.

Chapter 2

1   Older representations of Muslims and Muslim culture in Anglophone writing by Indian writers like Ahmed Ali in *Twilight in Delhi*, Attia Hosain in *Sunlight on a Broken Column* or, more recently, M.G. Vassanji and Anita Desai, have been ably discussed in terms of their Muslim characteristics. For discussion of Muslim representation in Ahmed Ali, Attia Hosain, and M.G. Vassanji, see Amin Malak (2005); on Anita Desai see Amina Yaqin (2006).

2   '[...] there has been very little place either in the culture generally or in discourse about non-Westerners in particular to speak or even think about, much less portray, Islam or anything Islamic sympathetically' (Said 1981: 6).

3   For Weldon's comments on Islam/Muslims in the context of the Rushdie see Lisa Appignanesi and Sara Maitland (1989); Kenan Malik (2009) quotes from Martin Amis's diatribe in *The Second Plane* (2008: 9) 'All over again the West confronts an irrationalist, agonistic, theocratic/ideocratic system which is essentially and unappeasably opposed to its [the West's] existence.'

4   Hanif Kureishi, 'The carnival of culture', *The Guardian*, 4 August 2005.

5   See Moore-Gilbert (2001: 103).

6   Kureishi links his mosque visits to the death of his father and the beginning of his research on *The Black Album*.

7   From 'they had access' to 'God had the answers', in 'The carnival of culture'; from 'I found ideology' to 'thought, was all', *My Ear at his Heart*, p. 168.

8   It is interesting, however, that with the exception of the potentially explosive Chad who brandishes a weapon over a white child during a skirmish outside the Bangladeshi family's flat, the group's violence exists more in the minds of others – Shahid for instance is in fear of their attacking him with 'machetes, carving knives, hammers' (239), and Brownlow is terrified of having his throat cut (244).

9   Ahmed is correct when she observes that Kureishi's placing of his father's racial struggles in the Powell/Thatcher era 'deflects attention away from the lack of a critique of present-day multiculturalism' (33).

10 'These elites, unlike those of the nineteenth and early twentieth centuries, mainly rejected the possibility that Islam would provide a gateway into the modern world. Moreover, they adopted notions such as nationalism, both as a governing ideology and as an alternative to the Islamic loyalties of the people' (Allawi 2009: 68).

11 Monica Ali, 'Where I'm coming from', *The Guardian*, 17 June 2003. Ali also writes in the article: 'I did not grow up like Nazneen (my protagonist) in a small Bangladeshi village, have an arranged marriage, and move to Tower Hamlets unable to speak a word of English.'

12 For example, Sukhdav Sandhu (2003): 'Chanu is a stock character, as many Asian men and women whose personalities have been determined by the stamp of caste and fixed religious and gender roles tend to be; it's impossible not to think of the yearnings of Mr Biswas or Karim's frustrated magus of a father in *The Buddha of Suburbia*. The character of Karim is somewhat less convincing, and to damaging effect [...] He is good-looking, 'walked a straight line while others turned and stumbled', and is very much the Millat character in Zadie Smith's *White Teeth*.'

13 Germaine Greer (2006), most notably, called into question the authenticity of *Brick Lane*: 'The fact that Ali's father is Bangladeshi was enough to give her authority in the eyes of the non-Asian British, but not in the eyes of British Bangladeshis [...] English readers were charmed by her Bengali characters, but some of the Sylhetis of Brick Lane did not recognise themselves.' On the other hand, in her review of Ali's novel Bedell (2003) takes it for granted that Ali is revealing a community 'of which most of us are entirely ignorant'.

14 See sura 2.256 – the *ayat al-kursi*.

15 Another faintly ridiculous image is the imam who attends the Tigers' meeting and is elected their spiritual leader. As opposed to the militantly masculine, home-grown Karim, he 'had only recently been imported', 'had not the slightest idea what was going on' and wears 'open-toe sandals with a plastic flower on the heel-strap': women's shoes (242). While making an obvious point about the disconnect between traditional Bangladeshi

and British Asian Islam, Ali may have had in mind the wheel-chair bound spiritual leader of Palestinian Hamas, Shaykh Yassin, who was assassinated by Israelis a year after the publication of *Brick Lane*.

16 'All you need is love', review of Nadeem Aslam, *Maps for Lost Lovers*, *The Guardian*, 26 June 2006.

17 The woman of forty was the Prophet's first wife Khadija whom he married at about the age of twenty-five. Most authorities say he was in his fifties when he consummated his marriage with Aisha whose age at marriage is disputed. Far from suffering through her life as a victim of paedophilia, Aisha rose to be a prominent member of the Muslim community in Medina: 'She witnessed and reminded others of the details of Muhammad's demeanour, from the smallest domestic encounters to the major public actions that shaped the Muslim community. It is thanks to this exceptional marriage, between a man near the end of his life and a woman still near the beginning of hers, that we know so much about both of them' (Lawrence 2006: 51).

18 In re-writing his 2008 article 'Leila Aboulela and the Ideology of Muslim Immigrant Fiction' (for his study, *Immigrant Narratives*), Waïl Hassan goes so far as to categorize Aboulela's work as a 'minor literature within a minor literature' where Anglophone Arab writing is the minor literature (within English literature) and her 'Islamically inspired fiction' is a minor literature within that. He also points out that modern Arabic fiction 'has been predominantly secular.'

19 'Keep the faith', *The Observer*, 5 June 2005.

20 'An Interview with Leila Aboulela', University of Aberdeen, 2007.

21 Ibid.

22 'Keeping the faith.'

23 See Aboulela's remark in introduction, n.9.

24 Hassan connects Aboulela's work with Tayeb Salih's, and sees her as setting out to fill the gap opened by Salih's forthright, resistant statement of the postcolonial predicament in *Season of Migration to the North* which Salih believed could only be filled by fulfilling the Islamist slogan 'the solution is Islam'. Hassan's approach rather confirms Aboulela's argument that postcolonial critics always read Islam in political/cultural rather than faith terms.

25 For example, 'The version of Islam propagated in Aboulela's fiction […] involves a complete disavowal of personal liberty as incompatible with Islam, of feminism as a secular and godless ideology, of individual agency in favour of an all-encompassing notion of predetermination, and consequently of political agency as well' (Hassan 2008: 313).

26 Aboulela's third novel *Lyrics Alley* is however situated in Sudan in the 1950s – a territory and chronology also visited by Jamal Mahjoub.

27 Neither do they become Jasmines who throw off their eastern lendings to embrace the many freedoms denied them at home, as the eponymous heroine of Bharati Mukherjee's novel.

Chapter 3

1 'The new feminist articulation of the concept of Islam as the "cause" of women's oppression was based on an eclectic choice of concepts […] The concept of patriarchy was a central one to this articulation […] the new wave of radical feminism in the late 1960s and 1970s, conceptualised "patriarchy" as the source of women's oppression […] It was in this context that a new criticism of Islam as the most patriarchal religion and an understanding of "Muslim women" as the most oppressed was constructed' (Paidar 1995: 18).

2 In her reading of Victorian women novelists Rosalind Coward warns us of the dangers of defining women by their sexual experience alone, thereby shortchanging the linkage of sexuality with social power (Coward 1989). She goes on to argue: 'The emphasis on sex as knowledge may well obscure the fact that sex is implicated in society as a whole, that sex has consequences and there are always other people to consider in sexual experience' (45).

3 This chapter is concerned with the construction of masculinity and oppression of women in texts focused mainly on national Islamic societies. However in the 2000s criticism in Britain began to discuss the issue with respect both to filmic and literary representations of indigenous Muslim communities. This is a large topic which I do not have space to go into in great depth here. See, for example, Rehana Ahmed (2009a) and Ruvani Ranasinha (2007).

4 For a discussion of the term 'Islamic Feminism' see Margot Badran (2002). In endorsing the position of feminists like Badran, Tariq Ramadan (2004) points out their awareness of the complexities of their position in being charged with 'belonging to the West', and upholds their wish to avoid these binaries: 'They [Islamic feminists] label themselves as Muslims, criticize erroneous interpretations, and use the scope of interpretation provided by the texts and the various opinions of the ulama of the reformist tradition to construct a discourse on Muslim women that calls them to an active, intelligent, and fair faithfulness – an Islamic faithfulness that sets them free before God and does not subject them to the masochistic imagery of either East or West' (141–2).

5 Nikki Keddie (2000–2001) opines: 'Today it is mostly nonspecialists who say that Islam is and will continue to be a barrier to equality. Even specialists highly critical of Islamic regimes' de facto record on women's rights [...] suggest that it is not Islam but those who use its name that limit the rights of women' (40).

6 Haider Moghissi (1999) is in contrast much more forthright in alerting us to the danger of what she calls relativist postmodern, anti-Orientalist scholarship converging with 'a fundamentalist conservatism'. She argues powerfully for the reinstitution of 'concepts of universality, equality, modernity and human rights' (47).

7 Gillian Whitlock includes *Reading* Lolita *in Tehran* within a category of Iranian émigré women's writing – 'the Iranian memoir boom' stemming from the late 1990s – that 'is writing by and about women; it revolves around the cosmopolitan elite privileged under the regime of the Shah and disinherited by the revolution' (Whitlock 2008: 10–11).

8 Whitlock notes that in the Iranian-American memoir 'the Islamic revolution continues to play out within and beyond Iran and impact upon thinking about gender, sexuality and identity' (16).

9 Parvin Paidar argues that while the 1967 Family Protection Act placed restrictions on males' exercise of their divorce and polygamy prerogatives, these were not abolished. The position of women in the last years of the Pahlavi state remained ambiguous: the man was still considered head of the household and divorce was considered his 'natural right' (Paidar 1995: 157).

10 Similar charges relating to Nafisi's politics and privileged social status are made by Marandi and Pirnojmuddin (2009).

11 Like Sasson while reporting on Gulf society, within the Khan household Seierstadt is situated in a highly favourable position. Privvy to family confidences revealed to her by the women to whom on account of shared gender she has the privilege of access, she is also the recipient of the kind of respect from the menfolk that upper class Victorian and Edwardian female travellers experienced among non-western peoples. She even enjoys the anonymity of wearing the burka although the novelty soon wears off.

12 In his authoritative narrative of the Taliban's rise to power in Afghanistan, Ahmed Rashid points out that the Americans had been warned by secular Arab regimes of the fanatical 'Arab-Afghans' who were involved in the internecine struggles of Afghanistan that followed on the ejection of the Russians; and that from 1992 to 1996 the USA ignored Afghanistan, 'while the Taliban were providing sanctuary to the most hostile and militant Islamic fundamentalist movement the world faced in the post-Cold War era' (Rashid 2001: 135, 140).

13 All of Nasreen's writings with a few exceptions are confined to Bengali. These are *Lajja* (Shame), her intentionally controversial account of Muslim mistreatment of the Hindu minority in Bangladesh which sparked off opposition to her when it was published in 1993; and *The French Lover*, both published by Penguin books, India. Of her four volume autobiography which is banned in Bangladesh, volume 1, *My Girlhood*, has been published in an English translation in New Delhi. The promotion of Nasreen by Indian newspapers, magazines and publishers speaks for itself.

14 See Irshad Manji Wikipedia entry (accessed 30/11/10).

15 On the oft-repeated hypothesis that the virgins promised believers in paradise were really raisons see Ibn Warraq (2002a; 2002b).
16 See Beverley Thomas McCloud and Marcia K. Hermansen's articles in Haddad (1991).
17 As found in a book like Ed Hussain, *The Islamist*. For a discussion of the genre, which he contends treats reformed Islamists largely in terms of psychological neurosis and eschews political or ideological analysis, see Stephen Howe (2008).

Chapter 4

1 Following the periodicity of Hourani (1983), Kurzman dates the decline of modernist Islam at roughly 1940, in the later twentieth century to be 'revived in a subset of modernist Islam I have labelled "liberal Islam," which sought to resuscitate the reputations and accomplishments of the earlier modernists' (4).
2 Tropes such as 'The Hour', 'the Last Day' etc., may be considered among the paraphernalia that Judaism and Christianity bequeathed to Islam. See Cook (2005: 6–9).
3 See Esposito (1983: 63–6) and (2003: 50–61). Other figures often invoked are the poet/philosopher Muhammad Iqbal and, especially in the context of the Iranian revolution, the sociologist Ali Shariati. On Iqbal, Shariati and Qutb together, see Robert Lee (1998). For Esposito (1983: 65), Iqbal and Shariati represent 'a more reformist Islam' in contradistinction to the revivalists, al-Banna, Mawdudi and Qutb.
4 A similar process, we should not forget, has happened in the Christian churches. George W. Stroup (1981) locates the loss of a distinctive Christian identity in the pressure sustained by what he believes to be the centrepiece of Christianity: revelation. 'The crisis in the church is that the personal identity of many Christians is no longer shaped by Christian faith and the narratives that articulate faith but by other communities and other narratives' (36).
5 On Muslim travel to the West see Nazik Saba Yared, *Arab Travellers and Western Civilization* (1996), and on Muslim travel in general, Dale F. Eickelman and James Piscatori, eds. *Muslim Travellers: Pilgrimage, migration, and the religious imagination* (1990).
6 On Muhammad Abdu see Albert Hourani (1983) and Malcolm Kerr (1966).
7 The implied opposite is the response of Sayyid Qutb to what he inscribes as the decadence of 1950s American in *Milestones*.
8 A contested term adopted by both Salafi ('fundamentalist') and liberal Modernists like the Iranian Shi'i thinker Abdulkarim Sorush. See Allawi (2009: 117–19, 127–9). On the integration of *ijtihad* and fatwa within Muslim thought see Ramadan (2004: 43–55). From a western perspective, Sim (2004: 63) sees *ijtihad* as a strategy of exit from fundamentalism and progress towards an Islamic Reformation.
9 Şemseddin Sami Frashëri (1850–1904).
10 See Naipaul, *India: A Million Mutinies Now* (1990)
11 The messianic/revivalist movement of the Sudanese Mahdi is frequently compared with the Wahhabi movement of the eighteenth and early nineteenth century; the attempted Babi revolution in mid-nineteenth-century Persia; and the Sanusiya or Senusis in Cyrenaica (modern Libya) in the 1840s.
12 Performed most histrionically by Lawrence Olivier in the film *Khartoum* (1964).
13 The story has some of the ingredients – a villain threatening Islamic holy war against Britain – present in John Buchan's *Greenmantle* (1916) to be revived eight decades later in A.J. Quinnell's *The Mahdi* – a novel of crime fiction with Iran this time as a backdrop. In fact the mahdi story can be inserted into a genre of popular fiction structured around a 'devious plan for the destruction of the hero, his country, [...] of Western civilization, itself' (Simon 2004: 280).
14 Confirmed by Jamal Mahjoub in an email to this author, 22 January 2001. See *The Memoirs of Babikr Bedri*, translated from the Arabic by Y. Bedri and G. Scott.
15 'The more, too, the Muslim masses have felt themselves oppressed and humiliated, either by their own rulers or by non-Muslims, the more fervent has been the longing for this ultimate restorer of the true Islam and conqueror of the world for Islam.' H.A.R Gibb

and J.H. Kramers, *Shorter Encyclopaedia of Islam* (1961: 313). Like other commentators Holt (1970) traced the 'Mahdist idea' back to Jewish, Christian and Iranian sources, referring to its 'classic formulation' in Ibn Khaldun's *al-Muqaddima*. He argued, however, that it took time for the idea of the Expected Deliverer and the eschatological context (i.e. his appearance at the End) to cohere (23–9). It is important to bear in mind though that, at least for Sunnis, the mahdi has no scriptural validity.

16　Timoth Furnish (2005) argues there is a distinction between the precise meanings of terms such as 'eschatology' and 'apocalypse', but agrees that they overlap. The terms *al-kiyama*, 'the arising of men at the Resurrection, and *al-sa'a*, "the Hour" (or Day of Judgement), come for theologians under the general term *al-ma'ad*, the "returning", i.e. the return to life after death'. 'For Muhammad, a revivalist preacher seeking to strike terror in his hearers, the doctrines of resurrection and of the judgement were of the first importance, and the Kur'an, in consequence, is full of references to them' (Gibb and Kramers 1961: 263).

17　Those acquainted with this kind of modernist reformist thinking might make the connection between Taha's approach and that of Fatima Mernissi, who has suggested that the Prophet's initial inclination towards a tolerant, egalitarian faith in Mecca had to be revised in the face of patriarchal pressures when Islam came to rule over a defined community in Medina. See her *Islam and Democracy*.

18　First in November in 1968, when at the Muslim brotherhood's instigation the Supreme Sharia Court judged him guilty of apostasy; and in January 1985 when he was found again guilty of apostasy and condemned to be executed by a special court. See Mahmoud (2007: 21–9).

19　Among the first women admitted to the University of Tehran in 1974, she later resigned from Iranian National Television and Radio in protest against the Shah's execution of two poets. Arrested by SAVAK secret police and imprisoned for a short time, she was imprisoned for over four years by the Iranian Revolutionary Government for her outspokenness over human rights. She now lives in California.

20　Interestingly, during the Constitutional Revolution the opportunist leader of the 'Moderate' Party in the Majles, Ayatollah Tabatabai, while he opposed giving women the vote nevertheless had his daughters educated to read and write (Paidar 1995: 67).

21　On Khiabani, who is best known for his leadership of a breakaway Azarbayjan in 1920 – whether under the influence of Bolshevism as rumoured in *Touba*, or not – see Katouzian (2003: ch.10). It is peculiar that Parsipur uses this historical figure to encapsulate Touba's awakening rather than his fellow Constitutional Democrats Taqizadeh and Dehkhoda both of whom were outspoken advocates of women's emancipation. The latter 'urged women to get together, open schools, establish organisations, become educated, break their ever-dirty pots and pans [...] and drive backward looking mollas out of their lives' (Paidar 1995: 63).

22　Touba's youthful negotiation of and self-extraction from her marriage contract are probably her most assertive acts in the novel. According to Farzaneh Milani, Parsipur had in mind the Babi preacher and poetess Tahireh Qurrat ul-Ain in staging the young Touba's 'first challenge to an aged-old, male-centered, male dominated belief system' (Milani 1992: 98). Tahireh left her clerical husband and two children to adopt her career as a Babi in the 1840s. Milani also quotes the daughter of Shah Nasir ud-Din, Taj O-Saltaneh, who like Tahireh unveiled herself in public, openly supported the Constitutional Revolution, and claimed her family stigmatized her as a Babi (Milani: 97).

23　Two daughters of Shah Nasir ud-Din actively supported the Constitutional Revolution. Malekeh Iran spoke at meetings unveiled and Taj o-Saltaneh authored memoirs about life in a Qajar haram. A divorcee, she founded a literary society criticizing polygamy, veiling and seclusion of women. The movement for national progress 'defined women's position in terms of national interest and saw it as one of the elements on which the nation depended [...] Women [...] were considered as significant to the nation because of their role as biological reproducers of the nation, educators of children, transmitters of culture and participants in the national life.' (Paidar 1995: 68, 71–3).

Chapter 5

1 The major difference between Palestinian and Muslim identity is that, as Khalidi argues, the former, in spite of its failure to find expression in a recognizable state, 'shows myriad features similar to those of other national movements' (xii).

2 On this incident, and the affect the 2003 invasion on Iraq has had on terrorist recruitment, see Steve Hewitt, *The British War on Terror*, Chapter 3.

3 In her study of his earlier 'terrorist novel' *Mao II*, Margaret Scanlan argues that DeLillo conflates the novelist and the terrorist, as well as the news media and the novel. The impact of the latter seems to be confirmed by his remark: 'The news is fiction, the news is the new narrative – particularly the dark news' which leads to the conclusion that the novel can only follow the news media, in fact has been replaced by it (Scanlan 2001: 13). In his 2007 *Guardian* review of DeLillo's *Falling Man*, Toby Litt appears slightly more confident about the novelist's agency: 'What *Falling Man* implicitly says to its audience is [...]: "OK, we saw the same thing, the same repeated footage of impact and explosion. But my job is words, and I've turned my seeing into saying."'

4 'Policies end up being made, wars even end up being fought, not in response to real conflicts in the realms of social relations and politics, but in reaction to the simulacra of conflict circulated in the media by way of a mythography of terror' Appelbaum and Paknadel (2008: 389).

5 Sara Upstone (2007b) has gone so far as to argue that Perowne's attitudes represent a validation of a liberal interventionist ideology of the Blair years.

6 DeLillo's long-term interest in strands that come together in the events of 9/11 such as terror, the twin towers, American hubris, the crossover from fact to fiction and vice versa, prompted Margaret Scanlan (2007) to remark that he 'almost invented 9/11 before it happened.'

7 'Updike appears as keen as Amis to optimise his research. Indeed, he seems to have visited the same websites of Koranic pseudo-scholarship. Invoking the raisin-virgin controversy, one of Updike's fanatical Muslim characters echoes Amis's little joke that the substitution of virgins with dry fruits "would make Paradise significantly less attractive for many young men" [...] Struggling to define cultural otherness, DeLillo, Updike and Amis fail to recognise that belief and ideology remain the unseen and overwhelming forces behind the gaudy fantasies about virgins' (Mishra 2007).

8 Hamid's sensitivity to the migrant's precarious position comes across in an interview he gave soon after the publication of *The Reluctant Fundamentalist*: 'I have lived much of my adult life in America and have enormous affection both for the country and my many, many friends there. I didn't want to write something that was gratuitously offensive or, even worse in today's environment of government-erected walls, could lead to my being prevented from visiting the United States.'

9 Such as are to be found in twentieth-century Arabic novels and short stories, most notably Tayeb Salih's *Season of Migration to the North* and Hanan al-Shaykh's *Only in London*, as well as in the Anglophone fiction of Anglo-Egyptian author Ahdaf Soueif (*In the Eye of the Sun*, *Map of Love*) and Arab-American Diana Abu-Jaber (*Crescent*).

Bibliography

Aboulela, Leila. *Coloured Lights*. Polygon: Edinburgh, 2001a.
— *The Translator*. London: Heinemann, 2001b.
— *Minaret*. London: Bloomsbury, 2005.
— 'An Interview with Leila Aboulela.' University of Aberdeen, 2007. http://www. abdn.ac.uk/sll/complit/leila.shtml (accessed 16/10/2010).
Abu-Lughod, Lila, ed. *Remaking Women, Feminism and Modernity in the Middle East*. Princeton: Princeton University Press, 1998.
— '*Orientalism* and Middle East Feminist Studies.' *Feminist Studies*, 27, 1 (Spring 2001): 101–13.
Ahmed, Akbar S. *Postmodernism and Islam: Predicament and Promise*. London: Routledge, 2004.
Ahmed, Leila. *Women and Gender in Islam*. New Haven and London: Yale University Press, 1992.
— *A Border Passage From Cairo to America – A Woman's Journey*. New York: Penguin, 2000.
Ahmed, Rehana. 'British Muslim Masculinities and Cultural Resistance in Simon Beaufoy's *Yasmin*.' *Journal of Postcolonial Writing*, 45, 3 (September 2009a): 285–96.
— 'Occluding Race in Selected Short Fiction by Hanif Kureishi.' *Wasifiri*, 58 (Summer 2009b): 27–34.
Akram, Ejaz. 'Negotiation of Modernity and Tradition within the Muslim World: The Case of the Sub-Continent.' In Seyed G Safavi, ed. *Dialogue Among Civilizations*. London: Institute of Islamic Studies, Salaman Azadeh Publication, 2003: 92–108.
Akhtar, Shabbir. *Be Careful with Muhammad!: The Salman Rushdie Affair*. London: Bellew Publishing, 1989.
Ali, Ayaan Hirsi. *The Caged Virgin: A Muslim Woman's Cry for Reason*. London: Pocket Books, 2007.
— *Infidel: My Life*. London: Pocket Books, 2008.
Ali, Monica. *Brick Lane*. London: Black Swan, 2004.
— 'Where I'm coming from'. *The Guardian*, 17 June 2003.
Allawi, Ali A. *The Crisis of Islamic Civilization*. New Haven and London: Yale University Press, 2009.
Almond, Ian. *The New Orientalists: Postmodern Representations of Islam from Foucault to Baudrillard*. London: I.B. Tauris, 2007.
Al-Mussawi, Muhsin J. *The Postcolonial Arabic Novel, Debating Ambivalence*. Leiden: Brill, 2003.

Amireh, Amal. 'Framing Nawal El Saadawi, Arab Feminism in a Transnational World.' In Lisa Suhair Mahjaj, Paula W. Sunderman and Therese Saliba, eds. *Intersections: Gender, Nation, and Community in Arab Women's Novels*. Syracuse, NY: Syracuse University Press, 2001: 33–67.

Amis, Martin. *The Second Plane: September 11: 2001–2007*. London: Jonathan Cape, 2008.

Amnesty International. 'Women in Afghanistan: Pawns in Men's Power Struggles.' November 1999. http://www.amnesty.org/en/library/asset/ASA11/011/1999/en/c80434b3-e035-11dd-865a-d728958ca30a/asa110111999en.pdf

Ansari, Humayun. *The Infidel Within: Muslims in Britain since 1800*. London: Hurst, 2004.

Appelbaum, Robert, and Paknadel, Alexis. 'Terrorism and the Novel, 1970–2001.' *Poetics Today* 29, 3 (Fall 2008): 387–436.

Appignanesi, Lisa and Sara Maitland, eds. *The Rushdie File*. London: Fourth Estate, 1989.

Aslam, Nadeem. *Maps for Lost Lovers*. London: Faber, 2004.

— 'God and Me.' *Granta* 93 (Spring 2006): 66–8.

Badran, Margot. 'Islamic feminism: what's in a name?' *Al-Ahram Weekly Online*, 17–23 January 2002, Issue No. 569. http://weekly.ahram.org.eg/2002/569/cul.htm

Bahramitash, Roksana. 'The War on Terror, Feminist Orientalism and Orientalist Feminism: Case Studies of Two North American Bestsellers.' *Critique: Critical Middle Eastern Studies*, 14, 2 (Summer 2005): 221–35.

Banita, Georgiana. 'Race, Risk, and Fiction in the War on Terror: Laila Halaby, Gayle Brandeis, and Michael Cunningham.' *Literature Interpretation Theory*, 21 (2010): 242–268.

Banville, John. 'A Day in the Life: Review of Ian McEwan's *Saturday*.' *New York Review of Books*, 26 May 2005.

Bedell, Geraldine. 'Full of East End Promise.' *The Observer*, 15 June 2003.

Brown, Malcom D. 'Comparative Analysis of Mainstream Discourses, Media Narratives and Representations of Islam in Britain and France Prior to 9/11.' *Journal of Muslim Minority Affairs*, 26, 3 (December 2006): 297–312.

Chambers, Claire. 'An Interview with Leila Aboulela.' *Contemporary Women's Writing*, 3, 1 (2009): 86–102.

Chaudhuri, Amit. 'Not Entirely Like Me.' Review of Mohsin Hamid, *The Reluctant Fundamentalist*. *London Review of Books*, 4 October 2007.

Cook, David. *Contemporary Muslim Apocalyptic Literature*. New York: Syracuse University Press, 2005.

cooke, miriam 'Feminist Transgressions in the Postcolonial Arab World.' *Journal of Arabic Literature* (Spring 1999): 93–105.

Cormack, Alistair. 'Migration and the Politics of Narrative Form: Realism and the Postcolonial Subject in *Brick Lane*.' *Contemporary Literature*, 43, 4 (Winter 2006): 695–721.

Coward, Rosalind. 'How I Became my own Person.' In Catherine Belsey and Jane Moore, eds. *The Feminist Reader, Essays in Gender and the Politics of Literary Criticism*, London: Macmillan, 1989: 37–47.

Cox, Harvey. *The Secular City: Secularization and Urbanization in Theological Perspective*. London: SCM, 1966.

Deen, Hanifa. *The Crescent and the Pen: The Strange Journey of Taslima Nasreen.* Westport, CT: Praeger, 2006.

DeLillo, Don. 'In the Ruins of the Future: Reflections on Terror and Loss in the Shadow of September.' *Harper's*, December 2001: 33–40.

— *Falling Man.* London: Picador, 2007.

Desai, Meghnad. *Rethinking Islamism: The Ideology of the New Terror.* London: I.B. Tauris, 2007.

Djebar, Assia. *Women of Algiers in Their Apartment.* Translated by Marjolijn de Jager, afterword by Clarissa Zimra. Charlottesville: University of Virginia Press, 1999.

Dunn, Ross E. *The Adventures of Ibn Battuta.* Berkeley: University of California Press, 1986.

Eaglestone, Robert. 'The Age of Reason is Over … an Age of Fury was Dawning: Contemporany Anglo-American Fiction and Terror.' *Wasafiri*, 51 (2007): 19–22.

Eickelman, Dale F. 'Islam and the Languages of Modernity.' *Daedalus*, 129, 1 (Winter 2000): 119–35.

Eickelman, Dale F., and Piscatori, James, eds. *Muslim Travellers: Pilgrimage, Migration, and the Religious Imagination.* London: Routledge, 1990.

Esposito, John L., ed. *Voices of Resurgent Islam.* New York: Oxford University Press, 1983.

— *The Islamic Threat: Myth or Reality?* New York: Oxford University Press, 2nd ed, 1995.

— *Unholy War: Terror in the Name of Islam.* Oxford: Oxford University Press, 2003.

Furnish, Timothy. *Holiest Wars: Islamic Mahdis, Their Jihads, and Osama bin Laden.* Westport, CT: Praeger, 2005.

Gellner, Ernest. *Postmodernism, Reason and Religion.* London: Routledge, 2002.

Ghose, Sheila. 'Brit Bomber: The Fundamentalist Trope in Hanif Kureishi's *The Black Album* and 'My Son the Fanatic'. In: MacPhee, Graham and Poddar, Prem, eds., *Empire and After: Englishness in Postcolonial Perspective.* New York: Berghahn, 2007: 121–38.

Gibb, H.A.R. *Studies on the Civilization of Islam.* London: Routledge and Kegan Paul, 1962.

Gibb, H.A.R and Kramers, J.H. *Shorter Encyclopaedia of Islam.* Leiden and London: E.J. Brill and Luzak, 1961.

Gottschalk, Peter, and Greenburg, Gabriel. *Islamophobia: Making Muslims the Enemy.* Lanham, MD: Rowland and Littlefield, 2008.

Gray, John. *Al Qaeda and What it Means to be Modern.* London: Faber & Faber, 2007.

Greer, Germaine. 'Reality Bites.' *The Guardian*, 24 July 2006.

Griffith, Glyne A. 'Travel Narrative as Cultural Critique: V. S. Naipaul's Travelling Theory.' *Journal of Commonwealth Literature*, 29 (1993): 87–92.

Gupta, Suman. *V. S. Naipaul.* Plymouth: Northcote House/British Council, 1999.

Haddad, Yvonne Yazbeck, ed. *The Muslims of America.* New York: Oxford University Press, 1991.

Halaby, Laila. *Once in a Promised Land.* Boston, MA: Beacon Press, 2007.

Hall, Stuart. 'Who needs "Identity"?' In Stuart Hall and Paul du Gay, eds. *Questions of Cultural Identity.* London: Sage, 1996: 1–17.

Halliday, Fred. *Two Hours that Shook the World: September 11, 2001: Causes and Consequences.* London: Saqi, 2002.

Hamid, Mohsin. *The Reluctant Fundamentalist.* London: Hamish Hamilton, 2007.
— 'Harcourt interview with Mohsin Hamid on *The Reluctant Fundamentalist*' (March 2007). mohsinhamid.com (accessed 16/3/2011).
Harris, Sam. *The End of Faith: Religion, Terror, and the Future of Reason.* London: The Free Press, 2005.
Hartnell, Anna. 'Moving Through America: Race, Place and Resistance in Mohsin Hamid's *The Reluctant Fundamentalist.*' Paper delivered at Terrorism and Migration conference, University of Southampton, 17–18 November 2007.
Harvey-Wood, Harriet and Antonia Susan Byatt. *Memory: An Anthology.* London: Chatto & Windus, 2008.
Hassan, Waïl S. 'Leila Aboulela and the Ideology of Muslim Immigrant Fiction.' *Novel* 41 (2008): 298–318.
— *Immigrant Narratives: Orientalism and Cultural Translation in Arab-American and Arab-British Literature.* New York: Oxford University Press, 2011.
Hellyer, H.A. 'Muslims and Multiculturalism in the European Union.' *Journal of Muslim Minority Affairs*, 26, 3 (December 2006): 329–51.
Hewitt, Steve. *The British War on Terror: Terrorism and Counter-Terrorism on the Home Front since 9/11.* London: Continuum, 2008.
Hiddleston, Jane. 'Shape and Shadows: (Un)veiling the Immigrant in Monica Ali's *Brick Lane.*' *Journal of Commonwealth Literature*, 40, 1 (2005): 57–72.
Holt, P.M. *The Mahdist State in the Sudan: A Study of its Origins, Development, and Overthrow.* Oxford: Oxford University Press, 1970.
Houen, Alex. *Terrorism and Modern Literature: From Conrad to Ciaran Carson.* Oxford: Oxford University Press, 2002.
Hourani, Albert. *Arabic Thought in the Liberal Age, 1798–1939.* Cambridge: Cambridge University Press, 1983.
Howe, Stephen. 'True Confessions.' *New Humanist*, 123, 2 (March–April 2008) http://newhumanist.org.uk/1730/true-confessions
Huband, Mark, *Warriors of the Prophet: The Struggle for Islam.* Boulder, Colorado: Westview, 1998.
Huggan, Graham. 'Perspectives on Postcolonial Europe.' *Journal of Postcolonial Writing*, 44, 3 (September 2008): 241–9.
Husain, Ed. *The Islamist: Why I Joined Radical Islam in Britain, What I saw Inside and Why I Left.* London: Penguin, 2007.
Ibn Battuta. *Travels in Asia and Africa 1325–1354.* Translated and selected by H.A.R. Gibb, London: Routledge and Kegan Paul, 1926; reprinted New Delhi: Oriental Books Reprint Corporation, 1986.
Ibn Warraq. *What the Koran Really Says.* Amherst, NY: Prometheus Books, 2002a.
— 'Virgins? What Virgins?' *The Guardian*, 12 January 2002b.
Jayyusi, Salma Khadra. 'Modernist Arab Women Writers: A Historical Overview', in Lisa Suhair Majaj, Paula W. Sunderman, and Therese Saliba, *Intersections, Gender, Nation, and Community in Arab Women's Novels.* Syracuse, NY: Syracuse University Press, 2002: 1–30.
Kabir, Nahid. 'Representations of Islam and Muslims in the Australian Media, 2001–2005.' *Journal of Muslim Minority Affairs* 26, 3 (December 2006): 313–28.
Kaleta, Kenneth. *Hanif Kureishi: Postcolonial Storyteller.* Austin, Texas: University of Texas Press, 1998.

Kandiyoti, Deniz, ed. *Gendering the Middle East: Emerging Perspectives.* London: I.B. Tauris, 1995.

Karim, Persis M. 'Biography of Shahrnush Persipur.' In Shahrnush Parsipur, *Touba and the Meaning of Night.* London: Marion Boyars, 2007: 407–14.

Katouzian, Homa. *Iranian History and Politics: The Dialectic of State and Society.* London: Routledge, 2003.

Keane, John. 'The Sacred in a Secular Age.' *Al-Ahram Weekly,* 7–13 January 1999.

Keddie, Nikki R. 'The Study of Muslim Women in the Middle East: Achievements and Remaining Problems.' *Harvard Middle Eastern and Islamic Review* 6 (2000–2001): 26–52.

— 'Women in the Limelight: Some Recent Books on Middle Eastern Women's History.' *International Journal of Middle East Studies,* 34, (2002): 553–73.

Kepel, Gilles. *Allah in the West: Islamic Movements in America and Europe* Cambridge: Polity, 1997.

Kerr, Malcolm H. *Islamic Reform: The Political and Legal Theories of Muhammad 'Abduh and Rashid Rida.* Berkeley. LA: University of California Press, 1966.

Keshavarz, Fatemeh. *Jasmin and Stars: Reading More than Lolita in Tehran.* Chapel Hill: University of North Carolina Press, 2007.

Khalidi, Rashid. *Palestinian Identity: The Construction of Modern National Consciousness.* New York: Columbia University Press, 1997.

Kureishi, Hanif. *The Black Album.* London: Faber, 1995.

— *My Beautiful Laundrette and Other Writings.* London: Faber, 1996.

— 'My Son the Fanatic.' In *Love in a Blue Time.* London: Faber, 1997.

— *My Ear at His Heart: Reading My Father.* London: Faber, 2004.

— 'The carnival of culture.' *The Guardian,* 4 August 2005.

Kurzman, Charles. *Modernist Islam, 1840–1940: A Sourcebook.* Oxford: Oxford University Press, 2002.

Lawrence, Bruce. *The Qur'an: A Biography.* Vancouver, BC: Douglas and McIntyre, 2006.

Lee, Robert D. *Overcoming Tradition and Modernity: The Search for Islamic Authenticity.* Boulder, Colorado: Westview, 1998.

Lewis, Bernard. 'Islam and Liberal Democracy.' *Atlantic Monthly,* February 1993.

Lewis, Philip. *Islamic Britain: Religion, Politics and Identity Among British Muslims.* London: I.B. Tauris, 2002.

Litt, Toby. 'The Trembling Air.' Review of Don DeLillo, *Falling Man,* The Guardian, 26 May 2007.

Mabro, Juliet, ed. *Veiled Half-Truths: Western Travellers' Perceptions of Middle Eastern Women.* London: I.B. Tauris, 1991.

Mahfouz, Naguib. *The Journey of Ibn Fattouma.* Translated by Denys Johnson-Davies, New York: Doubleday, 1992.

Mahjoub, Jamal. *In the Hour of Signs.* Oxford: Heinemann, 1996.

Mahmoud, Mohamed A. *Quest for Divinity: A Critical Examination of the Thought of Mahmud Muhammad Taha.* Syracuse, NY: Syracuse University Press, 2007.

Majeed, Javed. *Muhammad Iqbal: Islam, Aesthetics and Postcolonialism.* London and New Delhi: Routledge, 2009.

Majid, Anouar. *Unveiling Traditions: Postcolonial Islam in a Polycentric World.* Durham and London: Duke University Press, 2000.

Malak, Amin. *Muslim Narratives and the Discourse of English.* New York: State University of New York Press, 2005.

Malik, Kenan. *From Fatwa to Jihad: The Rushdie Affair and its Legacy.* London: Atlantic Books, 2009.

Manji, Irshad. *The Trouble with Islam Today: A Wake-Up Call For Honesty and Change.* Edinburgh: Mainstream, 2005.

Marandi, Syed Mohammed, and Pirnojmuddin, Hossein. 'Constructing an Axis of Evil: Iranian Memoirs in the "Land of the Free".' *American Journal of Islamic Sciences,* 26, 2 (Spring 2009): 23–47.

McEwan, Ian. *Saturday.* London: Jonathan Cape, 2005.

McPhee, Siobhán. 'Muslim Identity: The European Context.' Sussex Migration Working Paper No. 34. University of Sussex Centre for Migration Research, 2005. http://www.sussex.ac.uk/migration/documents/mwp34.pdf

Mernissi, Fatima *The Veil and the Male Elite, A Feminist Interpretation of Women's Rights in Islam.* Cambridge, MA: Perseus Books, 1991.

Midlarsky, Manus I. 'Democracy and Islam: Implications for Civilizational Conflict and Democratic Peace.' *International Studies Quarterly* 42 (1998): 485–511.

Milani, Farzaneh. *The Emerging Voices of Iranian Women Writers.* Syracus, NY: Syracuse University Press, 1992.

Mishra, Pankaj. 'The end of innocence.' *The Guardian,* 19 May 2007.

Modood, Tariq. *Multicultural Politics: Racism, Ethnicity and Muslims in Britain.* Edinburgh: Edinburgh University Press, 2005.

Moghissi, Haideh. *Feminism and Islamic Fundamentalism: The Limits of Postmodern Analysis.* London: Zed, 1999.

Mohanty, Chandra 'Under Western Eyes: Feminist Scholarship and Colonial Discourses', *Feminist Review,* 30 (Autumn 1988): 61–88. Repr. in Patrick Williams and Laura Chrisman. *Colonial Discourse and Post-Colonial Theory: A Reader.* Hemel Hempstead: Harvester Wheatsheaf, 1994: 199–220.

Mohsen, Caroline A. 'Narrating Identity and Conflict: History, Geography, and the Nation in Jamal Mahjoub's Portrayal of Modern-Day Sudan.' *World Literature Today,* 74, 3 (Summer 2000): 541–54.

Moore-Gilbert, Bart. *Hanif Kureishi.* Manchester: Manchester University Press, 2001.

Mortimer, Edward. 'Christianity and Islam.' *International Affairs,* 67, 1 (January 1991): 7–13.

Muir, Hugh, ed. *Islamophobia: Issues, Challenges and Action: A Report.* Runnymede Trust/Trentham Books: London, 2004.

Nafisi, Azar. *Reading Lolita in Tehran, a memoir in books.* London and New York: Harper Collins, 2003.

Naipaul, V. S. *Among the Believers: An Islamic Journey,* Harmondsworth: Penguin, 1981.

— *Beyond Belief: Islamic Excursions Among Converted Peoples,* London: Abacus, 1998.

Nandy, Ashis. 'The Return of the Sacred: the Language of Religion and the Fear of Democracy in a Post-Secular World.' Trans/forming Cultures Annual Lecture, University of Sydney, 12 September 2006. http://www.transforming.cultures.uts. edu. au/news_events/ashis_nandy.html (consulted 16/9/10).

Nash, Geoffrey. *From Empire to Orient: Travellers to the Middle East 1830–1926.* London: I.B. Tauris, 2005.

— *The Anglo-Arab Encounter, Fiction and Autobiography by Arabs Writing in English.* Bern: Peter Lang, 2007.

Nasr, Seyyid Hossein. *Traditional Islam in the Modern World,* London: Kegan Paul International, 1990.

Paidar, Parvin. *Women and the Political Process in Twentieth-Century Iran.* Cambridge: Cambridge University Press, 1995.

Parsipur, Shahrnush. *Touba and the Meaning of Night.* London: Marion Boyars, 2007.

Qutb, Sayyid. *Milestones.* New Delhi: Islamic Book Service, 2001.

Rahman, Fazlur. *Islam.* 2nd ed. Chicago: University of Chicago Press, 1979.

Rai, Bali. *(Un)arranged Marriage.* London: Corgi Books, 2001.

Ramadan, Tariq. *Western Muslims and The Future of Islam.* Oxford: Oxford University Press, 2004.

Ranasinha, Ruvani. *South Asian Writers in Twentieth-Century Britain: Culture in Translation.* Oxford: Oxford University Press, 2007.

— 'Racialized Masculinities and Postcolonial Critique in Contemporary British Asian Male-Authored Texts.' *Journal of Postcolonial Writing,* 45, 3 (September 2009): 297–307.

Rashid, Ahmed. *Taliban: The Story of the Afghan Warlords.* London: Pan Macmillan, 2001.

Roy, Olivier. *Globalised Islam: The Search for the New Umma.* London: Hurst, 2002.

— *Secularism Confronts Islam.* New York: Columbia University Press, 2007.

Ruthven, Malise. *Islam in the World.* London: Penguin Books, 1984.

— *A Satanic Affair: Salman Rushdie and the Wrath of Islam.* London: The Hogarth Press, 1991.

— *A Fury for God: The Islamist Attack on America.* London: Penguin, 2002.

— *Fundamentalism.* Oxford: Oxford University Press, 2004.

— 'How to Understand Islam.' *The New York Review,* 8 November 2007.

Said, Edward W. *Orientalism: Western Conceptions of the Orient.* Harmondsworth: Penguin, 1978.

— *Covering Islam: How the Media and the Experts Determine How We See the Rest of the World.* New York: Pantheon Books, 1981

— 'The Politics of Memory.' *Al-Ahram Weekly,* 26 September–2 October 1996.

Sandhu, Sukhdav. 'Come Hungry, Leave Edgy.' *London Review of Books,* 9 October 2003.

Sardar, Ziauddin. *Desperately Seeking Paradise: Journeys of a Sceptical Muslim.* London: Granta, 2004.

Sardar, Ziauddin, and Davies, Merryl Wyn. *Distorted Imagination: Lessons from the Rushdie Affair.* London: Grey Seal, 1990.

— *Why Do People Hate America?* Cambridge: Icon, 2003.

Sayyid, Bobby S. *A Fundamental Fear: Eurocentrism and the Emergence of Islamism.* London: Zed Books, 1997.

Scanlan, Margaret. *Plotting Terror: Novelists and Terrorists in Contemporary Fiction.* Charlottesville: University Press of Virginia, 2001.

— 'Migrating from Terror: The Postcolonial Novel after September 11.' Paper delivered at Terrorism and Migration conference, University of Southampton, 17–18 November 2007.

Seierstad, Asne. *The Bookseller of Kabul.* Translated by Ingrid Christophersen, London: Little Brown, 2003.

Shaked, Haim. *Life of The Sudanese Mahdi.* New Brunswick, NJ: Transaction Prublishers, [1978] 2008.

Shamsie, Kamila. 'All You Need is Love.' Review of Nadeem Aslam, *Maps for Lost Lovers. The Guardian,* 26 June 2006.

Sheikh, Farhana. *The Red Box.* London: The Women's Press, 1991.

Sim, Stuart. *Fundamentalist World: The New Dark Age of Dogma.* Cambridge: Icon, 2004.

Simon, Reeva Spector. 'The Tomb of the Twelfth Imam and Other Tales of Crime.' In Neguin Yavari, Lawrence G. Potter and Jean-Marc Ran Oppenheim, eds. *Views from the Edge: Essays in Honor of Richard W. Bulliet.* New York: Columbia University Press, 2004: 280–92

Smith, Wilfred Cantwell. *Islam in Modern History,* New York: Mentor, 1957.

Spurr, David. *The Rhetoric of Empire: Colonial Discourse in Journalism, Travel Writing, and Imperial Administration.* Durham, NC: Duke University Press, 1993.

Steiner, George. *In Bluebeard's Castle: Some Notes Towards the Redefinition of Culture.* London: Faber, 1971.

Stroll, Georg. 'Immigrant Writers in Germany.' In John Hawley, ed. *The Postcolonial Crescent: Islam's Impact on Contemporary Literature.* New York: Peter Lang, 1998: 266–84.

Stroup, George W. *The Promise of Narrative Theology.* London: SCM Press, 1984.

Taha, Mahmoud Mohamed [Mahmud Muhammad]. *The Second Message of Islam.* Translated and introduced by Abdullahi Ahmed An-Naim. Syracuse, NY: Syracuse University Press, 1987.

Talattof, Kamran. *The Politics of Writing in Iran: A History of Modern Persian Literature.* Syracuse, NY: Syracuse University Press, 2000.

Tibi, Bassam. *The Crisis of Modern Islam, A Preindustrial Culture in the Scientific-Technological Age.* Translated by Judith von Sivers, Salt Lake City: University of Utah Press, 1988.

Tucker, Judith E. *Arab Women, Old Boundaries, New Frontiers.* Bloomington and Indianapolis: Indiana University Press, 1993.

Turner, Bryan S. *Orientalism, Postmodernism, and Globalism.* London: Routledge, 1994.

Updike, John. *Terrorist.* London: Hamish Hamilton, 2006.

Upstone, Sara. '"Same Old, Same Old". Zadie Smith's White Teeth and Monica Ali's Brick Lane.' *Journal of Postcolonial Writing* 43, 3 (2007a): 336–49.

— 'The "Banal Terrorism" of Ian McEwan's *Saturday.*' Paper delivered at Terrorism and Migration conference, University of Southampton, 17–18 November 2007b.

Wasserman, Elizabeth. 'The Fiction of Life' (interview with Azar Nafisi). *Atlantic Unbound,* 7 May 2003. http://www.theatlantic.com/past/docs/unbound/inter-views/int2003-05-07.htm

Whitlock, Gillian. 'From Tehran to Tehrangeles: The Generic Fix of Iranian Exilic memoirs.' *Ariel,* 39, 1–2 (April 2008): 7–15.

Wiegers, Gerard. 'Dr Sayyid Mutawalli ad-Darsh's *fatwas* for Muslims in Great Britain: The Voice of Official Islam?' In Gerald MacLean, ed. *Britain and the Muslim World: Historical Perspectives.* Newcastle upon Tyne: Cambridge Scholars Publishing, 2011: 178–191.

Williams, Patrick. 'Inter-Nationalism: Diaspora and Gendered Identity in Farhana Sheikh's The Red Box.' *Journal of Commonwealth Literature*, 30, 1 (1995): 45–54.

Winter, Tim. 'Some Thoughts on the Formation of British Muslim Identity.' *Encounters: Journal of Inter-Cultural Perspectives*, 8, 1 (March 2002): 3–26.

Yaqin, Amina. 'The Communalization and Disintegration of Urdu in Anita Desai's In Custody.' In: Morey, Peter and Tickell, Alex, eds., *Alternative Indias: Writing, Nation and Communalism*. Amsterdam: Rodopi, 2006: 89–113.

Yared, Nazik Saba. *Arab Travellers and Western Civilization*. London: Saqi, 1996.

Yavari, Houra. 'Afterword: Touba: A Woman for All Seasons.' In Shahrnush Parsipur, *Touba and the Meaning of Night*. London: Marion Boyars, 2007: 383–406.

Young, Robert J.C. *Postcolonialism: A Very Short Introduction*. Oxford: Oxford University Press, 2003.

Žižek, Slavoj. *Living in the End Times*. London: Verso, 2010.

Index

Abbassid Caliphate 74
Abdu, Muhammad 70, 77, 84
Abdullahi, Khalifa 82–3
Aboulela, Leila 26–7, 44–9, 67, 118–19, 120n9
   articulation of Muslim identity within migrant experience 48–9
   Islam and postcolonialism 45–6
   migration to Britain and expression of faith 44–5
   postcolonial writer (Waïl Hassan) 45
   women characters in the West 47
Abraham 66
Abu-Lughod, Lila 52–5
Afghanistan 2, 24, 34, 55, 61, 64
   Amnesty International report on 62
Africans 75
Ahmad, Jalal Al-e 57
Ahmed, Akbar S. 48
Ahmed, Leila 52–4, 67
Ahmed, Rehana 31, 35, 43
Akhtar, Shabbir 23
al-Banna Hassan, 71, 125n3
Algerian war of independence 35
al-Gaddal, Mohammed
Ali, Ayaan Hirsi 66–9, 118
Ali, Monica 12, 26, 36–8, 40, 44, 49, 122n11
Ali, Sayyid Amir 86
Ali, Tariq 21
Allawi, Ali A. 1, 87
Almond, Ian 18, 24
al-Nejumi, Abdul-Rahman 83
Alzheimer's 95, 102–3
America, Americans 3, 101, 108, 110, 112, 113–15
American dream 106, 109, 111
American neo-conservatives 59, 68
Amis, Martin 17, 22, 27, 94, 95, 101, 106, 108
Among the Believers: An Islamic Journey 73

Ansari, Humayun 7, 22
al-Qaeda 14, 95
Appelbaum, Robert 96
Arabia, Arabs 3, 8, 81, 96, 101, 103, 112–13, 115
Arab-Americans 111–15
Arab nationalism 17
Arab women 54
Arkoun, Mohammed 72
Aslam, Nadeem 26, 41–4, 49, 83
'God and Me' 40
Ata, Muhammad 66, 95, 103
Austen, Jane 57
Australian media 20
autobiography 3

Badri, Babikr 82
Bahramitash, Roksana 55–6, 59, 63
Bangladesh 24, 37–8, 65
Bangladeshis of Tower Hamlets 36–7
Banville, John 101
baradarism 43
Baudrillard, Jean 18
Berlusconi, Silvio 10–11
Beyond Belief: Islamic Excursions Among Converted Peoples 73
Bin Laden, Osama 2, 62, 102
Bismarck, Otto von 1
Black Album, The 12, 26–7, 29, 30–2, 36–7
   from ethnicity to Muslim identity 33—5
   liberal discourse v Islamic fundamentalism 29, 30, 34–5
   postmodern message, 30

Bookseller of Kabul, The 55, 60–1, 63
Bosnia 9
Bradford 7, 20
Bradford book burning
Bradford City Council 7
Bradford Council of Mosques 22–3

Brick Lane 12, 26, 36–40
  (mis)representation of Bangladeshis of
    Tower Hamlets 36
  Nazneen – Muslim woman liberated
    from native culture 37
  two Islams: i. traditional, local, quietist,
    fatalist 38–9
  ii. new, radical, direct, authoritative
    39–40
British migrant Muslim fiction 26, 49
British Muslim Community 20–1
Brown, Malcolm D. 20
'brown sahib' 23, 26
Buddha of Suburbia, The 29–30
Buddhism/Buddhists 4, 75
Bungawalla, Inayat 24
Bush administration 59
Byzantium 75

Canada 65
Candide 68
capitalism 16
Cartland, Barbara 67
Central Asia 75
Chambers, Claire 44
Chechnya 9
China 75
Christianity 3, 13
Christians 10, 14
Christian Right 10
C.I.A. 2, 109
clash of cultures 3
clash of civilizations 12, 18, 26, 79 – *see
    also* Huntingdon, Samuel
Cold War 10
colonialism (western) 14
Coloured Lights 46
Communism/Communists 4, 9
Cook, David 83
cooke, miriam 51
Cox, Harvey 13
Crisis of Islamic Civilization, The 1

Daily Express 2
Daily Mail 2
dar al-harb (abode of war) 8, 74
dar al-islam 21, 73–6
dar al-kufr (abode of infidelity) 73
dar al-salaam (abode of peace) 8
Davies, Merryl Wyn 23, 26, 93
Day of Judgement 67
Deen, Hanifa 65

DeLillo, Don 94–6, 101, 103–5, 108, 110,
    118, 127n3
Derrida, Michel 18
Desai, Meghnad 14
*Desperately Seeking Paradise: Journeys of a
    Sceptical Muslim* 72–73
developmentalism 51, 117
Diary of Anne Frank, The 15
Dickens, Charles 37
*Distorted Imagination: Lessons from the
    Rushdie Affair* 23
Djebar, Assia 53
Dostum, General 61
Dreams of Trespass: Tales of a Harem Girlhood
    54
Dutch Labour Party 68

Egypt 35, 45
Eickelman, Dale 11–12
El-Sadaawi, Nawal 54, 59
'end times, the' 70–1
Enlightenment, The 3, 22
eschatology – *see* 'end times'
Esposito, John 10
ethnicity 27, 29
European Union 20

Falling Man, 94–6
  alienation from American civilization
    104
  post 9/11 trauma 101–2
  image of falling man 104
  memory loss and Alzheimer's 102–3,
    105
  motives of Arab terrorists 103
Faruqi, M. H. 24
Feminism/feminists 5, 51, 53, 119
  Colonial 52
  Middle Eastern 52
  see also Islamic feminism, and feminist
    Orientalism
Fire and Sword in the Sudan 82
Fitzgerald, F. Scott 57
Foucault, Michel 18
France 35
From Fatwa to Jihad 22
fitna (rebellion)
fundamentalism 15, 18, 72

Gellner, Ernest 13
German Muslim immigrant writers 64
Germany 67

Ghose, Sheila 3, 30
globalization 18
Globe and Mail, The (Canada) 65
Gordon, General 82
Gramsci, Antonio 71
Gray, John 14
Greer, Germaine 122n13
Gupta, Sumal 79
Gurnah, Abdelrazak 5

Haddad, Yvonne 72
haj 73, 75
Hall, Stuart 8
Halaby, Laila 96, 111–16, 118
Halliday, Fred 2, 93
Hamid, Mohsin 94–5, 108–11, 116, 118
Hassan, Waïl 45, 48, 119, 123
Hellyer, H. A. 20
Hicks, Colonel William 82
Hiddleston, Jane 36–7
hijab 3, 48, 50
Hindus 3–4, 10, 67, 75
Hindu pantheism 21
Holland 68
Holocaust 5, 16
Huband, Mark 62
Huggan, Graham 68
Huntingdon, Samuel 11, 16, 22, 81
Hussein, Saddam 9
Hyde Park demonstration (against *Satanic Verses*) 20

ibn Battuta 74–5
ibn Jubayr 76
ijtihad (independent reasoning) 77
imperialism, European 71, 82
In Bluebeard's Castle 14
Independent, The 65
India 3, 40, 62, 65–6, 79, 80, 120n3, n10
Indians 8
Indonesia 73, 79, 81
Infidel 66
In the Hour of Signs 82–3, 85–6
   linked to message of Mahmoud Taha 85–6
Iqbal, Muhammad 81, 86–7, 118
Iran 52, 55–60, 63, 65, 72–3, 75, 79, 80–1, 87, 89, 91–2
   Islamic Republic of 56–7, 63
   Iranian revolution (1977–79) 1, 36, 52, 56, 71, 81, 87

mushrutih, Constitutional revolution (1905–11) 87
Iranian women writers 56
Iraq 24
   invasion of 94, 97, 127n2
Islam 70, 117, 119 *see also* Muslim, Muslims
   confrontation with the West 10, 23, 106
   deterritorialization of 19, 21
   and globalization 19
   'high Islam' 13
   and human rights 67
   medieval presence in Europe 10
   and modernity 70, 117
   and theocracy, theocratic state, system 13, 22
   revivalist Islam – *see* also Islamism
   spiritual crisis of 74

Islamic
   civilization 70, 73
   feminism 51
   fundamentalism 13–14, 18, 25, 29, 41, 72, 81
   history 1, 23
   modernism 70, 77, 81, 118
   terror, terrorism, terrorist 2–3, 25, 69, 95, 97, 108, 115
   threat 16
Islamism 2, 13–14, 16–17, 19, 20, 24, 35–6, 52, 63
Islamophobia 59
Israel 15, 17, 65, 68

Jamaati Islami 14, 72
James, Henry 57
Jews 14–15
jihadists 1
Jordan 112
Journal of Muslim Minority Affairs 19
Journey of Ibn Fattouma 73, 76–8
   encounter with liberal Islam in Halba (America) 77
   five societies encountered 78
journey into the abode of impiety 76
   Muslim self-criticism 77
   Sufi motif of journey 76, 78

Kaleta, Kenneth, 30
Kabir, Nahid 20
Kandiyoti, Deniz 51, 53
Karim, Persis M. 89

Karzai, Hamid President 61
Kashmir, 34
Keddie, Nikki 52, 124
Kemal Atäturk, Kemalism 35–6
Kenya 67
Khalidi, Rashid 93
Khan, Nasrat Ali 40
Khan, Sayyid Ahmad 86
Khan, Sultan 60–3
Khartoum 82
Khiabani, Shaykh 88, 126n21
Khomeini, Ruhollah 14, 16, 56, 79, 92
Kitchener, General Herbert 82–3
Kulturkampf
    against Islam and Muslims 3–4, 6, 9, 11,
        24, 29, 64, 69, 71, 117
    Bismarck against German Catholics 1
    Naipaul against liberation narratives 79
Kureishi, Hanif 12, 21, 26, 27, 29–35,
        43–4, 49, 118, 122n6n9
Kureishi, Rafuishan 31–2

laïcism
Lee, Robert D. 71
Lewis, Bernard 11, 13, 59
Lewis, Philip 7
Levin, Bernard 78
London 101
London, East End 20
London Regent's Park Mosque 48

Mabro, Juliet 52
mahdi (guided one) 70, 86
Mahdi of Sudan (Muhammad Ahmad ibn
        Abdullah) 82–5, 125n11
Mahdi, The 125n13
Mahfouz, Naguib 72, 73, 76–8, 87, 92,
        120n12
Mahjoub, Jamal 82–3, 92
Mahmoud, Mohamed A. 83
Majeed, Javed 86
Majid, Anouar 5, 16, 119, 120
Malak, Amin 5, 23, 49, 119, 120n12
Malaysia 79, 81
Malik, Kenan 18, 21–3, 30
Manji, Irshad 65–6, 118
Maps for Lost Lovers 26, 36, 40–3, 83
    dark picture of Islam 41
    repetition of Orientalist, anti-Islamic
        detail 42
materialists, materialism 4
Mawdudi, Abul Ala 14, 71–2

McDonaldization 14
McEwan, Ian 93–101, 105, 108, 118
memoir 3
    American-Iranian female 55
memory loss 96, 102
Mernissi, Fatima 51, 53–4, 67
Midlarsky, Manus 11, 16
Midnight's Children 24
Minaret 46, 48
Mishra, Pankaj 94, 115
modernity 12, 35
modernization 11, 35
Modood, Tariq 7, 43, 121n2
Moghissi, Haider 54, 59, 124n6
Mohanty, Chandra 52
Mongols 74–5, 109
Moore-Gilbert, Bart 30
Moor's Last Sigh, The 24
More, Thomas 76
Morris, William 76
Mortimer, Edward 10
Mujahidin (Afghan) 62
multiculturalism 7, 13, 19, 20
Muslim, Muslims 1, 2, 9, 67, 93, 116–18
    apocalyptic literature 83
    identity 6–8, 24, 26–7, 48, 116–19
    images, stereotypes of 2–3, 20
    literature 119
    media representations of 3, 9, 20
    men and treatment of women 42, 50–1,
        53, 60, 62, 69, 117
    migrants, migration 1, 7, 21, 49, 108
    Other (of the West) 8
    radicals 72
    resistant subject 4
    South Asian 20–1
    world 2, 5, 9, 11, 18, 52, 71–2
    youth 22
    see also Islam, Islamic
Muslim Brotherhood 14, 72, 77, 84–5
*Muslim Narratives and the Discourse of
        English* 5
Mu'tazila 65
My Beautiful Laundrette 29–30, 32
My Ear at His Heart 31–2
'My Son the Fanatic' 33–4

Nabokov, Vladimir 57
Nafisi, Azar, 55–9, 63–4, 118
Naipaul V. S. 37, 46, 73, 78–81, 92
    Buddhist-Hindu history set against
        Islamic imperialism 80

fantasy of pure Islamic community 80
Third World liberation transferred to
    Islamic movement 79
unmasks Islamic fundamentalism,
    deconstructs Islamic modernism 81
Nandy, Ashis 15, 23, 26
Nasr, Seyyid Hossein 72, 74, 80, 120n7
Nasreen, Taslima 64–6
nationalism 35
native informant 4, 6, 23, 26–7
Nazis 9, 95
Nietzsche, Friedrich 71
New Orientalists, The 18, 24
New York 101
niqab 3
North American Muslim converts 66
Numeiri, Jaffar 85

Omar, Mullah 62
Omdurman, 1898 Battle of 82–3
Once in a Promised Land 96, 108, 111–16
    America's anti-Arab paranoia post 9/11
        114–15
    couple not quite at home in America
        or Jordan 112
    draw of American on Arab couple
        113–14
Orientalism 5, 11, 15, 23, 40, 45–6, 50,
    54–5, 117–18
    feminist Orientalism 38, 55–6, 60
'Orientalism in reverse' 40
Orientalism 15, 16, 18, 54
Ottomans, Ottoman empire 35, 74–5, 109

Paidar, Parvin 55, 124n9
Pahlavis 63, 88
Pakistan, 23, 40, 43, 62, 73, 81, 109
Pakistanis 8, 28–9
Paknadel, Alexis 96
Palestine, Palestinians 28, 34, 39, 93, 115
Pamuk, Orhan 72
Parsipur, Shahrnush 87–9, 91–2, 119
Philippines, The 3
Phillips, Caryl 46
Politics of Writing in Iran, The 56
postcolonialism, postcolonial theory 4–5,
    83, 118
postmodernism 5, 15, 45, 64, 118
Prophet Muhammad 22–3, 69, 84
Protestantism 12

Qajars 87–8

Quinnell, A. J.
    The Mahdi 125n13
Qur'an, 66, 70, 84–5, 107
Qutb, Sayyid 14, 71, 72, 81, 92

race, 7
racism 12, 23
Rahman, Fazlur 1
Rai, Bali, 27, 41
Ramadan, Tariq 8, 124n4
Ranasinha, Ruvani 29–30
Reading Lolita in Tehran 55
    criticisms of Islamic Republic 57–8
    portrayal of Iranian males 59–60
    women's rights in Iran 58–9
Red Box, The – *see* Sheikh, Farhana
Reformation, European 72
Reluctant Fundamentalist, The 94–95,
    108–111, 116
    ambivalent relationship with America
        109–10
    novel's purposive ambiguity 111
    rejection of American market
        fundamentalism 110–11
Republican Brotherhood (*al-ikhwan
    al-jumhuriyun*) 84–5 see also Taha,
    Mahmud M.*
revivalist Islam – *see* Islam
Reza Shah 88–9
romance fiction 67
Rousseau, Jean-Jacques 71
Roy, Olivier 12, 18–19, 21
Rushdie, Salman 5, 6, 9, 12, 26–7, 30, 37,
    65, 120n12, 122n3
Rushdie Affair 9, 13, 20–6, 29
Russia 1, 62, 120n10
Russian revolution, 56
Ruthven, Malise 14, 20–2, 67, 72, 93

Said, Edward 3, 6, 15–16, 23, 54, 69, 81,
    120n5
Salafis 77
Salih, Tayeb 45
Sandhu, Sukhdav 122n12
Sardar, Ziauddin 23, 26, 72–3, 93
Satanic Verses, The 9, 20, 22–3, 30, 36
Saturday 95–101
    Enlightenment reason v irrationality of
        terrorism 99
    fear of dementia 100
    influence of media on representation
        of terrorism 97

sickness and terrorism 98
Saudi Arabia 67, 72
Sayyid, Bobby 5, 15–16, 35
Scanlan, Margaret 23
Season of Migration to the North 46
Second Message of Islam, The 84–5
secularism 4, 12–13, 15, 35, 45
Secularism confronts Islam 12
secularization 11, 13, 35
Seierstad, Asne 55, 60–2, 64, 69
Selvon, Sam 46
September 9, 2001 (9/11) 2, 9, 19, 22, 24,
     55, 93–7, 101, 105, 109, 112, 118
shahada (declaration of Muslim faith) 8
Shame 24
Shamsie, Kamila 41, 43
Sheikh, Farhana 5, 21, 27, 28–9, 49
Shi'ism 91
Sim, Stuart 18, 121n8
Sikhs, Sikhism 3, 27, 67
Slatin, Rudolf Carl von 82
Smith, Wilfred Cantwell 74, 80
Smith, Zadie 37
Soroush, Abdul Karim 87
Soueif, Ahdaf 67
Somalia 67
Soviet Union 2
Spivak, Gayatri 26
Spurr, David 2, 120n1
Steele, Danielle 67
Steiner, George 14
Stoll, George 64
Sudan, 45–6, 83
Submission (film) 66
Sufism, Sufis 43, 72, 83, 84, 91, 119
Sun, The 2
Sweden 65
Swedish Foreign Ministry 64
Swedish PEN 65

Tablighi Jamaat 72
Taha, Mahmud Muhammad 82–6, 118
Talattof, Kamran 56, 58
Taliban 40, 60, 62
Taoist 4
taqlid (imitation) 70
Terrorist, The 95
  Ahmed's character as Muslim and
     would-be terrorist 105
  capitalist America's threat to faith 106,
     108
Thailand 3
Third World 4, 16, 54, 108
  women 51, 53, 64

Tibi, Bassam 75
Times of India 64
Touba and the Meaning of Night 87, 119
  apocalyptic and eschatological motifs
     emancipation of Iranian women 88,
     92
  esoteric and mystical strands 90–1
Translator, The 46–8
travel writing 3
Trouble With Islam Today, The 65
Turabi, Hassan 82, 85
Turkmenistan 62
Turner, Bryan 18

Uganda 65
ulama 53, 72, 75, 84
umma 18, 74–5
(un)arranged marriage 27
United States 1, 4, 62, 68
Updike, John 94–6, 105, 107–8, 118
Upstone, Sara 39–40, 127n5
Uzbekistan 62

van Gogh, Theo 66–8
Vattimo, Giorgio 15
veil, veiling, unveiling 53–4, 56 *see* also
     hijab, niqab

Wahhabi 74
'War of Terror' 55, 117–18
Wedding of Zein, The 46
Weldon, Fay 27, 122n3
West 14–16, 22
  v. the Rest 4
  treatment of immigrants 68
western civilization 3, 19, 95
westernisation 35
western secularism – see secularism
Whitlock, Gillian 57
Williams, Patrick 28–9
Wingate, Reginald 82
Winter, Tim 20
Winterson, Jeanette 27
Woking 20
Women – *see* Muslim, Third World
Women of Algiers in Their Apartment 53

Yavari, Houra 87
Young, Robert 15

Zionism 17, 83
Žižek, Slavoj 18, 35, 121n7